CW01261979

Changing Women's Lives
A BIOGRAPHY OF DAME ROSEMARY MURRAY

Portrait of Dame Rosemary Murray by Patrick Phillips.

Changing Women's Lives
A BIOGRAPHY OF DAME ROSEMARY MURRAY

ALISON WILSON

UNICORN PRESS LTD

William Wycliffe Spooner, M.A., M.I.C.E. (1882-1967)

The W.W. Spooner Charitable Trust is delighted to support this biography in celebration of the life of Dame Rosemary Murray, much loved and admired niece of William Wycliffe Spooner, M.A., M.I. C. E. (1882-1967)

Text Copyright © 2014 Alison Wilson
Images Copyright © 2014 as separately acknowledged

All rights reserved. No part of this publication may be reproduced or transmitted in any form or by any means, electronic or mechanical, including photocopying, recording or any other information storage and retrieval system, without prior permission in writing from the publisher.

First published in 2014 by
Unicorn Press
66 Charlotte Street
London W1T 4QE

www.unicornpress.org

ISBNs
978-1-910065-33-4
978-1-910065-34-1 e-book (epub)
978-1-910065-35-8 e-book (PDF)

Designed by Camilla Fellas

Printed and bound in Great Britain by TJ International Ltd. Padstow, Cornwall

– Contents –

Foreword by HRH Prince Philip, Duke of Edinburgh	7
Author's Preface	9
1: The Admiral's daughter	13
2: Early life and schooldays	27
3: Launching out: Neuchâtel and Oxford	45
4: Student days	65
5: Royal Holloway College and Sheffield University: the outbreak of war	81
6: Life in the WRNS	99
7: The Girton years	111
8: The Third Foundation for Women	123
9: New Hall: early days as a Limited Company	137
10: New Hall: from Approved Foundation to College	155
11: University responsibilities	175
12: Vice-Chancellor	193
13: The final years at New Hall	219
14: Retirement	233
Endnotes	251
Bibliography	261
List of Illustrations	266
Index	269

HRH Prince Philip, Duke of Edinburgh, KG, KT, OM, GBE.

BUCKINGHAM PALACE.

I am delighted that Alison Wilson has been persuaded to write this biography of Dame Rosemary Murray. Dame Rosemary came into my life when I opened a letter from her, as Vice Chancellor of Cambridge University, which informed me that I had been elected as Chancellor of that University. The war interfered with any plans I might have had to attend a university as a student, but in 1947 I was invited to become Chancellor of the University of Wales and then Chancellor of Edinburgh University in 1952, so I did, at least, have some experience as a Chancellor. Even so, the invitation from Dame Rosemary came as a major surprise and a great honour. Needless to say it gave me huge pleasure to accept.

Having been associated with four universities, I have the impression that, whatever the outward appearance, no two of them are quite the same. I soon discovered that Cambridge is even more different. However, I also discovered that they have one thing in common. One of the most valuable functions of a Chancellor is to provide a sympathetic shoulder for the Vice Chancellor to cry on – and in my experience, they have a lot to cry about.

I very soon discovered that Cambridge was also very different in the way it was governed and managed. Not that I was personally involved in the management process, but I felt it was important for me to know who was doing what – and why. As far as Cambridge was concerned, Dame Rosemary could not have been a better guide, philosopher and friend. However, in those days Cambridge changed its Vice Chancellor every two years, which made things fairly lively. Nevertheless, I valued that special relationship with Dame Rosemary until the day she left Cambridge.

Philip

*To my granddaughters, Hannah and Rebecca,
whose opportunities in life have been enlarged
thanks to pioneering women like Rosemary Murray*

– Author's Preface –

THE GENESIS OF THIS BOOK can be traced to a letter from Frances Crombie to Anne Lonsdale, then President of New Hall, in 2003. 'Do you think there is a possibility that someone, past or present, from New Hall might want to write a memoir of your first President, my sister Rosemary? … now would be the time for someone … to come and talk with her of her past life.' As it happened, the College Library had just started an oral history archive, so a small team recorded several hours of conversation with Dame Rosemary at her home in Oxford, to her obvious enjoyment. After that I began visiting her occasionally, but I was heavily involved with my work as Fellow Librarian and quite expected someone else to take up the challenge of the book. Instead, to celebrate the 50th anniversary of New Hall we turned some of our recordings into a film, which could not help being a celebration of Dame Rosemary too, as her life was so bound up with the development of the College.

Later, I wrote an article for the College magazine to mark Rosemary's 90th birthday, and when she died a year later I contributed a memorial and was asked to write an obituary for *The Independent*. Frances told me that the family had liked it best of the many tributes. In her will, Rosemary left New Hall first choice from her substantial book collection, and on a mission to make the selection I discovered that Frances and I had been thinking along the same lines: that I might write the biography. So the decision was quickly and informally made there and then. From that point on she and her husband, Ian, both in their nineties, gave me unstinting help, donating papers to the College archive and lending me Rosemary's precious diaries and journals and the enormous Murray family tree that Rosemary had drawn up. They invited me to visit them, and we chatted about Rosemary's life and looked at photograph albums. These visits were always accompanied by a delicious lunch prepared by Frances, and ended with a big hug. It was a great sadness when, in 2008, Frances had a severe stroke and was moved permanently to a nursing home where she died in 2013. Ian had predeceased her in 2010. Since then their daughter Marion has welcomed me to the house, done her best to answer my questions, and lent me a wonderful cache of hundreds of letters to and from Rosemary, without which this book would be much the poorer. Rosemary's brother, Richard Murray, and niece, Clare Crombie, also kindly contributed memories.

It was not possible to start on the biography in earnest until I retired as Librarian in 2010, but meanwhile I collected information, talking to alumnae, Fellows and staff of the College and interviewing founders and friends who had played an important part in the establishment of New Hall. I would like to thank all of them for being so willing to contribute their memories and opinions, especially those who agreed to be recorded, notably past and present Fellows Zara Steiner, Penny Wilson, Joanna Womack, Liz Acton, Janet Moore, Ruth Lynden-Bell, Joan Hinde, Kate Pretty, Catherine Belsey and George Levack; and from the staff, Mary Boothman, stalwart maid-of-all-work, Tony Norman, first Head of Maintenance, and Sister Jenny Hall, the College Nurse. Sheila Motley, Rosemary's secretary at New Hall and Mary Philpott, her cleaner, explained Rosemary's daily routine. I have enjoyed talking to many alumnae, including those from the Silver Street years: Annabel Rathbone, Jenny Moody, Angela Holder, Dinah Hutchinson, Elizabeth Waldram, Pat Houghton, Valerie Hess, Isabel Raphael, and Caro Barker-Bennett. From later years I am indebted to Caroline Postgate, Patricia Acres, Patricia Rogers, Ida Williamson, Gillian Martin, Patricia Williams, Rosemary Charles, Suzanne Irwin, Eleanor O'Gorman, and many more.

I was fortunate to be able to interview some of Rosemary's colleagues before they passed away: Robin Hammond, who had such an important influence on the shaping of the College, Ian Nicol, Secretary-General to the Faculties, Richard Barlow-Poole her Esquire Bedell, Sarah Newman, Emeritus Fellow and first Librarian of New Hall, and Peter Laslett, historian, who remembered racy discussions in Trinity about the new women's college. I am very pleased to have their words on record for future historians to consult in the College Archive.

Those who worked or advised the College on its buildings include John Honer, Frank Woods, Victor Bugg, Geoffrey Trickey, Richard Noble, and David Todd-Jones from Estates Management. They taught me a lot about construction and Rosemary's involvement in the planning and building on the Huntingdon Road site. Horace Barlow told me about 'The Orchard', his mother's home, and a visit he made to Cadlington. I am most grateful to Jeremy and Louise Sanders for introducing me to several Chemists who knew Rosemary: David Cohen and Cedric Hassall, and Ian Fleming, who gave me a particularly good overview of the Chemistry Department in the 1950s and 1960s. John Martin contributed a student's perspective. Of the many people who have worked directly with Rosemary I would particularly like to thank Alan Clark and Geoffrey Skelsey of the Old Schools, who assisted her as Vice-Chancellor. Both have excellent and long memories. George Reid, Sir David Harrison, Christopher Johnson and Owen Chadwick also provided recollections of that period. Charmian Gladstone commented on the vicissitudes of schooldays at Downe House. Michael Fish gave me some insights into the WRNS when he came to the Library as a reader. Janet Harker, a friend of Rosemary at Girton, told me how they dashed to the coast to help flood victims. The Librarian of LMH remembered how Rosemary used to catch up on college news over lunch with her in hall after her move to Oxford. My friend Elke Pollard entertained Rosemary in her garden, drawing her out on the subject of being a Dame. We could see that Rosemary would have liked to climb up to the tree-house! In her last years Rosemary was greatly helped by Shirley Smith, a secretary and friend, whom I consulted by telephone. I met in person Tony Price, the Vicar of Old Marston, and read his blog about visiting her in hospital, which I feel encapsulates all Rosemary's sterling Christian qualities. Ros Edwards, whose gift has transformed the College, told me about her first, and only, meeting with Rosemary since student days, when she talked to her about the re-naming.

I have been generously assisted by librarians and archivists while undertaking this research. Firstly I would like to thank the staff of the Rosemary Murray Library, Kirstie Preest, Jan Waller and Agnieska Ochal and most of all Joan Bullock-Anderson, who went out of her way to find material and check sources both at Murray Edwards and Girton Colleges. Kathy McVittie's past voluntary work on indexing the oral history videos also proved very useful. Elsewhere in Cambridge I would like to thank the staff of the University Library Rare Books Reading Room; the Librarian of Girton College, Frances Gandy, and Archivists Kate Perry and Hannah Westall; and the Senior Tutor and Keeper of Archives at Homerton College, Peter Warner. I was ably guided to cuttings and microfilms at the Cambridgeshire Collection in the central library and greatly helped by Mike Petty, its former Librarian, in obtaining photographs. In Oxford I visited the archives of New College and was advised by their Archivist, Jennifer Thorp, on Warden Spooner's Diary, and Lady Margaret Hall Library where the Librarian, Roberta Staples, and Archivist, Oliver Mahony, produced valuable references and photographs. I visited Downe House School and was greeted with enthusiasm by Kate Finlay and the

Archivist, Jennifer Kingsland, who also supplied images. I am obliged to all those who have given me permission to publish quotations and illustrations.

A number of friends read and commented on chapters of the book, notably David Adamson, Richard Buxton, Kathleen Cann and Jennifer Barnes. Christine Penney read it all in first draft as it came off the computer, encouraging me to keep going. Heather Glen, Penny Wilson, Rita McWilliams Tullberg and Dame Barbara Stocking read a near-final draft. I am immensely grateful to all of them for their suggestions and improvements.

I am especially indebted to Mrs Anne Lonsdale and Dr Jennifer Barnes, the third and fourth presidents of Murray Edwards College, for their understanding of the importance of this biographical project and support throughout, and to the College Council of that era who extended my Fellowship partly so that I could work on it, using the Archive and entertaining interviewees in the SCR. I hope I have justified their faith in me. I would also like to thank the Goldsmiths' Foundation for a generous grant to cover my expenses during this period, when I followed in Rosemary's tracks to Oxford, Emsworth and Downe House. It was a great relief when the Spooner Trust, set up by Rosemary's uncle, William Wycliffe Spooner, agreed to a request to fund the pre-publication costs of the book. The Trustees felt that William Spooner would have been pleased to see the niece he admired commemorated in this way. Michael Broughton has been my contact and he could not have been more kind and helpful. I am very grateful to Hugh Tempest-Radford of Unicorn Press for approaching me about publication and taking much care with the production of the book, and the College for publicising it. Finally, I would like to thank H.R.H. Prince Philip, Duke of Edinburgh for contributing such a charming Foreword.

– 1 –
The Admiral's daughter

IN THE VERY CENTRE of the City of Cambridge stands the Senate House, an imposing white stone building dating from 1722, which has been described as 'A most elegant blend of the English Wren tradition and the new Palladianism'[1] . This is the heart of the University, formerly the meeting place of its Council, and still the hall where all degrees are conferred. It is an impressive setting for ceremonies, a single galleried room with an ornate plaster ceiling and chequered marble floor, and at the front a dais backed by wooden panelling, featuring four Doric columns which frame the action.

One day in June 1977 the room was packed with people, predominantly men, in the academic dress appropriate to great occasions, gowns and hoods. Those with doctorates wore scarlet bands edging their black gowns; others with higher degrees had scarlet gowns faced with grey silk or clashing pink. They were assembled for the installation of a new Chancellor, a rare occasion since the term of office is not limited. The subdued conversation quickly subsided, and all stood as the Vice-Chancellor's procession entered from the East, preceded by a mace bearer. Two Esquire Bedells[2] conducted the Chancellor to a grand chair on the dais, and meanwhile a second procession made its way to the South Door. The Duke of Edinburgh, wearing a scarlet gown and carrying a velvet bonnet, escorted by two senior Heads of House, was greeted by the Vice-Chancellor and shown by the Esquire Bedells to his seat. After a performance of music he was greeted formally by the Vice-Chancellor.

It was a remarkable occasion, because Cambridge University had not chosen a royal Chancellor since 1847, when Prince Albert was elected. Moreover, the Vice-Chancellor, who had been deeply involved in the negotiations and every detail of the arrangements, was a woman, Rosemary Murray. She was nearing the end of her two years of office as the first female head of the University, and was consequently the first woman to lead the ceremony of admission of a Chancellor. Taking the Duke by the right hand she asked him in Latin to swear fidelity to the University and he replied 'Ita do fidem'[3]. He was then robed in the Chancellor's gown, black with lavish gold ornament, and a train carried by a page. After more

Installation of the Chancellor, 1976. Prince Philip leaving the Senate House after the ceremony.

speeches, the congregation was dissolved and a procession formed up, led by the Chancellor, now splendidly arrayed, and the Vice-Chancellor, a tall distinguished woman with white hair and sparkling blue eyes, standing out from the crowd of men.

How did Rosemary Murray come to be in this exalted position? Although many honours and achievements were to follow, this day marked the pinnacle of a long career of public service, academic endeavour, administrative excellence and a triumph over personal difficulties.

Rosemary had been in Cambridge over thirty years. She had come straight from wartime service in the WRNS to a rather lowly post at Girton College, one of only two colleges for women. It was hardly a step up in her career, because from 1939-42 she had been a Lecturer in Chemistry at Royal Holloway College in London and then briefly at Sheffield University. She needed great determination to integrate into the daunting social group of scholarly women and to revise her knowledge of chemistry, which had been put aside during the war years. Life in a women's college was familiar to her – she had studied as an undergraduate and doctoral student at Lady Margaret Hall in Oxford – but Cambridge was largely unknown and was different in many respects from her *alma mater*. As a fundamentally shy person she had difficulty in putting herself forward, but slowly she made her way up the ladder, becoming a Fellow and then a Tutor, which in Cambridge is a person responsible for the welfare of a group of students in a college. As a Fellow she was appointed to a number of College committees where her attention to detail and good judgement were recognised, and all the time she informed herself about University affairs; how the institution was governed, how the University and Colleges functioned together, what decisions were being taken at every level. This curiosity stemmed from her experience as a senior administrator in the forces, and also a character trait that was almost a compulsion, to dig deep into the facts of any situation she was presented with.

Rosemary eventually had tenure at Girton, and was increasingly respected, and there she might have remained had she not become involved in a movement to found a third college for women in Cambridge. She entirely shared the views of a group of senior women, and some men, who thought it shameful that there were so few places for girls at Cambridge University. As an Oxford graduate she would have registered the fact that those who did gain a place had not yet been granted the right to receive degrees.[4] Rosemary joined the Third Foundation Association as soon as it was set up, probably encouraged by some of the Girton Fellows who had been attending informal meetings for years, and was elected to the first Committee in 1952. The Chairman was the formidable Myra Curtis, Principal of Newnham College, whose organisational skills had been honed in the civil service.[5] She pushed the project ahead at great speed, aiming to open the new college for the Michaelmas Term 1954. A site was found and the method of admissions for the first year decided, but then came the question of identifying a Tutor-in-Charge who could manage the small institution. Prompted by a friend, Rosemary put her name forward and after some rigorous interviews was chosen.

It was as if Rosemary had been preparing for this post all her life. She had the academic credentials and teaching experience; she had been in charge of large numbers of women in the WRNS, where her administrative skills were developed; she had already been a Tutor; she knew personally the supporters (and detractors) of the scheme; and she understood the workings of the University. Later it was to emerge that practical ability, which ran in the family, was also very relevant to the job. Under her guidance, the new hall rapidly grew and flourished, becoming first an Approved Foundation and then, in 1972, a full College with its own buildings. Rosemary, in harmonious partnership with the second

Tutor, Robin Hammond, was during this period making decisions on admissions, rules, expenditure and the treatment of individual students, which would all cumulatively create the ethos of the future college. She threw herself into the task with enormous energy and, despite closely supervising every aspect, still found time to take on outside appointments as a Justice of the Peace in Cambridge, governor of several schools and colleges, membership of the Armed Forces Pay Revue Board and of the Lockwood Committee, set up to advise on a new university for Northern Ireland. She was invited on to committees of the University, sometimes as token woman but increasingly because of her useful contributions. This led naturally to election to the Council of the Senate in 1969, by which time her potential for high office was becoming clear. When New Hall achieved collegiate status, and Rosemary became its first President, the way was open for her to rise to the top job, since only Heads of Houses were eligible for the post of Vice-Chancellor. Nevertheless, she was greatly surprised to find herself in the running. One of her endearing qualities was a general humility and lack of personal ambition. In old age she described her career as a matter of luck, of being in the right place at the right time, but it had more to do with her outstanding qualities being recognised in whatever she undertook. She succeeded in a man's world by refusing to acknowledge any difference in ability between the sexes or even to notice gender. She was, however, by her middle years, a most attractive woman who turned many male heads and she developed a gentle, feminine style of diplomacy that made her friends and alienated no-one.

Some people were astonished when a woman was elected Vice-Chancellor and may have expected her to be just a figurehead. Those who already knew Rosemary were not surprised when she managed University business with great efficiency and pushed through many initiatives against the odds during her two years of office. The award of a DBE at the end of her tenure was truly well-earned. Still at the height of her powers, she returned full-time to New Hall for another six years until retirement age, contending with the difficulties of competition for women applicants from the newly mixed colleges and seeking to put New Hall on a better financial footing. Her retirement was a very active one, as she still participated in a host of committees, mostly external, but some, like the Botanic Gardens and the Veterinary School, connected to the University. Moving to Oxford in 1994 provided a new set of opportunities and the great pleasure of being near several members of her family. Until challenged by blindness she continued to serve the community in any way that she could find.

The attitude of service, which was at the heart of Rosemary Murray's character, had been deeply engrained on both sides of her family. Her father, Arthur John Layard Murray, joined the navy at the age of sixteen and worked his way up to become an admiral. Some of his relatives were in the armed forces, but Arthur's father was a partner in the publishing firm, John Murray, run by Arthur's uncle John Murray IV. The Murrays could trace a direct line back to John Murray I (previously MacMurray) who founded the firm in 1768, and ultimately to the Dukes of Atholl. One of Rosemary's great-great-grandmothers on the Murray side was Lady Charlotte Guest, an intellectual and philanthropist who translated the Welsh *Mabinogion*[6] into English and taught herself Arabic, Hebrew and Persian. She also showed herself to be a good businesswoman when she ran her husband's ironworks for several years. One of Charlotte's daughters married into the French émigré family Du Cane (originally Du Quesne), and her granddaughter Alicia Du Cane was Arthur Murray's mother. In the previous generation the eldest son of the Guests, a baronet, had married the daughter of the Duke of Marlborough. Arthur's sister Betty also married a baronet, Sir Richard Proby of Elton Hall Peterborough, so Rosemary Murray's family were always on the fringes of the aristocracy. The youngest sister of Arthur Murray, Rosemary's Aunt Barbara, worked for St Margaret's, at that time a Ladies Settlement in Bethnal Green, but during the War risked her life escorting Jewish people out of Germany and found homes and jobs for them in England. She was back in London during the Blitz, and after the War helped displaced persons in Vienna and volunteered for Relief Service in Greece, delivering food to villages in the mountains. Described as brave and indomitable, she was another model of selfless service for Rosemary. Both passed their 90th birthdays, were keen gardeners and never married.

Rosemary's mother was Ellen Spooner, the third daughter of Revd William Spooner, Warden of New College, Oxford, and Frances Wycliffe Goodwin. Many of the Spooner men were in holy orders, and the Spooner women had a tendency to marry vicars. William's grandfather was Archdeacon of Coventry and his godfather and uncle by marriage was Archibald Campbell Tait, later Archbishop of Canterbury. Frances Goodwin's father (Rosemary's great-grandfather) was Harvey Goodwin, who had to relinquish his Cambridge Fellowship when he married Ellen King, because in those days all dons were supposed to be celibate. He became Vicar of St Edward's Church, behind King's Parade in Cambridge and was a highly popular preacher and Principal of a Working Men's College started by Trinity men. He left to become Dean of Ely and finally Bishop of Carlisle. An avenue in Cambridge bears his name. The Goodwin family traced their lineage back to John Wycliffe the reformer through Bishop Harvey Goodwin's mother. They and the Murrays perpetuated the name: Warden Spooner's only son was christened William Wycliffe and Rosemary's youngest brother was Richard Wycliffe.

William Spooner is the best known of Rosemary's forbears, but for a quaint reason; his use of metathesis, colloquially known as 'Spoonerisms', such as 'the town drain' for down train. His wife did her best to forbid mention of these slips, but naturally the undergraduates enjoyed making up new examples. Rosemary knew some of the originals and did not mind quoting them in a speech to boys at his old school, Oswestry: 'kinkering kongs' instead of conquering kings, 'Will nobody pat my hiccup' (pick up my hat) and of the housemaid who fell out of a window and was miraculously unhurt, like a cat she 'popped on her drawers and walked away'[7]. Spooner was an albino with very poor eyesight, who nevertheless became a classical scholar at New College and then a Fellow. He never made a big contribution to his subject and he did not enjoy lecturing, but he was very good at supervising students one-to-one. In all these respects his granddaughter resembled him. Rosemary also inherited his acute observation of people and ability to summarise their character in a pen portrait. After twenty years in Oxford, Spooner chastised himself in his diary: 'none of it spent quite idly yet nothing I fear wholly mastered and made my own'[8]. A similar train of thought appears in letters of both Rosemary and her sister Frances written in their twenties. They had 'done nothing yet'. Clearly they all took to heart the saying, 'of those to whom much is given, much is expected'[9]. As Head of a College, Spooner was a huge success, chiefly because he was so likeable and such a generous host. He had an innocent appearance, disguising his shrewd insights – Rosemary may have learnt from this. Outside the college he was active in charitable works, trying to improve the lives of beggars, visiting the Workhouse school and supporting the University Mission in Bethnal Green. He enjoyed the variety, and in this Rosemary resembled him too. Mrs Spooner pioneered a successful scheme for teaching crafts

Frances and William Spooner, Rosemary's maternal grandparents.

to long-term hospital patients. They were an unusual looking couple because 'Frank', as he called her, was rather tall and towered over her husband. Rosemary resembled her in being dignified and composed and having 'good sense and plenty of determination'.[10] She described her grandmother as very human and sympathetic to the young – but she did think that it was not done to play cards on Sunday, or even to go on the river.

William Spooner was very close to his elder brother, Maxwell, who became a vicar and married William's sister-in-law, Catherine Goodwin. Their only son died of diphtheria in childhood, leaving them with two daughters, Ruth and Kitty, favourite cousins of Rosemary's mother Ellen. The two families stayed close, despite the physical distance from Oxford to Kent, where Maxwell had several parishes before becoming Chaplain to the Archbishop of Canterbury. They had much in common. They were products of 'that cultured, public spirited and godly society firmly rooted in the Church of England which was responsible for so much that was best in the life of the time'.[11] They visited each other's houses, loved parties, charades and practical jokes, and went for long walks together taking picnics. When Maxwell retired in 1921, the family returned to Oxford. Their daughter Ruth and Ellen's sister Rosemary both remained spinsters, channelling their amazing energy into good works. Eventually they kept house together in Polstead Road, Oxford, and Rosemary Murray was Ruth's lodger for some of her student years. Kitty married Ralph Inge, who became Lady Margaret Professor of Divinity in Cambridge and they lived in Trumpington Road with their four children until Ralph was unexpectedly invited to be Dean of St Paul's Cathedral. As Dean's wife, Kitty took on the social duties. In December 1924 the Dean wrote:

> 'Kitty has arranged several Christmas parties, and on this evening we entertained, to turkey, etc., all the virgers and guides and their wives. Our children, who are really very good actors, gave theatricals...'[12]

In the same month Warden Spooner was recording in his diary a visit from the Murrays:

> 'On Boxing Day Nellie, Arthur and their little girls came and we had our usual Boxing Day Feast and Charades...'[13]

He mentions that his brother Maxwell and family, his daughter Cath, and other friends and family were present. Rosemary, aged 11, would have remembered this and similar visits to the New College Lodgings. She became very fond of organising and acting in charades and was indispensable in helping with the big children's parties which the Murrays put on in their home at Christmas. The visit to the Lodge was the last before Spooner reluctantly moved out to No.1, Canterbury Road and handed it on to the next Warden. The children had loved playing in the narrow passageways, and being hoisted up in the basket on ropes that was the luggage lift. In summer they had the run of the Warden's large garden. They came to appreciate New College Chapel and its accomplished choir when they were older: as a student Rosemary frequently accompanied her grandmother to Evensong and helped with a Sunday School class for the choristers.

When Rosemary was born in 1913 the Murrays were still functioning very much like a Victorian family. They had servants: cook, housemaids and gardeners, soon joined by a nanny, a situation which gave them considerable freedom and leisure.[14] They read a great deal, exchanging and recommending books, they kept diaries, and when they went on holiday wrote journals that were passed around the relatives. Reading aloud was still very much part of their entertainment and remained so into the 1930s. Lengthy books such as Dickens novels were continued in daily instalments, exactly as the author intended. It was usually mother who chose and read the books, and she made sure to have one with her when they were travelling. In Grandfather Spooner's household, morning prayers were held with the servants and attendance at church on Sunday was a matter of course for all the family. If prevented from going to church for some reason, Ellen Murray would read a portion of scripture and instruct the children in it. By the time she was a teenager, Rosemary had a good grounding in Bible studies and was a critical listener to sermons. Although the earlier Spooners had been evangelicals, Warden Spooner and his extended family were middle-of-the-road Anglicans, not showy in their faith but striving to live a good Christian life, exhibiting hospitality, concern for any in their care and working especially for the under-privileged. William was an extremely popular Warden, and as he confided to his diary, 'I have had a certain gift for making friends with the men, convincing them that I really thought of them and cared for their interests ... cared for every side of College life'[15].

The Spooner women used their free time to become involved in what we would now call social work. As a young girl Catherine Goodwin accompanied her father, Bishop Harvey, to the Ely Workhouse and was able to institute some improvements. This led to her lifelong interest in 'moral welfare', which inspired her daughter Ruth and nieces, Rosemary and Ellen Spooner (Murray), all extremely active in their communities. Rosemary Spooner became a local councillor and was awarded the OBE for her hospital work. After her marriage, Ellen Murray was involved in a scheme called '100 Mothers' in Portsmouth, visiting slum families and doing preventative and rescue work with wives and young girls in trouble. She was an excellent organiser of people, something that the young Rosemary Murray quickly learned from her. Rosemary was used to being asked for help with her projects and naturally absorbed the idea that one should be useful to others in whatever circumstances one found oneself. This is what led her to be, at various times, a helper at a baby clinic, an ambulance driver, a canteen worker for the YWCA, a lecturer for the WEA, an appeal organiser for the Samaritans, a committee member of

'Henry Ford' on the way to Oxford; Rosemary in the driving seat.

Cancer Research, and a volunteer in a primary school, to name only a selection of voluntary rôles.

In Rosemary's youth, evenings were often spent playing cards or other games such as Mah Jong and Lexicon. Whist and Bridge were popular and she was particularly good at 'Racing demon', a competitive type of Patience where speed is of the essence. She learned to knit at an early age and continued all her life, taking orders for sweaters from members of the family and knitting squares for Oxfam. Amateur dramatics with other families resulted in plays, using home-made scenery and costumes, being taken into nearby schools or institutions. These plays may sometimes have been specially written: a fragment exists in which Rosemary acted Lady Clara Butt in "The Mysterious Pot", a Christmas tale performed with members of the neighbouring Wickham family in the cast.[16] The Murrays were keen filmgoers by the 1930s. Rosemary often went to the cinema with student friends in Oxford, sometimes seeing the same film more than once. Her favourites were adventures, such as *The Bengal Lancers*, a story of the Raj starring Gary Cooper, and detective films like *Bulldog Drummond* and Hitchcock's *The Man who knew too much*. During the War, Egham cinema provided one of the few entertainments near

Royal Holloway College and it was there that she saw her first colour film, *The Drum*, also about the Raj, and of course the latest bulletins of Pathé News. In the absence of television there was more emphasis on reading and throughout her life Rosemary's diaries recorded lists of books she had read or intended to read. She was a life-long member of the London Library, having joined in her teens, and while studying at Oxford went regularly to the public library to change her books. In Northern Ireland during the War she joined the Times Book Club. Arthur Murray was very left wing for a naval man and read the *New Statesman* from cover to cover, a habit which Rosemary copied in her teens and twenties.

There were still hansom cabs on the streets of London when Rosemary was young and she would be met at Oxford station by her grandfather's horse and carriage. The motor car revolutionised transport during Rosemary's lifetime, and again the Murrays were quick to take advantage. By the 1920s they had a capacious Ford named Henry, whose average speed was 20 m.p.h. Ellen Murray was the chief driver, taking the children to see her family in Oxford, a journey that took all day, and later ferrying them to and from boarding schools. She knew how to change the plugs, but sometimes had to get help with cranking the starting handle. Flat tyres and over-heating were not unusual and sometimes they helped out other motorists, towing cars that had stalled on hills. Treasure hunts in cars were a novel diversion in these days of little traffic. Rosemary learned to drive as soon as she was seventeen, largely by trial and error, with some instruction from her parents, and without having to take a test. They found it very useful to have another driver in the family who could chauffeur the younger children. In Oxford she regularly took Granny Spooner out in her own car. Rosemary kept lists of her longer journeys with precise mileage and times, soon becoming keen to break her own speed records. She could also change a wheel when necessary. It was not long before the Murrays ventured abroad in the car for holidays, first to France, and when Rosemary lived in Neuchâtel, to Switzerland. They were indefatigable as tourists, sightseeing with determined thoroughness and prepared to put up with considerable discomfort. They bought provisions for picnics rather than eating in restaurants and found accommodation as they went, often sharing beds. Rosemary did not travel in style until she went on official missions in her forties.

In an age when the telephone service was in its infancy, and the telephone used for urgent communications rather than chatting, letter-writing was universal amongst the middle and upper classes. The Murrays and Spooners maintained their close network by regularly exchanging letters, and the postal service was so good that they used it sometimes for people only a few streets away, expecting a reply next day. Rosemary never liked the telephone. She kept messages as concise as possible and abruptly said 'good-bye' when the business was done. Because it was such a large family, letters were often written to be read aloud or passed on; consequently not very many confidences or critical remarks were included, except when a warning was given at the beginning that the contents were private. The servants were not part of the reading circle, so their behaviour was often commented on and amusing anecdotes about people well outside the family clan were recounted. Ellen Murray was at the centre of this network: she wrote letters every day, often in odd moments waiting for a train or a visitor, and she frequently enclosed letters that she had received and was not averse to opening those addressed to her children before forwarding them. Favourite correspondents were her mother and her sisters, Rosemary and Cath. She wrote to her husband several times a week when he was at sea. As the six children grew up and went away to school the task became more arduous and she would ask the addressee to pass the letter on to a sister or brother. At Rosemary's school the girls were expected to write to their parents every Sunday and messages sent during the week were about items left behind and urgently needed, visits to the 'San' and arrangements for going out at the weekend. Ellen wrote mainly about domestic and social topics, her letters bubbling with energy. Even after the children left home she was highly influential in their lives and was the chief organiser of the family occasions which kept them all in touch. Rosemary's father communicated with his children in short, often didactic but kindly letters. He was very interested in their doings and their enthusiasms. To Rosemary, as she grew up, he liked to discourse on scientific matters, either explanations or just something he had read, such as a book on newly-invented plastics. He tried gamely to understand her research subject at Oxford. Eventually he acquired a typewriter and sent long, duplicated letters with added postscripts for each person, and while the family was in China he produced a regular journal for those back home, circulated to his mother as well as the children, aunts and cousins. Arthur's passion for sailing was passed on to Rosemary and her brothers, so they all wrote many accounts of races they took part in, expeditions around Chichester harbour in their dinghy and plans for sailing holidays.

Ellen and Arthur Murray; Silver Wedding, 1937.

John and Rosemary often corresponded about carpentry and mechanical equipment, subjects which they both found fascinating.

Echoes of past speech are heard in some words and expressions used by the Murrays; little signals that they were part of a group with a shared history. Rosemary and her mother, when asking a favour, write 'would you sweetly...?' They use 'eat' as a past tense instead of 'ate' and have certain unusual words such as 'tigging', probably of naval origin, for putting boats, rooms, clothes etc. in order. An expression Rosemary copied with amusement was 'How is the dear boy, bless'm', perhaps a favourite of one of the servants. The children often called their mother 'Mommon', a corruption of Maman, also found in other branches of the Spooner clan. Like every family they had nicknames. Ellen is 'Nel', her daughter Frances is usually 'Puss', Grandmother Du Cane is 'Nonna', Rosemary is often abbreviated to 'Rose', while initials are routinely used for identification, partly to avoid confusion because so many of the Christian names were passed down through the generations. Second names were often preferred: Alice Rosemary Murray (A.R. or A.R.M.) never used her first name. The Murrays had the upper class accent common to their circle; clipped phrases with lengthened vowels, the women speaking in quite a high register. Before the War, most of the members of Oxford and Cambridge universities would have spoken in the same way. Rosemary retained this cut-glass accent throughout her life, into an age when

Rosemary, Frances, Ann and John on Selsey Beach, early 1920s.

it sounded distinctly old-fashioned, but, being both superior and very audible, it served her well as an instrument of command.

A large family develops its own private world and becomes self-sufficient. Rosemary was fortunate to grow up in this kind of sheltered environment, but the experience of War service forced her, perhaps beneficially, to become detached from it. Once she achieved independence, she made her own way in the world with increasing decisiveness. Her life spanned a century of rapid change, in which women's lives evolved from being centred on domesticity to sharing in men's occupations. Though never a Feminist, Rosemary had an unshakeable belief in equal opportunities and led the way by example.

– 2 –
Early life and schooldays

Ellen Maxwell Spooner and Lieutenant Arthur John Layard Murray R.N. were married in the chapel of New College, Oxford in September 1912 by the Archbishop of Canterbury, Randall Davidson. The bridegroom wore full dress uniform of blue and gold, and the wedding cake was cut with his sword. The bride, attended by six bridesmaids, wore ivory satin with a lace train. She was described by the Archbishop as the prettiest bride he had ever married. Some 300 guests attended the ceremony and had tea in the quadrangle afterwards, and the list of wedding presents filled several columns of the newspaper. It was a grand start to married life, but the Murrays initially lived in fairly simple circumstances in an unpretentious house.

Rosemary was born on 28th July 1913 at South Leigh Cottage in the Saxon village of Warblington on the Hampshire coast, but not long afterwards her parents moved the short distance to Emsworth, a small town with a natural harbour, part of the extensive Chichester harbour. Arthur Murray was stationed at the large naval base at Portsmouth, though frequently away at sea. During the First World War he served in the Dardanelles. Then, as now, Emsworth was popular with sailors and walkers and had its own sailing club, a focus for social activity. Fishing, and especially oyster catching, was an important trade into the twentieth century, with boat-building an associated activity. The Murrays bought a house called 'Brookfield', destined to be their family home for nearly thirty years. It was a short distance west of the centre of Emsworth, set back from the Havant Road. The house was rambling, not overly grand, built of red brick with prominent gables and a veranda at the back overlooking a large garden. Here they could enjoy a rural life, in an area of natural beauty, but still within easy reach of the busy centre of Portsmouth by train from Havant, three miles away.

Emsworth offered a healthy seaside environment for bringing up children, and ready access to the harbour where the family could keep boats and go out sailing, either to explore the coastline or to take part in races at the local regattas. Hayling Island, with its sand and shingle beaches, proved an excellent spot for camping holidays and the Murrays eventually had a hut there. As keen walkers they appreciated the many footpaths and longer trails across the South Downs. Rosemary and her sister Ann developed a life-long interest in birdwatching from visiting Emsworth's two tidal ponds and the saltmarshes along the coast which attract migrating birds. The garden and various outhouses gave the children every opportunity for imaginative play, and one of Rosemary's early memories was of a donkey they owned called Jinny.

We are fortunate to have an account of Rosemary's birth, given by her grandmother Spooner in an emotional letter of congratulation on her twenty-first birthday.

> 'Bless you my dear child. I shall think of you on 28th and recall all the anxious time I spent the morning 21 years ago at South Leigh Cottage, waiting and waiting … to know whether you could be 'smacked' into life – and when Nurse Martin brought you to me in a bundle I was almost too overcome to hold you! … 21 years has not made me regret that 'smacking' but has made me even a little more thankful.'[17]

It seems that the baby was a good weight, because she refers to her as 'a delicious little fat lump of a girl for me to hold and love.' In the fashion of the times Ellen and Arthur Murray would probably have hoped that their first-born would be a son, but as they were young and anticipating having more children, the arrival of a daughter was greatly welcomed. It was only a matter of months before Ellen fell pregnant again. Rosemary was just one and a quarter when her sister Frances, later known as "Puss", was born, but she had, and retained, all the advantages of the eldest child: the parents' delight in each new achievement, their encouragement and teaching and their high expectations that she was somehow 'special'. She was considered 'the nicest thing ever hatched', admired by the extended family and the many visitors to the house. There is a glimpse of Rosemary as a toddler on a visit to 10, Keble Road, the original home of her maternal grandparents, which had been passed to Mary Goodwin, Harvey Goodwin's youngest, unmarried daughter, and his widow Ellen, (Rosemary's great grandmother whom she called 'Armoo').

> 'Yesterday was an epoch in A.R.'s life. She came out with our babes quite alone, adored by Cath and Paula – nursing their dolls – taking their hands – riding in Paula's chair – and having tea with them entirely unattended – and happier than words can say…'[18]

Catherine and Paula were the daughters of Dean Inge and Kitty Spooner, and the writer is Kitty's mother, Catharine Spooner, Rosemary's great aunt. Another account of the same visit, by Frances Spooner, recounted how Rosemary 'came up into the Nursery like Apollo, and at once attacked the Powber [sic], smeared me over with it – and herself – and was all honey-pot'[19]. Just a month before her second birthday, Rosemary was clearly a spirited and independent child. The relatives noticed her 'seeking eye' which took in everything around her. Meanwhile her baby sister Frances was happy and undemanding.

Cousin Ruth Spooner wrote perceptively,

'She is quite the most remarkable little girl I have ever seen – that preternatural gravity & the indescribable gleam glint glow of the smile when it does come'.[20]

Rosemary did not take to Ruth, who 'bore the repulsion bravely'. Being a musician she was alert to the sound of Rosemary's baby-talk in a low monotone. 'I wd Yike to sit on yr Yap Armoo'. Ellen Murray's sister Catharine, wife of Campbell Dodgson, the Keeper of Prints and Drawings at the British Museum, was equally captivated by Rosemary and took her to meet the former Prime Minister, Arthur Balfour. She dashed off a letter to Ellen, 'I must write to tell you how I admire A.R. She is so vivid & brilliant & alive – Mr Balfour couldn't take his eyes off her face & I'm not surprised.'[21] Certainly 'admire' is an unusual word to use of a small child and Rosemary clearly had qualities which made her stand out. Many years later she was to admit a young member of the Balfour family as one of her first students at New Hall.

According to Frances, Rosemary was told, 'Now that you have a little sister you must be a good example to her', and Rosemary, anxious to please her parents, always was good. It was not easy for Frances living with such a paragon and finding her continually favoured. She remembered that when they went to the Observatory in Oxford it was Rosemary who was taken by Granny's friend the Professor of Astronomy to look through the telescope: 'It was always Rosemary'. The Murrays had to wait seven years for a son – their third child Ann Olivia arrived in 1917 – and the birth of John Hallam Murray in 1920 was greeted with great rejoicing by the whole family. Then came two more boys, David and Richard. Rosemary may have felt up-staged, but by then she had established herself as leader of

Ellen Murray with Frances.

Rosemary Spooner ('Aunt Rose') with Rosemary.

Rosemary aged about 9.

The Murray children with their mother and nanny, minus Rosemary, who probably took the photograph.

the children and almost a substitute son. Her father, in particular, treated her exactly as he would have done a boy, encouraging scientific interests and teaching her sailing, painting and carpentry, and she responded by trying to excel in these activities. Both parents had confidence in her: at the age of eight she was allowed to escort Frances alone on the train to have their photograph taken in Portsmouth. At twelve she harnessed the donkey to a cart and took her little brothers for quite long drives. At thirteen, 'Daddy' gave her an air gun, news meriting ten exclamation marks when she wrote to tell Aunt Rosemary.

Life in the Murray family was never dull. Both parents were energetic, industrious and sociable. Ellen Murray was much involved in 'moral welfare' and used to cycle off to Havant *en route* for meetings in Portsmouth, leaving the children in the care of a live-in nanny. A bishop once described her as 'competent, dedicated and formidable', adjectives which could later be applied to her eldest daughter.[22] When her husband had his own ship, she felt it was a duty to visit all the sailors' wives in their homes to check that they were coping while the men were at sea. She opened 'Brookfield' for entertainments for many different local groups, especially the disadvantaged. Following her parents' example of hospitality to the poor, she put on a large children's party every Christmas, with presents, carefully chosen and wrapped, for each child. Groups of girls from institutions were invited for tea and games and she even took them for joy-rides in her car. An extensive network of relations on both sides of the family engendered a constant stream of visitors to the house. Ellen's favourite sister, Rosemary, came often and the two would talk and laugh together for hours. They had much in common because Rosemary was heavily involved in social work, carrying on an institution for the deaf which their mother had started in Oxford. She had been a Red Cross nurse in France in the First World War, mentioned in despatches. The young Rosemary absorbed the philanthropic outlook of these and other women in the family without question.

Return visits to their relatives took the Murrays to some impressive houses, chief among them the Warden's Lodge at New College, where William and Frances Spooner had lived since 1903. On becoming Warden, William had thoroughly renovated his lodgings, contributing £3,000 of his own money to the scheme, putting in a sitting room for himself over the arched gateway and building attic rooms for eleven servants. The front door opened on to a magnificent black and white tiled hall with a massive oak staircase leading to sixteen bedrooms. Downstairs were several grand reception rooms furnished in Victorian style with heavy mahogany furniture and drapes. The family breakfasted in one of these. Visitors were received in the drawing room, which had a Tudor ceiling, and the dining room was the setting for large formal dinner parties. One guest described the table: 'elaborate flower piece, two enormous silver mugs ... little clear glass pitchers of water, old silver, large salt cellars and pepper mills, silver dishes with the dessert around the flowers, candles and silver mugs'.[23] Uniformed maids waited on the diners, bringing soup, fish, partridges, omelette, jelly and fruit. This was prepared in a huge medieval kitchen, dating from the College's foundation, connected to larders, pantry, scullery and servants' hall. Outside there was stabling for four horses and the Warden's private walled garden. They would stay for a week at a time in Oxford, visiting all the relatives and close friends of the family.[24] Ninety-year-old Frances Murray still recalled the luxury of water bubbling up in the gigantic bath with bone-handled levers for taps, the narrow stairway leading to a room in the turret and the noise of the bells that summoned them to College Chapel.

Elton Hall, a grand house near Peterborough, belonged to Sir Richard Proby, who had married Arthur Murray's sister Betty. Visits here were infrequent as the families were not close, but their six children were similar in age to the Murray children; the eldest, Peter, two years older than Rosemary. He was to play a part in her life when she moved to Cambridge, and Claud, four years younger, was a companion on a visit to Austria in the 1930s. Elton Hall was a rambling, part-Gothic house, set in delightful gardens bordered by 200 acres of parkland. It was full of treasures including Old Masters, paintings by Gainsborough and Constable, and French furniture and clocks. Rosemary may have been allowed to see the fine library, full of rare books including a book of prayers annotated by Henry VIII.

Aunt Catharine's town house, at 11, Montagu Square, was a convenient pied à terre in the West End of London. Campbell Dodgson and Catharine Spooner[25] married in 1913 and lived in some style, entertaining the wide artistic circle in which they moved and always having time for family. Catharine studied at the Royal Academy Schools and liked to take her nieces to the summer shows, where in 1923 her portrait of Dean Inge was exhibited. She was an accomplished artist, known particularly for portrait drawings; the best, according to the Dictionary of National

Biography, were of her family and friends.[26] Ellen Murray always turned to her sister for fashion advice, and as the girls grew up they were taken clothes shopping by Aunt Cath. In the 1930s Rosemary usually stayed with her when she needed a bed in London. Having no children of her own, Catharine was particularly fond of Ellen's.

As young children, Rosemary, Frances and Ann had to be on their best behaviour when paying visits. They were particularly constrained when they went over to see their paternal grandmother at Fittleworth, near Midhurst, as she was very severe and particular about manners. 'Nonna', as they called her, lived in a big house with a brother and some of her sisters. To prepare for the ordeal, the children would sing in the car a disrespectful rhyme called Fittleworth Fair, made up by Ann, about 'the Iz and the Jule', their great aunts Isabel and Julia Du Cane. Rosemary and Frances once had to stay with them for a week, looked after by the cook. Frances also remembered staying with a friend of their grandmother's at Trengwainton, Cornwall, a property of 25 acres now owned by the National Trust. She and Rosemary were allowed to go for a walk in the gardens but warned not to pick anything. They came upon a particularly beautiful leaf, lying on the ground, and had an intense discussion about the correctness of taking it back to the house. Such was the rigour of their moral upbringing. Late in life Rosemary was still examining her conscience about decisions that she had made years earlier.

Rosemary did not go to school until she was seven. It was a private school in Havant with only a handful of teachers, but classes were small – five or six pupils in each – so she received plenty of individual attention. She already knew her letters and numbers and soon progressed to joined-up writing, keeping a note in her diary of the number of words written each day, 24 being a record. This is an early example of Rosemary's almost compulsive desire to tabulate facts: she loved making lists. She made friends at school and the diary records an endless round of tea parties with other children. The school served her well: in fact she often said that she had better Maths teaching from Miss Porter, a lady who wore a long skirt with a watch on a chain tucked into it, than at any other time in her life. Her school reports were carefully preserved. The teachers' remarks suggest that she developed rapidly in application and ability over the first three years and was marked out as a problem-solver in mathematics. Her appreciation of literature improved, but the English teacher concluded she was 'not greatly moved by language'; her compositions were 'a little commonplace in style' and her spelling weak. By 1925 when Maths was divided into Arithmetic, Geometry and Algebra, she was top in all three; considerably ahead of the other girls, if hampered by careless mistakes. Her mother found it exciting to have a daughter 'who may arrive somewhere'. There is an interesting observation on Rosemary's character at age eleven from the new Headmistress:

> 'Rosemary has a strong sense of justice and is beginning to develop a sense of responsibility but she is sometimes inclined to be a little self-assertive'.[27]

She was allowed to be assertive at home, where she was by then the undisputed leader of the five children, soon to be six when baby Richard arrived in 1925. They did not mind taking orders from Rosemary because she could make activities as mundane as clearing an outhouse seem fun. She always claimed that the boys and girls were treated equally by her parents.

At the age of nine, Rosemary discovered the Scout movement, thanks to the chance purchase of a book at a jumble sale. 'Scouting for Boys' introduced her to a world of camping, tracking and making fires. From then on she acquired the Boy Scouts Diary and filled in the certificate of membership inside, giving herself the rank of Scoutmaster of 'Our Society'. It was full of practical knowledge, and Rosemary learnt all 29 useful knots from the diagrams and spent her time obsessively practising them, much to the irritation of Frances, who refused to take an interest in scouting. Rosemary devised secret signs for her patrol to indicate messages such as 'war', 'good water' and 'I have gone home'. At the end of January 1923 she wrote in the diary, 'We went to Lucei's [sic] house for the afternoon we dressed up as boys and we were scouts it was lovely'. Rosemary had already bought herself a scout belt and lanyard and her teacher remarked that she was more interested in scouting than in Nature Study. So Rosemary's first great enthusiasm was for a male activity and she much preferred boys' adventure stories to the tamer novels written for girls.[28]

In the 1920s the school leaving age was 14: only 14% of girls went on to secondary education. Some of the Emsworth and Havant neighbours sent their daughters to the Girls Public Day School Trust (GPDST) High School in Portsmouth, but the Murrays looked round for a boarding school for Rosemary, and eventually her sisters, perhaps because they believed the teaching and range of activities would be better. Frances suspected it was convenient to send the children away, so that Ellen could spend more time on her social work. In July 1926 Rosemary, Ann and their parents visited Downe House, a girls' school in Berkshire. Rosemary immediately took to the Headmistress, Olive Willis, and the feeling seems to have been mutual. They were in some ways kindred spirits. They settled on the school and in November the Murrays had a trip to London to buy the distinctive uniform, staying with Aunt Cath. The main item was a green djibbah, a kind of knee-length tunic with a V-neck, under which was worn a long-sleeved Viyella blouse or thick white jersey. Long brown stockings and green woollen pants, also worn for gym, completed the ensemble. Outerwear was a woollen purple coat, a felt hat and a purple blazer. Can it have been a coincidence that these were the colours of the suffragettes, who had recently won the right for women over 30 to vote and were still campaigning for it to be extended to those over 21? In summer the girls wore lighter cotton tunics of any colour, and all the year round they could change out of uniform after Games.

Downe House had started at Charles Darwin's house in Kent and then moved to a large site at Cold Ash near Newbury, Berkshire in 1922. Miss Willis was a somewhat eccentric woman, with strong views on education. She regarded the school as an extended family where every individual was valued and given as much freedom as was consistent with the good order of the society. She believed in long walks and fresh air, gymnastics and dancing, and she disliked regimentation and exams. Pupils were encouraged to explore and experiment and become rounded personalities. Christianity was central to the school's ethos. Each day started with compulsory school prayers before breakfast. The Headmistress usually took the services and preached a sermon on Sundays, concluding, Frances remembered, with a 'tear-jerking hymn'. Her religion was somewhat vague and mystical: in her own words, 'I tried to lead the girls to find their own spiritual way'.[29] Above all, the ideal of service was uppermost. As most of the pupils were from well-to-do families, Olive wanted to make them aware of their good fortune and encourage them to give something back to any community in which they lived. This was entirely in accord with the Murray/Spooner philosophy, and would have been a compelling reason to choose the school for their daughters. Rosemary started in the Upper IIIrd in January 1927.

There is no doubt that Olive Willis was a rôle model for the young teenager. She exerted a strange power over the girls and had strong likes and dislikes: some pupils could be quite neglected and misunderstood. Rosemary fitted her preferred mould – obedient, self-sufficient, energetic – and rapidly became one of her favourites. Olive was a hardy character who seemed to be stimulated by adversity. She wrote that she 'rather welcomed any emergency, such as lack of light or water, as good for both staff and children'. In the early days water from the well turned brown in the hot summer, so she pronounced it good for the health. When Downe moved to Cold Ash many girls had to sleep outside because the dormitories were not ready, and this became an accepted tradition for the summer term. For the first three years, before a chapel was built, services were held in the open cloisters throughout the year. The food was poor, stodgy suet puddings and bread which sometimes contained 'strange bodies'. In winter the school buildings were always cold: the electric generator, never very efficient, had a habit of breaking down. Rosemary was soon used to lack of hot water, resulting in cold baths. In March 1931 she recorded, 'Last night the temperature of our room went down to 8 degrees below freezing ... The water in my jug froze ...' Olive Willis, working in an unheated room, would keep the window open, just as Rosemary did later at New Hall.

Though not exactly a pioneer, because a number of girls' boarding schools had been founded in the nineteenth century, attracting formidable heads like Dorothea Beale at Cheltenham Ladies College and Frances Buss at the North London Collegiate School, Olive Willis needed some courage to found a new school. Together with a friend from Oxford she raised the money to buy a house and over two years built up the number of pupils to 30. They moved to get more space, and by Rosemary's time the school housed over 100 girls. It was still small enough for everyone to know each other and Olive deliberately arranged a lot of interaction between the different age groups. Cold Ash had been built on a hilltop for a religious order called 'The School of Silence' who embraced the simple life. All the buildings were white with red pantiles; there was a large three-storey house with two halls and 36 bedrooms and a three-sided cloister and small amphitheatre. Two houses in the grounds were used for staff or for dormitories. By the time Rosemary arrived, a gym, sanatorium, laboratory and six classrooms had been added and the chapel transported from Kent and reconstructed. To her delight a library was added in 1929.

Downe House in the 1920s. Main building with cloisters in the foreground.

'You can go and read in there whenever you like and there is no talking allowed there'. Rosemary did not object to the plain, monastic style of the buildings; in fact they may have influenced her taste, because when it came to writing a brief for New Hall's architects she was looking for simplicity, light and a place where concentration was not disturbed by too much decoration.

Rosemary settled into Downe very happily and was quickly promoted by Miss Willis. She wrote to tell her parents the thrilling news:

> 'Now!! Here is the thing which I long to tell you most, so much that as I write I quiver all over and little squiggles go all down my back. Last night when Miss Willis came in to say goodnight she said to me, "Do you find the work fairly easy in your form?" and I said "Yes, I think so, *so* far…" "Then I am going to move you up to the *lower fourth*" '.[30]

Rosemary's excitement was tempered by anxiety because she would be the youngest in the class and would have to work '*awfully hard*'. Meanwhile Miss Willis was writing flatteringly to the Murrays, concluding that of the new intake 'Rosemary is quite the most promising – and in fact the nicest'[31]. In March, despite being in the 'San' with a sore throat, she wrote to Aunt Rosemary, 'I still think school is lovely

I am glad to say'. Her reports for the first year were encouraging but not brilliant. Her mathematical talent was soon recognised, and in the second year her work was described as exceedingly promising, 'always thoughtful and interesting'. However her conduct came in for some criticism: she was accused of unnecessary prattle, being argumentative and asserting herself too much in the Maths class. The teaching at Downe was variable in quality, and a couple of years earlier the School Inspector had criticised the lack of time devoted to Science. In her first two terms Rosemary did none at all. There was definitely a bias towards the Arts subjects, unluckily for Rosemary since she was already a scientist at heart. Plentiful opportunities for Music and Art seem to have passed her by, but she did participate in dramatic productions, preferring to be backstage. She soon became bored with history and was not very good at literature or languages. Her first science reports in 1928 described her as 'decidedly good'. Her schoolmates soon began to respect her talent and she acquired the nickname 'Archie', short for Archimedes. From the Lower Vth onwards all the reports are about chemistry and she had little tuition in physics.

Olive Willis seemed to attract, and easily tolerate, eccentrics. Rosemary's favourite teacher was Miss Maria Nickel, a gifted but very strange European lady, reputed to be an aristocrat, who came to teach geography and chemistry. She was a mannish person, dressed usually in a long brown serge overall and wide-brimmed felt hat and speaking in a deep voice with a strong accent. Somehow she had acquired skills in architecture and construction which she put to good use in ambitious building projects for classrooms and the chapel. Her methods were unconventional and she built with concrete blocks, doing some of the heavy work herself. She taught carpentry to any girls who were interested and did most of the school's maintenance work. Rosemary, fascinated to see this woman doing the work of a man, became her devoted slave, following her around in her free time, learning about plumbing and roofing and scaffolding, and probably also how to give orders to workmen. It was a most unlikely opportunity for a girl.

Arthur Murray was equally intrigued by Miss Nickel. He searched her out one Seniors' Weekend, hoping to see her in Sunday clothes: 'not in workshop – tried new building – found there a refrigerating plant she'd just put in ... then at last found her in the kitchen putting cream into 100s of meringues ... & smoking a cigarette the while ...'[32]

Parents were always welcome at Downe: Miss Willis liked to get to know them and to have an audience for dramatic, musical and other events. The Murrays drove the 60 miles from Emsworth two or three times a term, a three-hour journey, bringing with them substantial picnics. Frances joined the school a year after Rosemary when she was 14. Frances was good at games and keen to get into the choir and orchestra: she felt she had simply been wasting her time until she went to Downe, where there were so many activities filling the days. The two of them greatly looked forward to the outings with their mother and siblings, often taking friends along with them. Occasionally they were invited to tea in Newbury by the parents of other girls. There were exeats too, keenly anticipated. For Rosemary the best were visits to Aunt Rose in Oxford, who took her swimming and on the river. The two became firm friends as Rosemary matured, despite the generation gap. Frances described Rosemary as 'terrifyingly duteous' and rebelled against school discipline herself, getting a reputation for disobedience which must have pained her sister. Unlike Rosemary she had little respect for the headmistress.

Miss Willis valued physical activity highly. Gymnastics and a kind of statuesque Greek dancing took up a lot of time, culminating in massed outdoor displays by the whole school at the end of term. Rosemary was tall for her age and too stiff and inaccurate in her footwork to please the dancing teacher. A life-long dislike of dancing may be traced back to these classes! On the other hand Frances, with her petite frame, was a 'natural'. Team games – lacrosse, netball and cricket – were not really to Rosemary's taste either, although she played in school teams. She persevered at tennis because her mother was anxious that she should be able to join tennis parties in the summer: it was a necessary social accomplishment. Best of all she liked walking, which was much encouraged. So long as they went in threes, the girls could roam in over 100 acres of woodland and on a grassy hillside with extensive views over the Kennet Valley.

One of Olive Willis's methods was to assign the girls to frequently-changing groups for both dining and boarding. They were accommodated in small dormitories, usually of four girls of different ages, and switched round each term. In this way they learned to appreciate others, or at least tolerate them. There was always much chat about who was rooming with whom, and gossip sounding much like a schoolgirl novel. 'P----- is infernally cheeky and bumptious and lazy and untidy to the last degree. And I can't squash her… It will be lovely when you come back to

Parents and friends watching mass dancing at Downe House, c. 1930.

sleeping in that lovely room in Bolton West'[33], wrote one of Rosemary's friends. Rosemary was a popular room-mate because she was tidy and companionable and helpful to the younger children. Inevitably the teenage girls occasionally had crushes on each other. Rosemary's superior talents made her a subject for hero-worship, especially as a Senior in her final year, and one girl wrote in 1929, '…even though I have, I think, no longer got a pash on Archie I still think she is quite the most wonderful person here. And very far from being ordinary, so there.'[34] Rosemary developed a great affection for an older girl in her class, Marjorie Verney, and was gently reminded by Matron how silly it was to have 'pashes'. Nevertheless she continued to admire Marjorie long after they left school and was especially happy in her company. Of a rather boring skiing party in 1937 she wrote, 'Marjorie makes up for everything'.

Rosemary must have been delighted to discover that Downe had a Girl Guide troop. Scouting and Guiding (she didn't make much distinction) continued to be an absorbing interest throughout her school life. As a member of the 3rd and 4th Cold Ash company she rose from Tenderfoot to Troop Leader by 1930, when Miss Willis advised her to take a break while preparing for her exams. By then she had an impressive range of badges, all carefully listed in the diary. At the age of sixteen she was taking Guides in the absence of the Captain, a teacher. She was very good at devising games for them: it was not so different from playing with her brothers and sisters or helping her mother with the groups she entertained at home, and she knew how to make it fun while maintaining authority. She had high standards for the guides and for herself: one day in 1930 she recorded 'Guides very slovenly and I took them very badly and laid an Indian trail for them – very unobservant they are.' In what was really her first teaching role she coached them for their badges, inspected them, led marches and supervised lighting fires on which they cooked breakfast or supper. The surroundings of Cold Ash were perfect for these pursuits.

A retired army colonel who lived nearby set up a small-bore shooting range in his garden and offered to teach the Guides to shoot. Rosemary took full advantage of this opportunity and became one of the best shots, averaging 73% for 10 attempts. In an early letter Rosemary described with great excitement how Col. Leicester prepared a nature trail for which they had to spot broken branches to find their way, and afterwards provided an enormous tea at his house. Later on he taught them signalling and prepared them for the Ambulance badge. He took the Cadets, including Rosemary, to a Berkshire County rally, where they were inspected by Queen Mary. Clearly he was quite a hero for Rosemary and they kept in touch for years after she left school.

In March 1929 Rosemary spent ten days in the Sanatorium with measles. The interruption to her studies came at a bad time, because she was due to take the School Certificate exams in mid-July. It seems that revision was not properly supervised, for in May Rosemary was still busy with the Guides, collecting more badges and captaining the shooting team, though 'almost in despair' about chemistry. In June she was in the Guard of Honour for Princess Mary, honorary President of the Girl Guide Association, at another County Rally. Predictably she struggled with the examination papers – theoretical chemistry was 'absolutely beastly'– and emerged with Third Class Honours, a disappointing result that did not reflect her ability. There were credits in chemistry, algebra and geometry, but she failed trigonometry. Her best results were in the English papers, for which the students had been thoroughly prepared. It is interesting to note that Frances, who was not singled out as 'clever', in her turn achieved Third Class Honours, with credits in all subjects except maths, and so did better than her elder sister.

The pressure was still on for Rosemary, as it was decided that she would take the Oxford Entrance exams the following year and apply to read chemistry at Lady Margaret Hall (LMH). The school considered her keen, methodical and hard-working but they could not provide the standard of teaching she required, except in mathematics which was taught in the VIth Form by the Deputy Headmistress, Lilian Heather. Everyone loved Miss Heather, who had a friendly and sympathetic nature and was well-qualified, having studied maths and chemistry at Holloway College. Unfortunately she had many demands on her time and was not infrequently called away from Rosemary's lessons. Rosemary found herself stretched by the maths syllabus but Miss Heather was not too concerned, writing in summer 1930, 'Rosemary always works splendidly, with great concentration and determination. Her analytical mind makes her most interesting to teach'. She expressed the hope that Rosemary would be able to spend more time on maths next term. Meanwhile Miss Willis, who was on record as saying 'exams are only a sideline', praised Rosemary for being a great help to the school. Clearly no-one was helping *her* to prioritise her activities and organise her exam preparation. Consequently in the Michaelmas Term, with exams looming, Miss Heather was forced to admit, 'She is having to hurry over the very long syllabus for the College Entrance examination, and is not finding it easy to assimilate her work thoroughly'.[35] Things were no better with chemistry, for which she had an external tutor and worked in a shed with inadequate equipment.

In January 1931 Rosemary began her final term at Downe. When she filled in her application to LMH she left out '3rd class honours', but was eventually required to admit to it. Then came a terrible setback: a major 'flu epidemic swept through the school, at its peak confining 100 girls to bed. Rosemary was told that she was to be sent home to avoid the infection, or at least to get it over before the exams. It was devastating.

> 'It gave me such a shock and it seems so awful to go home in the middle of the term and also to miss twelve lessons a week with Miss Heather.'

She was sent schoolwork, which she got through in the mornings, and was then pressed into service by her mother, running errands and trying to operate a hectograph to print posters supporting the miners' strike. On return to school the three scholarship candidates were quarantined in a house in the grounds and teachers came to them, but by mid-February they were allowed back into the main school and Rosemary resumed her prefectorial and Guide duties. Miss Willis advised them against cramming: far from it – Rosemary played in matches, read the lesson in Chapel and worked the epidiascope for evening lectures.

On March 2nd she sat the first maths paper. 'It was an absolutely awful paper and I could hardly do any of it, even Miss H. did not think it was very nice.' The second one was not so bad and general knowledge went quite well, with questions on education, the press, wireless and monarchies. (It may have been this experience that gave her the idea for New Hall's general entrance paper.) Rosemary was very lucky with the chemistry paper as two questions she had prepared came up, on the commercial preparation of chlorine and the Periodic Table. Practical chemistry followed; an analysis estimating the percentage of water of crystallisation in blue copper sulphate. Next day the external chemistry teacher, Miss Rippon, decided to drive her to Oxford to see the laboratories where she would shortly be taking more practical exams. It was Rosemary's first sight of the new Dyson Perrins Laboratory where she was to spend so much time in the coming years. It also seems to have been the first time she encountered a Bunsen burner: 'it was all most exciting'. They also visited the physical chemistry labs at Balliol, which were underground, with moss growing on the damp walls, 'like an alchemist's cellars', thought Rosemary.

The interviews and practical in Oxford were spread over two days. Rosemary was able to stay with her grandmother at her substantial North Oxford villa in Canterbury Road, a short walk from Lady Margaret Hall. The examinees had lunch together in Hall, and Rosemary discovered that there was only one other girl taking chemistry, (who in the event was unsuccessful), but for the examination they were joined by several Somerville candidates. Rosemary had no success in analysing the white substance they were given. She did better with volumetric analysis. The same day she had an interview with the Principal of LMH, Lynda Grier, whose opening remarks were about William Spooner, Rosemary's grandfather, who had been one of the Founders of the College. In those days it must have been an advantage to have such an eminent connection. The second interview was with Miss Orr-Ewing, Tutor for science subjects. She advised Rosemary to learn some physics before starting the course. The third interview was more testing and technical. The two examiners went over her paper and asked 'the most awful questions'. It appeared that she had made a lot of mistakes in the calculations. However, afterwards she maintained that the script they had on the desk was not hers – but she was too shy to point out the error![36] When she became an interviewer herself she drew the conclusion that you never know what the candidate is thinking.

There was no time to dwell on the unsettling experience, because the very next day she was to appear before the Queen, representing Downe House at the opening of a Settlement in Peckham for which the girls had raised money. Rosemary was wearing her purple school uniform, but when they arrived they found the girls from all the other schools wearing white. Her teacher rushed her to a nearby shop to buy a white frock and she was back in time to see the Queen arrive and declare the Settlement open. A bishop read the names of the schools and 'we went up in twos and made our curtsies one by one'. Rosemary took all this in her stride: it was not her family's way to be overawed by royalty.

At last the Oxford entrance results came in a telephone call from LMH. Rosemary was offered a vacancy for 1932. 'It was the most extraordinary thing that has ever happened,' she declared. Miss Heather clasped her round the waist and jigged up and down, her schoolmates shouted acclaim and congratulations came from all sides. All three candidates had been successful, so Miss Willis awarded the school a half holiday.

There was some question about what further exams Rosemary would have to take for LMH, but her mother eventually managed to see Miss Grier and it was agreed that she need not re-take Maths, which she had failed. Rosemary could therefore look forward to an eighteen month gap between school and university. The Murrays were soon busy deciding how she might use it profitably by improving her languages and widening her horizons as well as preparing for her studies.

– 3 –

Launching out: Neuchâtel and Oxford

ONE DAY MISS WILLIS CALLED ROSEMARY into her study and asked her if she would be able to go to Switzerland with the Verney family, should they invite her. 'I was so taken aback that I hardly knew what to say', was Rosemary's diary entry, but of course she wanted to go. She adored Marjorie Verney, a musical and artistic girl who like Rosemary was a Senior,[37] and she had met her parents, Sir Harry and Lady Rachel, quite recently when they came over to visit Downe. They had taken her and a couple of other girls out to supper with Marjorie. Her first impressions were that 'the Verney parents are awfully nice and papa is very amusing. Lady R. is very sort of quiet'. They were an aristocratic family with an estate beside the Menai Straits in Anglesey. Sir Henry, the 4th baronet, had been brought up at Claydon House in Buckinghamshire where Florence Nightingale, his great aunt and sister to his grandmother Lady Parthenope Verney, had spent many years. The holiday in Switzerland would prove to be a memorable one: the start of a lifetime friendship between Rosemary and Sir Harry and perhaps the first time she was truly treated as an adult.

Meanwhile, Ellen Murray had been making enquiries about places where Rosemary could spend some time abroad. The Murrays were not the sort of people who patronised finishing schools, but it was usual for girls in their set to have a few months in Europe after their schooling to round off their education. Some near neighbours, the Selwyns, had sent their daughter Lucy to Colombiers in Switzerland where she stayed with a family as a paying guest and took some French courses at the nearby University of Neuchâtel. It was arranged that Rosemary should overlap with her there, spending the summer improving her French and German and enrolling in the Autumn Term for a course of physics. The invitation to join the Verneys on holiday fitted in very well with this plan. They were to depart for Geneva and the village of Chateau d'Oex in mid-May and stay for a month. From there it was an easy journey to Neuchâtel, then a town of some 22,000 inhabitants, on the shores of the lake of the same name. Initially it was planned that Rosemary would return home for Christmas.

Sir Harry Calvert Williams Verney, 4th Baronet.

Rosemary hardly had time to reflect on the sadness of leaving Downe. She was pleased with her final 'jaw'[38] with Miss Willis, who said complimentary things about her, and her last school report in which she had 'excellent' for conduct: 'There have only been about four others in the history of the school', she recorded proudly. The end of an era only really sank in when they went to Paddington to see the school train depart for the Summer Term. '...it did make me long to go back to Downe', she wrote. Living at home, she kept herself busy taking the local Guide troop, with whom she became very popular. Her father, who had just arrived back from Gibraltar, took her to see HMS *Victory*, and then to dinner aboard his ship, HMS *Montrose*, lying in Portsmouth harbour. She also accompanied him when he went to see his Uncle Louis and the three aunts at Fittleworth. The Murrays put on a dinner party at 'Brookfield' as a prelude to the local Sailing Club dance, inviting three of Arthur's officers. Rosemary was being gently introduced into society. Her father explained how to divide her time between the guests sitting on each side, making sure to talk to one during the first course and the other during the second, and because she was shy, they devised topics of conversation in advance. When one of them successfully introduced a subject, they would put out a breadcrumb as a signal to the other. This training served her well in later life. Aunt Barbara, anxious that she should develop an interest in social welfare, invited Rosemary to the St Margaret Settlement, Bethnal Green, to see the work they were involved in: a babies' play centre, a vocational school where boys were learning technical drawing and girls dressmaking and cooking, an experimental day nursery and two elementary schools. Rosemary was genuinely interested in these initiatives.

Arthur Murray felt it appropriate to give his daughter some advice when 'starting a fresh stage in furrin parts'[39]. She was to remember that quite a few people she would meet would not have seen an English person before, and would 'unconsciously judge England by the impression they get of YOU'. With the Verneys, Rosemary took the Newhaven to Dieppe crossing, priding herself on eating sandwiches while they were all feeling sick. They travelled by train to Paris and were whisked in a taxi past the Louvre and Notre Dame to the Gare du Lyon for the overnight journey to Geneva. Here they stayed for a few days. Sir Harry Verney's status as a Liberal MP gave him contacts at the League of Nations and he took the party in twice to listen to debates featuring Lord David Cecil, on the prevention of war, and M. Briand, the retiring President of the Commission. He was impressed by Rosemary's interest in current affairs and discussed with her a report he was reading on Britain's Industrial Future.[40] They had many conversations about politics in the weeks ahead. A steamer trip on the lake relieved the summer heat and they wandered round the cathedral, botanic gardens and Jardins Anglais, stopping for the occasional ice. On the final day Sir Harry decided that he wanted to ascend the Salève, a mountain just over the border in France. Rosemary was the only one who volunteered to go with him, so together they took a tram to the foot of the cog-wheel railway, something new to her. 'It goes up so slowly with awful bumps and creaks… in some places the line is about 35 degrees sloping upward'. At the top a panorama of mountain peaks surrounded them. Mont Blanc was identifiable through the clouds, but Rosemary seems to have been more impressed by the wild flowers: 'hundreds of blue gentians … lots of cowslips'. It may have been the first time she saw gentians in the wild. They were to become one of her favourite flowers, and at the end of her life she was growing them in her Oxford garden. The excursion à deux seems to have cemented her friendship with Sir Harry. He was *in loco parentis* and everyone called him 'Par' (pater) but his relationship with Rosemary was more than paternal. There was a true meeting of minds, with respect on both sides.

Next stop was Lausanne, to call on an acquaintance of the Verneys and then catch the steamer to Montreux, and finally the train, winding through the hills and across fields of white narcissi to Chateau d'Oex, a picturesque hamlet of chalets. The Verneys had stayed at Pension Morier before and were good at joining in village life, even singing in the church choir. They were keen flower collectors, a hobby which led them to explore paths all over the region, often through steep and rocky terrain. Rosemary delighted in the scenery and the plant-hunting, learning a great deal from the family about botany. In her usual fashion she made a list of the flowers they found, giving the Latin and common name, date and location. She was not the most observant in the party, though she made some finds, but she was certainly the most energetic, with considerable stamina. 'I feel as if I could go on walking for ever without getting tired', she said happily. Lady Rachel stopped for frequent rests and was 'fearfully tired' after walks, while Marjorie suffered from hayfever which sometimes kept her indoors, so Rosemary had some excursions on her own with Sir Harry, who had difficulty keeping up with her. They made a strange pair, the portly, sweating baronet puffing up hills, and the 18-year-old girl rushing ahead to search for flowers while he rested and changed into a dry shirt. Up above the snowline walking could be perilous. They experienced falling stones, dislodged from higher up and one day heard the thundering of an avalanche and saw 'clumps of snow go bouncing down splitting into two or three pieces at every bounce.' Rosemary followed Sir Harry blindly over a bridge of ice: 'The snow looked quite safe and Sir Harry went across with me following in his footsteps. I was absolutely terrified of going through because of the snow giving way'. For both of them it was a very special holiday. Letters which he wrote in later life show Sir Harry's great admiration and affection for Rosemary.

The holiday ended with a brief stop at Berne, where they linked up with Rosemary's mother, who had come out to make sure all arrangements for her stay in Neuchâtel were in place. Next morning the Murrays and Verneys departed almost simultaneously on trains in different directions; there was hardly time to say goodbye. 'I could easily have sobbed if I ever had, but it was mostly inward', wrote Rosemary. She had struggled to hide her strong emotions. Sir Harry recalled, 'I cried and you nearly did.

Not often does a scheme work out so perfectly'.[41] He had given her his precious barometer, which had belonged to his father, as a memento.

Rosemary and Ellen were met at Neuchâtel by Lucy Selwyn, the girl with whom Rosemary was to share a room. They went straight to the University to confirm Rosemary's registration for French classes, followed by Physics, and then went rowing on the lake. At supper in the large villa, 'Sambacour', Rosemary met the family she was to live with: Monsieur and Madame Pasquier, Madame's two brothers and sister (the Berthouds), Ebba, the Swedish fiancée of the Pasquier's son, Alphonse, and Mme Dubied, bosom friend of Mlle Berthoud, who was to give Rosemary extra French tuition. Rosemary was used to living in a large household and fitting in without fuss. She was quietly observant, and after a few days made an assessment of each person in her journal; '... then I can see how it changes as I get to know them better'[42]. This is an early example of Rosemary's rather detached interest in analysing character. She found Madame very kind, Mlle Berthoud 'a very managing body' and her friend 'a rather non-descript sort of person'. Rosemary was very ready to assist and was soon running errands, helping in the kitchen and picking fruit and flowers from the garden. Lucy helped her to settle in, showing her the village of Colombiers and the Planeyse, a grassy plain behind their villa that had been used as a runway since the early days of aviation. Here Rosemary was fascinated to see an 'autogyro', or early helicopter, demonstrated, 'most extraordinary to watch'. They played all kinds of games together, and with the family, went to the cinema and a sewing class and bathed in the lake. French lessons with Mme Dubied started straight away. German tuition had been arranged at the École Bénédick in the town. Rosemary went to the first lesson with 'much fear and trembling', and was relieved to find the teacher 'quite a nice old thing'. Although she had done some German at school, she took the easy way out and started again *ab initio*.

Rosemary had a little wobble of home-sickness, not for her family but for Downe, knowing that she was missing Seniors' Weekend. She so much wished she was there, in any capacity, but especially as an active Senior. 'To have missed being a Senior in the Summer Term is to have missed half the joy', she thought. The Murrays had obviously calculated that the school fees would be better spent on broadening her education. At the beginning of July, Lucy passed her French exams and prepared to depart. Always disorganised, she relied on others to do her packing, label her luggage and deliver her to the train, and she left several jobs for Rosemary to complete. Madame thought Rosemary would be very homesick without Lucy: on the contrary, she breathed a sigh of relief and moved into a single room with 'a lovely view of the garden and the sound of the fountain every night'.

Soon the University 'cours de vacances' began. Lectures occupied every morning, including Saturday, from 8 a.m. to 11 a.m., so Rosemary breakfasted alone and caught the tram to Neuchâtel at 7.30 a.m. At first she had some difficulty understanding the lectures. 'Interpretation' was comprehensible and very interesting, the tutor examining texts and explaining the meaning of words. 'Composition' she couldn't bear and soon dropped. 'Improvisation' was designed to get the students talking and Rosemary dreaded the thought that she might have to speak in front of the class. She was forced into it when an English boy gave a talk on public schools and the lecturer asked for a mademoiselle to explain the mysteries of English girls' schools. Despite the help of Mme Dubied and hours of preparation, Rosemary 'dried' and hadn't the courage to continue. 'How I blushed, and how my hands and knees shook!', she recalled. It was many years before she could overcome this shyness. Two sessions a week were 'conferences' with visiting speakers, and Rosemary had the good fortune to hear M. Piaget, a native of Neuchâtel and the first psychologist to make a systematic study of cognitive development in children. By 1931 he had formulated his theories on their judgement, reasoning and language. Rosemary went to all four sessions and was fascinated by the topic. 'He regards the child rather as a machine', she concluded. The University also arranged some charabanc trips for the students, and once they went by motor boat across Lake Leman to explore the wooded Île Rousseau. Rosemary was impressed by the Alpine scenery and enjoyed mingling with young people from many European countries. By the beginning of August when the course ended she felt she had made good progress with French, although people still commented on her terribly English accent.

During the vacation her private lessons continued, but there was plenty of free time. Rosemary found Ebba, the Swedish fiancée, a congenial companion for walks and swimming, and spent her evenings with the Pasquier family, often playing bridge and listening to the gramophone or to their newly-acquired radio. Monsieur liked to frighten them with stories of his Alpine climbing adventures. In the middle of the evening she would be dispatched to fetch the Benedictine from the sitting room. 'I really am becoming quite intimate with those little glasses', she wrote. A visit from her parents, Puss (Frances) and Granny Spooner enlivened the August holiday, despite unseasonal weather. The floods rose, the water of the lake was high and muddy and the clouds hid the mountains. The Murrays, in their usual intrepid fashion, carried on with their plans, making excursions to see glaciers and driving through the mountains round hair-pin bends to admire waterfalls and gorges and the snow-capped peaks of the Finsteraarhorn and Jungfrau. They ate picnics, sheltering under umbrellas: Rosemary recorded 'a freezing lunch in the wind'. Eventually they reached the pension at Chateau d'Oex where Rosemary had so recently stayed with the Verneys. 'I wish that they were here now', she thought, but instead she had the pleasure of Puss's company, the two of them talking in bed until late and laughing so much they 'nearly burst'. Puss brought all the latest school news, which is probably what motivated Rosemary to write and congratulate the new Seniors, 'an absolutely awful lot', she confided to her diary. Puss sketched whenever the weather relented: 'she really does draw very well', thought Rosemary and wondered what she would do in future. In fact, despite getting the grades for university, Frances had no interest in pursuing an academic career and took an art course at Ruskin College instead.

Returning to 'Sambacour' after the family holiday, Rosemary still had a month to fill. She did not take to two Swedish girls who came as lodgers, but she was quite capable of amusing herself, going for long solitary walks, arranging flowers and putting out bedding plants, sewing and knitting, and as October approached, studying physics books in French. The family were fond of her, calling her pet names: 'Rosalie' from a popular song and 'Mistinguet' after a dancer. 'C'est fou comme elle est gentile', they said. She wondered why they did not tutoyer her, but it didn't occur to her to propose it. As her French improved she was able to participate in the family's discussions of economics and current affairs. Uneasiness in European politics was reflected in the household. In discussions the Swedish girls always took the side of the Germans, while the Pasquiers were fervent supporters of the French. Madame would mutter 'sales Boches' if they passed a German car. Although Switzerland was a neutral country, plenty of soldiers were stationed there. An assault course ran beside the road near Colombiers, cavalry soldiers were billeted in the farm opposite the villa and the Planeyse was used for army exercises. On the roads they encountered groups of soldiers with pack-horses or on manoeuvres. Anxiety about renewed conflict was in the air, but Rosemary seems to have been unperturbed. What affected her more directly was the economic crisis, leading to a sudden run on the banks in September. 'All the bourses have been closed, and they all (the Pasquiers and Berthouds) were feeling as if it was the end of the world ... and everything was going to crash'. The Berthoud brothers were bankers and the family faced financial ruin. Reality impinged as Rosemary found that she could not change a cheque at the bank, and so was very short of money. Soon she read in the newspaper that England had come off the gold standard, which would lead to a very unfavourable exchange rate: the pound dropped by 25%. Ellen Murray wrote to warn that Rosemary might have to return home. Arthur Murray explained that his pay had gone down by £50 a year because of Admiralty cuts, and tax had gone up an extra £60 a year. He was also worried that there would be a revolution in Germany. To save expense they immediately cut down her French lessons from five to three a week. All the other tuition was pre-paid.

Many young women would have been anxious to return to the security of their families, but Rosemary was remarkably unfazed by the situation. She did not want to go home, and luckily the financial pressure was relieved by Aunt Cath sending a 'fat cheque'. The University term began and Rosemary had physics lectures every morning and a practical on one afternoon a week for which she was paired with a French girl. She also enrolled for 'Mineralogie' on Saturday mornings and fitted in more French lectures. She was disappointed to find that the physics was mainly mechanics, which she had covered with Miss Heather at Downe. However the practical work, such as verification of Boyle's Law, and use of the barometer and 'balance de precision' did become quite challenging and was a useful preparation for her undergraduate studies. The week before Christmas she proudly collected two certificates from the University. It was time to leave, but Madame Pasquier encouraged her to stay on over Christmas. Her family must have been surprised that she preferred to do this rather than join in the usual festivities at Emsworth. In the end she delayed until mid-January and was very sorry to depart, after a round of good-byes and a last 'sad supper' together. She left herself only a week to get ready for the next trip, a visit to the Home Fleet at Gibraltar, where her father was serving on the flagship HMS *Nelson*.

Aided by fashionable Aunt Cath, Rosemary shopped in London for dresses for the voyage and suitable underwear. 'Behind enormously thinned by corset!' she exclaimed. Dressmakers were called in to carry out alterations to clothes donated by her aunt and to make up material bought by her mother, who pointed out that she was 'over stock size'. Rosemary reacted without much enthusiasm to the new wardrobe ('quite nice'), and even less to the obligatory permanent wave, which made her 'look just like any [one] else'. Mrs Murray was the driving force, anxious that her eldest daughter, now of marriageable age, should shine in company and that the whole family should be a credit to Captain Murray. She organised the trip with great thoroughness. Rosemary was detailed to look after her younger brothers, David and Richard, and to give them lessons in writing and arithmetic, history, geography (of Spain), Latin and French. The necessary books were sent in advance, along with Trevelyan's 'History of England' for reading aloud in the evening. Marjorie Verney was invited as a companion to Rosemary, but in the end her place was taken by another friend, Alice Stainer. They went out in the elderly liner *Orsova*, taking four cabins on the lower deck. No account of the stay has been preserved, but we can be sure that Rosemary was well-prepared for the many formal dinners in Gibraltar, where her father would have hosted some on his battleship. Recent experience had given her plenty of topics of conversation. Several gold-crested invitations to dances at Government House were received. Rosemary still disliked dancing but did her duty, partnering Lieutenants, Captains and Commanders. Her dance card was usually full. The Fox Trot, Waltz and One Step were the dances in vogue, set to sentimental tunes such as 'Apple Blossom Time' and 'Goodnight Sweetheart'.

Rosemary was probably not sorry to return to Emsworth for the summer of 1932. There was the usual pleasant round of parties and dinners, tennis matches and practical activities. She greatly enjoyed the opportunity to sail again and took part in the Hayling Regatta. A mark of her grown-up status was an invitation from the Proby relatives to a dance at Elton Hall. Aunt Cath also invited her to stay and began to introduce her into London society, including her in the many dinner parties she hosted and still keeping an eye on her outfits. When Rosemary and Frances went to a private view at the Royal Academy, 'Aunt C. had to stop on the way to buy us gloves'. Trips to the hairdresser became a standard chore. In June Rosemary went back to the Seniors' Weekend at Downe for the first time. Old members and their parents were always given a warm welcome by the school, and she no doubt experienced the adulation of her former

Matriculation of the 1932 intake at Lady Margaret Hall, Rosemary in the centre.

schoolmates, many of whom had written in sycophantic terms when she was at Neuchâtel: 'Darling Archi ... willingly would I come and grovel at your feet' gushed one of them. In July Rosemary stayed in London for ten days and fitted in some chemistry and physics coaching in an effort to prepare for the coming term. She had a month in Grasmere with the family and then it was time for the younger children to go back to school and for a quick dash to London to buy two hats and a coat before travelling to Oxford.

Rosemary matriculated on Saturday, 8th October 1932, wearing the new cap and gown which had cost her 10/6. It was the start of six happy years at Oxford, although at the time she thought no further than the first three, which would lead to a B.A. degree. Oxford had been awarding degrees to women since 1920, the same year in which Cambridge voted to remain 'a men's University – though of a mixed kind'[43]. Becoming an undergraduate was an easy transition for Rosemary after the Neuchâtel experience, and Oxford had been almost a second home since her youth. Granny Spooner's large house on the corner of Canterbury Road was conveniently close to Lady Margaret Hall, and since 1929 Aunt Ruth had lived nearby at 9, Polstead Road, where Aunt Rosemary joined her in 1940. Rosemary frequently had meals with one or other relative, meeting a much wider circle of people than the average undergraduate. The widowed Frances Spooner still moved in the higher echelons of Oxford academic society, offering generous entertainment to dons and visitors and old friends as she had done when mistress of New College Lodge. She particularly liked the company of young people. Ruth and Rosemary were very active in good works and determined egalitarians, involved in Ruskin College, which had been set up to provide educational opportunities for working men. They were noted for their hospitality to these students, and indeed to any needy people they came across: during the War they filled their home with refugees.

When Rosemary left for Oxford, her father sent an encouraging letter of advice mixed with praise. Using a naval metaphor, he wrote:

'…it was rather a serious & exciting occasion, launching out in your frail bark (I don't think!) into the ocean of University life. But as a matter of fact you have no cause for alarm – you have a good compass, plenty of common sense and savoir faire, & good brains. So I'm sure you'll find it all plain sailing. Think out any questions of conduct for yourself & having decided what's right, stick to it. … And go "all out" at anything you're doing – work or play or anything.

My dear, you may not be "out earning" yet, but you are "pulling your pound" on the rope – your Mother has told me – I forget the words – that when you're about the place she feels she's got someone to fall back on: and we're very proud of you.'[44]

Rosemary had probably expressed some concern about being dependent on her parents. It was still the case in many families that boys' education was thought to be more important than their sisters' and she must have been conscious that she was the first girl in her family to go to university. Her allowance was rather small, about £21 a month plus travel expenses, and nothing in the vacations. Looking back she did not find it generous, but at the time it sufficed and she kept meticulous records of income and expenditure to avoid over-spending. The Murrays were quite parsimonious – Ellen hated being asked for a 'sub.' – and scrupulous about paying back small sums that they owed each other, the women even buying each other's second hand clothes. This early appreciation of the value of money made Rosemary frugal all her life, though generous in her gifts to others.

It had been a foregone conclusion that Rosemary would go to Lady Margaret Hall, rather than Somerville, the other women's college. After all, her grandfather had helped to found it in 1878, though he was not in favour of awarding degrees to women, or even allowing them to take the same examinations as men; nor did he encourage his daughters to go to university[45]. Set in attractive gardens with an abundance of trees, the College was situated in a quiet corner of North Oxford next to the University Parks, with the River Cherwell running along its boundary. 'Talbot', designed by the architect Basil Champneys, was the main building, housing the elegant dining hall and library. There were four student residences, built in brick with stone facings, all with spacious rooms, comfortably furnished. An army of maids, cleaning, carrying coal for the fires and serving meals, made life easy for the girls. Rosemary was one of the first inhabitants of 'Deneke', the work of Giles Gilbert Scott, named after the choir master of LMH, Margaret Deneke. The building was part-funded by an American benefactress and newly opened in 1932. Rosemary had to take her own linen and eiderdown and went out to buy crockery as soon as she arrived: cocoa and coffee parties were an important way of getting to know her fellow students. There were only 150 in College, roughly the same number as at Downe, so it was quite possible to know everyone. She had not entirely conquered her shyness, but she did get on with most people and gradually acquired friends who were prepared to join in her many activities. Among these were the Junior Science Club, which held weekly lectures on topics as varied as Eugenics, viruses and X-Rays, and the Boat Club.

Students had to be equipped with a dark coat and skirt, worn with a white blouse and black shoes and stockings, for formal occasions. Gowns were obligatory in Hall and for lectures. They were invited in turn to sit on High Table with the Fellows, which was not a huge ordeal for Rosemary, who was accustomed to formal dinners. Rules of the Hall were very strict, especially concerning men.

> 'Students may not receive visits in their rooms from men other than fathers, uncles, and brothers.'

> 'Students are expected to obtain permission from the Principal or Vice Principal before going out to a mixed party or dinner or a dance… Permission to go to dinner or any form of mixed party in men's rooms, whether in College or outside, after 7p.m., will not as a rule be given unless some senior woman is a member of the party'[46].

A student room in Deneke, Rosemary's residence at Lady Margaret Hall, in the 1930s.

Oxford University had set a cap of 840 on the number of women students admitted, roughly 25%, and it was still very much a male-dominated institution. This was especially true in the sciences. In the Dyson Perrins Laboratory women were heavily outnumbered and would not have found many rôle models. Mild harassment by some of the male teachers was not considered unusual. The women students naturally tended to stick together, working conscientiously, and to centre their social life on the College. Rosemary would have met other young men through her family, and according to her sister she fell in love with one of them while in Oxford. Since her diaries are missing between 1933 and 1935, it seems likely that she destroyed the evidence of a failed romance. By the third year there is just a hint of condescension in Rosemary's attitude to her male tutor. In a teaching session she 'managed to keep him going' and on another occasion he could hardly stay awake, which she guessed was because, of necessity, 'he tuts too many people ... apparently demonstrators are paid very little'.

Rosemary saw her Tutor, Jean Orr-Ewing, the day after she arrived. She was a thirty-five year-old College Lecturer who had been a medical student at LMH during the First World War and Tutor in Natural Sciences since 1929[47]. She was to become an official Fellow in 1937. It has been said that 'the high standard she required of her pupils inspired the strong and scared the indolent into activity'. A perceptive and friendly person, she probably realised that Rosemary was unlikely to have problems. They had common interests, since Miss Orr-Ewing was a keen ornithologist and loved to climb in Switzerland, and it may have been her enthusiasm for the game that encouraged Rosemary to take up hockey in her second year. There were five natural scientists among the fifty-four Freshers: Wilma Hessey and Nancy Litt were the other chemists; Patricia Lupton and Ursula Wykes were zoologists. Rosemary studied chemistry, mechanics and physics for Prelims, which she passed at the end of the academic year. The time commitment in the first year was not great – about six hours a week in lectures and laboratories and a weekly tutorial, all requiring additional private study. The Principal, Lynda Grier, kept a close eye on her students, calling them in for a chat three times a term. She too was very approachable and tolerant of minor infringements of the rules. Staff and students alike described her as 'magnificent' and 'dignified'. A good administrator, Grier was much respected for her University work and active on various external boards and committees. At LMH she had used her business sense to manage the expansion of the College despite shortage of capital. Subconsciously Rosemary would have taken this in, and realised that one did not have to be a brilliant academic to succeed as a woman in the University.

Rosemary quickly gravitated towards the river, literally in her back garden. She was out sculling in the first week and was passed 'competent' for punting. Canoeing was another possibility she explored. In the Summer Term she was usually on the river several times a week, and was soon training other girls. When the Murrays came to visit, a favourite pastime was a punting picnic, with John or her father taking a second boat. Sometimes they would find a place to bathe. On one of Arthur's visits to Oxford they were out on the river when they saw two boys in trouble, and according to the grateful letters from relatives, saved their lives in a 'courageous act'.

Rosemary also went with friends to watch the rowing. The Torpids in April and the Eights in May were exciting bumps races, at that time restricted to men only, where college crews competed to become Head of the River. On Sundays Rosemary frequently attended St Mary's, the University Church, in the morning, listening critically to the sermons, and usually had lunch or tea with her grandmother. The days passed swiftly in the society of new friends and the Oxford relatives, who frequently entertained other members of the extended family. One of these was Rosemary's Uncle William, with his wife Maidie and son Bill. He liked to see the labs and pick Rosemary's brains about chemical processes related to his factory.

Rosemary loved going for long walks and bike rides in Port Meadow or out to Wytham Woods, always observing, and often recording in her diary the birds, animals and flowers she saw. Mary Odgers, a mathematician, referred to by her surname, was generally happy to go with her. In the evenings there were trips to the cinema and theatre and sometimes to concerts featuring famous visiting musicians. Her companion for these in the third year was Rosamund (Rosie) Jenkinson, a student of English whose father was a don at Brasenose college. The two became close friends and Rosemary was often at Rosie's house and treated almost as part of the family. Rosie took her to look at the college and some of its treasures, and it was in Brasenose Library that Rosemary first encountered rare Italian books and admired the Greek typeface of the printer Aldus Manutius. Later in life she would attempt to conserve similar books after the Florence floods.

After the end of her first Michaelmas term Rosemary went to help at the LMH Settlement in Kennington Road, Lambeth, following in a long tradition of educated Christian women, like her own relatives, who tried to improve social conditions in impoverished areas. The students were shown the slums and the various clubs and groups set up to help the inhabitants. Rosemary became a firm supporter.

Rosemary celebrated her 21st birthday on July 28th 1934 with a family luncheon. Several members of the family clubbed together to buy her a bureau, a fitting present for someone who was clearly going to be scholarly. Most of the other gifts were heirloom pieces of jewellery, money and books. Good wishes came from near and far. She would have been particularly pleased to hear from her old Nanny, who had moved on after many years with the Murray children. Granny wrote affectionately to tell her of the anxious wait at Rosemary's birth to hear a cry. Rosemary was not one for introspection, but she must have realised that she could now be more independent if she wished. She was beginning to organise her own life, arranging visits to friends and planning holidays without so much reference to her parents. Nevertheless, they remained close, and she saw them several times a term, either in Oxford or on weekends at home.

There was more pressure of work in the third year, and Rosemary's supervisor, Dr Brewer, was quite hard on her.

'He was very scathing over my manner of writing. What were yr ancestors – surely they were literary – is it necessary in science to write so badly? etc.'

This rather knocked Rosemary's confidence, but she concluded stoutly, '... I think that it is a very good thing to be blown up': it would make her more careful in future. By Hilary Term 1935, Rosemary was starting revision for Finals and doing practice papers. At the half-way tutorial meeting Miss Orr-Ewing commented that she was not looking well, and should take a break from work in the vacation because it was important to be fresh for next term. Although she did not follow the advice to the letter, continuing to revise her notebooks when at home, Rosemary had quite an eventful Easter holiday. She had a day at Downe, catching up with Miss Willis and Miss Heather and a day in Winchester, where John was at school. 'The craze at the moment is boat-building', she heard, and it was not long before John had started an ambitious project, eventually to involve all the family. She fetched David from school in the Austin and then went to London to stay with friends in Smith Square, among them a young man prepared to talk about economics and unemployment, a pastime which she much preferred to dancing. It was a particularly wet April, but the Murrays stoically carried on with plans for a cycling and horse riding holiday in the West of England. In preparation, Rosemary cut up mackintoshes to make aprons to wear under their waterproof ponchos. Averaging about thirty miles a day, Rosemary, Ann, John, David and their mother cycled via Wimbourne and Dorchester to Honiton, staying in bed and breakfast places where they had to share beds, and buying food to eat on the way. Eventually, after taking the bikes on a train, they met Arthur Murray at Plymouth, on board his new command HMS *Dorsetshire*. Rosemary and her mother were shown over the ship by the Sub-Lieutenant and returned, chauffeur driven, in the evening for a dinner party. The next five days were spent riding horses on Dartmoor, which was 'superb'.

Returning refreshed to Oxford, Rosemary put her best efforts into revision, setting her sights on a good class in the Part I examination. She was already on a short list to stay on a year and take Part II, which would lead to a BSc. if she passed. Deciding this had been the subject of much soul-searching and discussion with parents. Whether her anxiety about being a burden on them was genuine, or just a polite way of showing that she did not take their support for granted, is hard to tell. In March Miss Orr-Ewing wrote to ask Dr T.W.J. Taylor, a demonstrator noted for his enthusiasm and teaching ability, if he would be Rosemary's research supervisor. He came to see her in the lab and said that next term he would write to the Head of Department, Professor Robinson, on her behalf, '(which is a great comfort as I should not have any idea how to do same)'. Robinson was a very dominant character in the world of organic chemistry who had influence beyond Oxford, as Rosemary was to discover in the 1940s. Taylor talked vaguely about research on isomerisation with different catalysts and Rosemary showed an interest. At a second meeting, in April, they agreed that the proposed subject would be isostilbene isomerism. She explained to her father that the first stage would involve making some complicated glass apparatus, which might take many attempts, but sounded a most exciting thing to do.

Rosemary did much of her revision with Nancy Litt, who was a good friend and calm influence. They worked in each other's rooms by the fire when it was cold; in the science library in the Radcliffe Camera and in the lab, practising analysis. The other LMH chemist, Wilma Hussey, on the contrary, was sometimes despairing and 'needed a lot of reassuring'. Rosemary began to feel a little superior in the lab because Wilma was messy and Nancy 'always seems to get stuck & her methods are primitive in the extreme'. Wilma told her that Taylor had asked if Rosemary was good at lab work, and hearing that she was, said he would probably give her his best research topic. Unlike some of her friends, who could not settle to anything, Rosemary worked systematically to a revision timetable, and snatched some exercise punting, and playing tennis and squash. She tried not to be disconcerted by awkward questions from Brewer, though 'It was awful knowing so little when so near schools'.

Revision was briefly interrupted by the Silver Jubilee celebrations of George V on May 6th. Rosemary listened to a thanksgiving service on the wireless with Granny. In the evening she, Rosie and 'Odgers' climbed St Mary's church tower and looked across at the lights of Oxford, the floodlit towers of Magdalen and Christ Church on their level, and the headlamps of a queue of cars down below in the High, 'like a great caterpillar'. They could see a firework display at Headington and the beacons being lit on high points near and far in all directions. The Jubilee helped to raise the spirits of the English nation, hard hit by the Great Depression. This had not really touched Rosemary since her Neuchâtel experience of currency deflation, because Oxford was thriving, thanks to the booming motor industry.

Rosemary made the rather extraordinary decision to take a short excursion on the river before exams started on Thursday June 20th. She and Mary Odgers picked up a college canoe, the *Optimist*, at Lechlade on the Sunday and paddled it back along the Thames to the college boathouse, arriving on Tuesday afternoon. Rosemary used her Guiding skills to cook meals al fresco, and they found lodgings as they went, sharing a double bed. There were no mishaps, apart from Odgers getting sunburnt: 'it was a very nice trip and we really quarrelled not at all'. It is quite surprising that such an adventure was sanctioned by the College, assuming they knew about it.

There were three days of written exams, Physical, Organic and Inorganic Chemistry. None of Rosemary's pet questions came up and the elementary Organic, in which she had expected to do well, was 'disgusting', while advanced Inorganic was 'impossible', but she kept her head and 'managed to write if only quantity'. John had arrived at 1, Canterbury Road to recuperate from measles, so as soon as the exams were over she rushed to LMH to change and took him out for a supper picnic on the river. At fifteen he was becoming a good companion, keen to learn physics from Rosemary and always ready for excursions on the water. He tried his hand at punting and was a natural, 'easily competent'. A week later came the practical exams. The first two went quite well, but Rosemary got into a muddle analysing two products and was not helped by Brewer interrupting to talk about a question in her written exams. She also blamed him for lack of success in the second half, on absorption indicators: '…if only he had not been so officious in the term I should already have done something with them as I had wanted to'. Poor Wilma was very much upset when he told her in the middle of the practical that she had written on the wrong topic for her main organic question. One can sense the misogynist in this man, undermining the young women at every opportunity.

The results were out within a fortnight: Rosemary had a Second, and found out when she saw Dr Taylor in August that she was in the top half of that class with several alpha papers. He had thought she was well

The Dyson Perrins Laboratory, Oxford.

in the running for a First. 'If only I had known how near a 1st I was perhaps I might have been spurred on', she lamented. However it was still possible that research in the fourth year could push her up a class. The other scientists in Miss Orr-Ewing's group who stayed on to do research were Peter (Patricia) Lupton, who was awarded a Third in Zoology in 1936, and Ursula Wykes, who dropped out to take up a Henry Fellowship at Radcliffe College. Most of the cohort of 1932 left, including Wilma and Nancy. Rosemary was the remaining high flier.

Passport photograph of Rosemary, aged 25.

Finstergrun castle.

– 4 –
Student life

IMMEDIATELY AFTER THE EXAMS FINISHED, Rosemary and her friend Joyce set out for Austria by train, crossing from Dover to Ostende and taking a sleeper from Cologne to Munich. The final leg was by bus over the 'marvellous' high Alpine Tauern Pass. Rosemary loved the snow-capped mountains and could not wait to explore. They were making for Finstergrun Castle, a commanding edifice on a steep crag above Mauterndorf, where her Aunt Issie normally spent the summer months with her friend Gräfin Szápáry, the owner. She liked to encourage other friends and relatives to join her as paying guests, especially the younger members of the family. The castle was run like a rather select hotel with a house party atmosphere, offering scenic walks and tennis. In the evening the guests made their own entertainment, with card games, charades and occasional dances in the Rittersaal, a vaulted room with a massive open fireplace. Rosemary and Joyce went for long walks in the hot sunshine, sometimes stopping to bathe in the Alpine lakes. One afternoon, with Rosemary's cousin Claud Proby, they climbed up behind the castle for three hours to a log hut, where they lit the stoves and made supper, eating it outside while the sun went down across the valley and the moon rose. Claud and Rosemary talked Austrian politics: Dolfuss had been assassinated the previous year and anti-Nazi feeling ran high in Finstergrun. Very early next morning Rosemary was up lighting fires and making tea before the party set off to see the sun rise from the top of the mountain. 'The Gross Glockner was marvellously white & completely covered with snow', she wrote. They walked to the top of the Königstuhl, over 7,600 feet in height, and had breakfast enjoying the panoramic view.

Joyce had to leave after ten days, but Rosemary was happy walking on her own. She even ascended the Königstuhl again, confidently trying a new path across a boggy area. One of the guests told her that she had felt obliged to cling on to a fir tree while she summoned the courage to go along a precipitous path beyond the castle: 'I must go there', thought Rosemary. Other members of the party were impressed by the length and speed of her walks. Even cousin Claud was 'rather fatigued' as he tried to keep up. It was Rosemary's idea of a perfect holiday and she said sad farewells when the time came to leave. She was due to spend a week in Dresden with an elderly lady whom Frances had lodged with for six months while studying violin. Travelling alone, back to Munich and on to Dresden overnight, she had one or two alarms about customs and luggage but dealt with them like a seasoned traveller. Her landlady had arranged a very full programme taking in picture galleries, the Meissen porcelain factory and local beauty spots such as the mountainous Bastei. It has to be said that Rosemary was ungrateful for the old lady's efforts to entertain her and took every opportunity to escape her company. Disgust at her snoring and 'grunts and humming' and the general obesity of the Germans was confided to the diary. She also noted the presence of Nazis, marshalling people into groups, and an exhibition of defences against poison gas, chilling portents of war. 'The whole of Dresden was swarming with people in uniform, police, post office, army, navy, airforce, black and brown Nazis and "Hitler Jugend" everywhere', she told Joyce[48].

This time Rosemary was not sorry to leave. After an exhausting 36-hour journey across Europe she was met from Havant station and found everybody at home and a cake waiting for her belated birthday celebration. She only had one day to turn around before setting off for Scotland with Frances to visit friends. The Macklehoses lived in Lamington in Lanarkshire and the connection with the Murrays seems to have been their son, Alec. Again Rosemary was one of a house party, mainly of young people, playing tennis nearly every day and table games after supper. Rosemary was enormously impressed by Alec's speed at card games and his 'phenomenal' memory, as he swept the board every time they played Pelman patience. With an older man, presumably as chaperone, Alec, Rosemary and Frances made a great excursion into the Highlands by car, taking it in turns to drive along the shores of Loch Lomond and Loch Fyne, with the mountains of Arran in the distance, to Inverary and thence to the little fishing village of Tarbert where they went rowing and stayed the night. Next day they took out a sailing boat. There was only time to 'sniff the open sea' and identify Islay and Jura in the distance. This was the beginning of Rosemary's love of the Highlands and the West Coast, home of her Murray ancestors the Dukes of Atholl, and much later a regular summer destination for sailing holidays with John or Richard. She resolved to read more about the history of Scotland. At the end of the holiday Rosemary concluded, 'Alec is very nice and much more human'. Whether there was any romantic interest we can only guess. Certainly

Alec's mother made an effort to get to know Rosemary, and she and Alec 'went a walk in the twilight' on one of the last evenings. Writing a 'bread and butter' letter to her hostess, Rosemary struggled to find words to express how much she had enjoyed herself.

Rosemary and Frances travelled directly back to Oxford and met up with their mother and the other children. Rosemary moved straight into 1, Canterbury Road, where she was to stay with Granny for her fourth year. The family enjoyed a few days of relaxation in perfect weather, taking picnics on the river, the boys swimming at Parsons' Pleasure and fishing. One evening they took Granny's five maids with them for their annual treat, providing an enormous tea with masses of iced cakes. Alec Macklehose joined them for a day walking on the Downs. There were also shopping trips to prepare for a camping holiday in the West of England. They bought six yards of hessian and 'lots of things from Woolworths'. Their destination was a farm site on the side of a hill near Falmouth. Unfortunately the heatwave broke and it started to rain the day they left and hardly stopped during the holiday. Rosemary was in charge of the camp, deciding on the layout of the tents and making a windbreak from the hessian and some pea sticks she had cut. Most nights it 'absolutely poured' and much time was spent drying out mattresses and blankets in the sunny intervals. Rosemary was startled by a rat running over her feet in bed; 'Mom' woke to find a big pool in her tent. Hail as big as cherry stones beat down on the site one day and sometimes there was fog and sea mist. At any opportunity they went for walks along the cliffs and bathed in the cold September sea, even when the waves made great rollers. On occasional fine nights the girls slept out under the stars, waking covered with dew: 'with five rugs and a sweater it was alright', said Rosemary. It took a lot to deter the Murrays. Fortunately they were back home before a great gale hit the South coast on the night of 16-17th September.

It was time to go back to Oxford, and 'with much fear and trepidation' to the Dyson Perrins laboratory. Rosemary was still nervous of new ventures. She felt happier once she had cleared a bench and a cupboard for herself and obtained a key to the building: 'It is superb to have the key like that and to be able to go in & out when you like'. There was only one other female student in the organic chemistry lab, Nancy Newman, also supervised by Dr Taylor. He told them 'finding jobs for women is no easy matter'. After a fortnight he became a little too familiar. While Rosemary was occupied he 'came in & put his hand most affectionately like on the back'. Rosie Jenkinson told her that Taylor, a Brasenose man like her father, had stayed with her family 'and one night had come in to talk to Rosie when she was in bed!' This behaviour was rather innocently recorded and does not seem to have damaged Rosemary's relationship with her supervisor. She also tolerated personal remarks about her hair and clothes, which today would be off-limits: 'That's a damn pretty frock you've got on, nice stuff!!'

Rosemary's usual routine was to spend the morning in the lab, take a long break to go out cycling or walking, then return to the lab until 6.00 or 7.00 p.m. Often she went in again after supper to check experiments or turn off the Bunsen. The first term was spent in alternate hope and despair as she set up experiments that failed completely (recorded as 'washout') or produced puzzling results. Taylor was in the lab almost every day, closely supervising her, helping to make apparatus and putting forward suggestions for fresh approaches. Rosemary soon decided that she was glad to be researching with him, because he was always so kind and interested. Her patience and long hours of work (including evenings and weekends) were at last rewarded when, shortly before Christmas, the product she was seeking was produced. It was dicyclohexyl succinic ester, never before synthesised.

During this first term there was a dramatic incident in the lab, when the apparatus of Nancy Newman, whom Rosemary had already identified as 'not very good at practical', exploded and shattered glass everywhere. Sixty years later Rosemary recalled, 'One afternoon, bang, and there was Nancy with blood streaming down her face together with some chemical solvent'[49]. It was Rosemary who took charge, mopping up and taking Nancy to the Radcliffe Hospital in a taxi, waiting with her and badgering the nurses to get a blanket for the patient. The doctors found glass in Nancy's eye and she was lucky not to lose her sight. Rosemary visited her nearly every day for the rest of term, taking playing cards and solitaire and doing her best to keep Nancy cheerful. Dr and Mrs Taylor were also frequent visitors, reading aloud to her. Rosemary crossed paths with the Taylors socially in many other ways, because the University members all went to the same concerts, especially of visiting artists, and the same theatrical productions, took part in the University choir and orchestra, met at each other's lunch and dinner parties and passed each other in the street or on the river. It was a small and privileged world.

Meanwhile Ellen Murray, Frances and Ann were preparing to depart for Wei Hai Wei in North East China where Arthur Murray was stationed with the Eastern Fleet, captaining the cruiser, *Dorchester*. Rosemary had also been invited, and it says much for her dedication to chemistry that she did not disrupt her studies. All the same, she spent a weekend helping the others to pack up 'Brookfield', ready for incoming tenants. Sorting, tidying, packing trunks and making an inventory was the sort of activity Rosemary enjoyed. Aunt Rosemary was to look after the Murrays' financial affairs in England (she reported a significant overdraft before long) and Rosemary was clearly chief carer for her brothers, with Granny providing a base. After some delays the China party set off in mid-October on the S.S. *Franken*, 'too super for words' as Ann said. Rosemary must have had a few qualms as she read Ann's entertaining letter about the fun she was having with Puss and the eccentricities of the other passengers, especially when she wrote about passing Gibraltar. It was Rosemary's task to meet David and Richard off the train from their school at Seaford, and together with John, keep them busy over the Christmas holidays. She was left to buy all the presents, following her mother's directions, at Hamleys and Selfridges. The boys loved the London Underground and the Mickey Mouse films she took them to, and John appreciated a visit to the Chinese Exhibition. They were staying with Aunt Cath, who helped Rosemary fill the boys' stockings. Aunt Barbara and the Byam Shaws (notable artists) came for Christmas dinner, making a festive party. On Boxing Day they flew David's new aeroplane in Regent's Park and played family games in the evening.

Rosemary left the boys with Ethel the maid while she went down to Fittleworth for a ball at Goodwood House. This was arranged by Aunt Nela, who provided supper for two young men Rosemary had never met and cousin Claud. '…such a queer party', Rosemary thought, and sidestepped her aunt's questions next morning because she had failed to dance with one of them. Rosemary's mother was always encouraging her to go to dances in Oxford and it seems that other female members of the clan were looking out for a suitable partner for her too. Many of her friends were already engaged and Lucy Selwyn, her Neuchâtel companion, was married. Rosemary was not exactly a blue-stocking, but she was already a rather formidable person, inclined to be critical and reserved, and she did not get on with young men easily. Her mother once described Rosemary's long silences as 'terrifying'. In private she could be quite scathing about male contemporaries, for example 'P- D- has become a horror, rather typical of one sort of undergraduate, boasting in a loud voice…' Rosemary also suffered from being a 'Daddy's girl': it was difficult to find a man who measured up to her multi-talented father.

After Christmas, plans to stay at Fittleworth with Nonna fell through and Rosemary and Richard were shunted off to their elderly Aunt Annie in Shepway. Her household was dull at the best of times, it rained incessantly and Richard was very bored. They were back in Oxford by January 4th and Rosemary was able to fit in some hours at the lab between buying the boys clothes for the coming term, going for walks and taking them to the pantomime. Granny clearly found the disruption a little trying and wrote to her daughter an account of 'How we send our Boys to School' in the form of a play.

> 'Clothes of every description – under and upper – fill every table and shelf. – Front Hall heaving with every description of parcel cardboard boxes, hat box, innumerable parcels of shoes'.
>
> 'Evening – Drawing Room – floor strewn with collars, handkerchiefs, sweaters etc. ARM at table pen in hand … murmuring "I love marking".'[50]

Granny reported that Rosemary had been marvellous, morning, noon and eve, and a mother to them all.

Once the boys left, Rosemary could work intensively again on the experiments with isostilbene. She needed to make more of the compound she had synthesized in order to try the next stage: the yield was poor, but she kept going and found herself enjoying the work enormously. By mid-March she had decided that she wanted to make research her career, rather than teaching, which was the only option for most educated women in the 1930s. She wrote to ask her parents if she might go on to read for a D.Phil, another six terms of research after the end of the current academic year. She was backed by Dr Taylor, who said she was just the sort of person required. He recommended her to Professor Robinson, the Head of Department. Rosemary had applied for the LMH Research Scholarship but was unsuccessful and consequently anxious about paying the fees: £5 a term to the University and £6.6s.0d to the laboratories. She wrote persuasively to her parents:

'I feel that I really ought to get a job having been educated for 15 years on the other hand I should adore to do more research, and of the more theoretical sort, and not having to apply what I was doing directly to some industrial problem [i.e. in a commercial lab.]'[51]

She did not rule out teaching eventually,

'But I think that I don't want to teach directly because I think that unless you had already done some research you would never be able to start research again, and that I just couldn't bear'.

She seems to have persuaded Aunt Ruth to offer her free board and lodging and she held out the possibility of earning some money from coaching.

Her parents, however, had another suggestion. Rosemary could go out to Hong Kong for a while after completing the BSc.and spend some time with her father. Her mother, in particular, seems to have put on some pressure for her to take that course, perhaps thinking of all the eligible young naval officers she would meet. Rosemary agonised over the choice. 'I can't bear to think of Daddy being in H-K all alone when I might be there too', she lamented. Was it her duty to go? It 'has driven me nearly distracted trying to decide', she wrote in May. It was particularly difficult having her parents so far away, with letters taking weeks to reach their destination. She was influenced by Dr Taylor, who said that 'from the pure science point of view' it would be better to go straight on and not have a gap. Rosemary eventually concluded that if she wanted to do research she had better get on with it, because to secure one of the few really good research posts 'you must get more or less to the top of the tree'.

'So I think that it really all hangs on whether I really do want to do chemistry or whether I will do something else, such as teaching. And I am sure that I want to do Chemistry'.[52]

Making this first career decision had stirred up some ambition in Rosemary. It forced her to set a goal and commit to it, breaking free of parental control despite the strong attachment.

While handling this dilemma, Rosemary was in the middle of writing up her thesis – all 116 pages - on a typewriter borrowed from Mrs Taylor.

She had enough to write about and it was 'rather longer than it should be'. She had not managed to synthesise the compound dicyclohexyl ethylene, but she was half way there, and the experiments on the rate of change of isostilbene to stilbene were satisfactory. She handed in the thesis, which typically she bound herself, on June 3rd, but continued to work hard, hoping to produce more results before her viva. Taylor was clearly worried by the lack of success ('hope I haven't let you down') and wondered if he should have explored the problem more thoroughly. Rosemary only took time off to go and see the boys at their respective schools. She had misgivings about attending the Winchester v. Eton cricket match the weekend before her viva, but dutifully talked to John's Housemaster, then drove back and went into the lab after supper.

Rosemary was probably unlucky to have Brewer as one of her examiners since she found him intimidating. Afterwards she castigated herself for giving an 'abominable' explanation of her recent results. Flustered, she was then unable to answer their questions on the thesis. 'Oh it was so awful and I am so angry at having been such a fool'. The agony of re-living the disastrous interview kept her awake until three in the morning. She felt she had wasted her last chance to improve on her degree class. Three days later her friend Rosie broke the news that she had indeed been awarded a Second. 'Alas, I did so long just to squeak in to the 1sts it would have been so glorious', she wrote. Everyone tried to console her – Taylor said he had hoped she would pull it off; Mrs Taylor was sorry for her, but thought a second seemed marvellous and not a cause of commiseration. Miss Grier, always so sensible, said that Rosemary's class would be forgotten when superseded by a D.Phil, and the only cure for disappointment was to get back to work as soon as possible. Dr Taylor had some paid work for her, writing abstracts of chemical papers in English, French and German, and she threw herself into it, while still doing some research.

In the middle of July Rosemary took Rosie to stay at Aunt Annie's for a short seaside holiday and then spent a week with Marjorie Verney at Rhoscolyn, her home in Anglesey, doing all the things she liked best – walking, sailing and bathing in the sea, and having serious conversations with Marjorie and her brother Ralph on topics ranging from free will to marriage. Sir Harry was only there for a few days, but joined in their activities enthusiastically. In August the tenants at 'Brookfield' departed and the Murrays were able to move back to their home. Rosemary energetically began to set it right, roping the boys in to help. Unpacking the lock-up room took several days, interspersed with tarring their boat *Kelpie* and sailing her in Hayling Regatta. Anticipating her mother's return from China, Rosemary was very busy cleaning and tidying the house and weeding the garden. Ellen Murray was sailing into Southampton on the *Potsdam*, alone, because Frances and Ann were following later. Rosemary made a very early start with the boys to catch the tender out to the ship at 6 a.m. She must have been disappointed by her mother's first reaction, which was that they looked 'most unrespectable'. Ellen may have secretly resented Rosemary's competence and the close relationship that had developed between her and the boys. John and Rosemary in particular had much in common and became good companions as he matured into an intelligent, charming young man, outstandingly good at any kind of practical work. Rosemary had been looking after her brothers for eleven months and it must have been a difficult transition when her mother took control once more.

Rosemary was home until mid-September, sailing every day when it was not too windy with the boys and local friends. She and John put a lot of effort into reclaiming the garden, scything and tackling nettles and thistles. Rosemary liked nothing better than a 'roaring bonfire'. Returning to Oxford she moved into 9, Polstead Road, the house bought by Ruth Spooner when her father died. She did not find Ruth easy to get on with, considering her 'dotty about Russia'. The feeling was mutual: sometimes Ruth 'invited' Rosemary to go and work in her own room. It was better when another lodger her own age arrived: this was May Crum, daughter of friends of the Murrays in Canterbury. She and her brother Michael became frequent companions for Rosemary at concerts and church services. Dr Taylor was back from an extended trip to Spitzbergen and had not given any thought to Rosemary's D.Phil research topic beyond assuming that she would continue with geometric isomers. Eventually he set out some ideas that she could explore, but at the end of October she summed up, 'The general impression of these days is that I work very hard and make no progress'. She was also coaching her first pupil, a girl who was applying to LMH. Most of her friends had left Oxford, so she had a lot of time to herself, often going on long bike rides in the afternoon. She was becoming increasingly interested in birdwatching, a hobby she shared with Mrs Taylor. She enrolled in a First Aid class ('boring') and helped her friend Rosie Jenkinson's mother at a baby clinic in Cowley on Friday afternoons. Her interest in music grew as she attended concerts featuring famous artists such as Thomas Beecham, Jelly d'Aranyi, the Hungarian violinist and the Griller String Quartet. She was a faithful follower of New College Choir because Granny liked to go to the services, and they ran a Sunday School for the choirboys. Rosemary was not musically talented like Frances, but she was thrilled to join her in the Bach Choir in her final year. 'I am so elated at having got in that I cd shout with joy', she wrote, in a rare burst of emotion.[53] From then on the practices were a highlight of her week. She also acquired a clarinet and took lessons. In late November 1936 she made a quick trip home to see Frances and Ann, who had just arrived back from China, but otherwise continued working right up until Christmas. She was looking forward to a skiing holiday in the Tyrol with the Wigrams, friends from Emsworth, John, Ann and cousins Catherine and Peter Inge.

By now, Rosemary was an old hand at crossing Europe by train. She watched the frosty scenery give way to the snowy valleys of the Oetztal. The mountains grew steeper and the final transport was by sleigh. Ann sent her parents a descriptive letter about the exciting journey to Vent.

> 'Then we started along a tiny winding snowy track. John and I wedged behind the plumlike horse's backside. Rose [ARM] in the front one. Away we went, so that we could see all the snow and icicles...'
>
> 'We went on and on, up and down, over precipices with a black and green frozen river below, thro rock tunnels, pine woods, on and on...'
>
> '...The luggage sleigh fell over the edge once, but by all of us pushing we got it up again... At last at 2 we saw the great mountain ahead, which we knew was above Vent, and after a few more turns we saw it, looking superb with a church & few houses & hotels'.[54]

Ann's lively prose is in complete contrast to Rosemary's dry and factual account. The two sisters had very different talents.

Sadly for Rosemary she developed a temperature which kept her off the slopes for three days. An ominous pain in her right side was the precursor to appendicitis. It was frustrating to have to sit reading in the sun while the others went on excursions.

Rosemary was well enough to continue her research in Oxford, but the appendix grumbled on and eventually two doctors agreed that she should have it removed. The operation was in a private hospital, Wray House in

Havant, where she stayed for sixteen days, missing the spectacle of the *Dorchester* coming in to Devonport, band playing, pennants streaming, the men lined up on deck and her father on the bridge. She continued convalescing at home, too weak to finish out the Hilary Term and recovering only just in time for a planned 3-week Mediterranean cruise. This was an Hellenic Tour with lectures on board from Uncle Campbell Dodgson, the young architect Hugh Casson and Naomi Mitcheson, and excursions to famous sites in Greece and the islands, Crete, Cyprus and Rhodes. On the way back, Rosemary was able to meet up with Miss Willis and Miss Heather in Athens, and they talked about Ann's success in the Oxford entrance exam. She had rather unexpectedly won an award as an Exhibitioner, surpassing Rosemary's achievement.

Rosemary was anxious to get back to Oxford, because it was two months since she had done any chemistry. At her first meeting with Dr Taylor he said he felt they were rather stuck. Rosemary battled on with end-to-end experiments on which he commented, investigating isomers and polymers. She was rather pleased to find that he thought it was worth writing a paper based on her BSc. thesis results. Her first pupil had been low on the waiting list for LMH and failed to get in. She took on three more, teaching a total of four hours a week, and became a more confident coach. Work was interrupted for a day to celebrate the coronation of George VI. Oxford was decorated with flags and banners on the lampposts and a floodlit fountain in St Giles. Granny put out decorations painted by Frances. In the evening Rosemary went up New College tower with the choirboys to see the lights and fireworks, then walked about the crowded streets.

In the summer of 1937 Rosemary spent some weeks at home, taking part in all the local regattas with various combinations of family and friends as crew. She also played tennis, rather less enthusiastically. She had a long weekend sailing around Portsmouth with Ann and her father, who was stationed at the Signal School in Devonport. They had the use of the *Zelda*, a larger boat than Rosemary had sailed before. She took the opportunity to sleep on deck: 'So super – to hear the sea birds paddling about and feeding on the mud'. On this trip Ann developed a bad asthmatic cough and in early July Rosemary was called back home for a week to look after her and do the cooking because the maids were on holiday. Ann had suffered from asthma since the year in China: it became very serious in 1938, in fact so worrying that her mother took her to a clinic in Lausanne for consultation with several specialists and treatment. They spent several weeks there in the spring, while Rosemary and Puss managed the household, their brothers and the many moral welfare activities that Ellen delegated. Ann had an operation, followed by convalescence at Chateau d'Oex and made a partial recovery, but she had to defer entrance to Oxford until 1939. Asthma continued to curtail her activities, (she often writes of being in a 'parlous state') and it was thanks to great determination that she achieved a second class degree in Natural Sciences. She suffered continual bouts of chronic ill-health, leading to a rather desperate attempt to find a cure by moving to the hot climate of southern Africa, and eventually died at the age of forty.

In September 1937 Rosemary was back in Oxford, where Granny arranged a 'great party' for Captain Murray, perhaps a belated 50th birthday celebration. The family converged from all over the country, enjoying a supper prepared by the New College chef. Afterwards William Spooner proposed Arthur's health and Rosemary seconded. As a lodger at Polstead Road Rosemary had felt she was trying her best with cousin Ruth, despite radical disagreements on subjects like the value of the House of Lords. However, Ruth decided that she wanted Rosemary to move out for the second year and told her that the room was needed for another visitor. For the first time Rosemary had to live in lodgings on her own, though Ruth relented and took her back after one term. An action-packed seven weeks at home, mainly sailing, bathing and playing tennis, had left little time for thinking about chemistry, apart from correcting proofs of the paper Taylor had written. She had built up a good body of material, but 'I wish I could make something of all these results, but so many things seem so arbitrary'. She was now more than half way through the allotted period and was particularly rattled when Taylor said they must start a systematic investigation: 'What the hell have I been doing all this time?' she wondered. However, by Christmas she had monochlorostilbene results that he thought were worth publishing.

Dr Taylor asked what Rosemary was going to do next: was she going to 'shove off' after getting her D.Phil? The only possibility of continuing research seemed to be a scholarship to an American University. Miss Grier enthused about the Henry Fellowship which had been awarded to another LMH student, Ursula Wykes, and Dr Taylor agreed, writing Rosemary a glowing testimonial in which he said he had no doubt that she would obtain the D.Phil.

'I have a very high opinion of Miss Murray's capabilities and hope very much that she may have the opportunity of widening her experience by working for a year in the United States. She is a thoroughly competent worker with the virtues of perseverance, balance of judgement and independance [sic] of thought, and since she hopes to devote herself to a scientific career, such an opportunity would be especially valuable to her'.[55]

Rosemary became increasingly keen on the prospect: 'How I long to go to America', she wrote at Christmas as she filled in the forms, but sadly she was not successful with any of her applications for funding.

There was a holiday in Aosta with the Wigrams, John and others, where she significantly improved her skiing, and then she headed back to Oxford. Apart from the pressure of work on the thesis she had seven pupils, some for University entrance and some for Schools, and was teaching at least five hours a week. She also had to prepare a paper for the Chemistry Colloquium, on 'Stereoisomerism in the stilbene series'. This went rather well and she was able to speak from notes, 'It makes a lot of difference talking of something one really knows about', she concluded. In April she started typing her thesis, again borrowing Mrs Taylor's typewriter, and for once she worked through the Easter vacation, even while at home. She seemed more concerned about her English style than the technical details.

Rosemary knew she must start thinking about jobs, reluctantly, because she hated the thought of leaving. Frances had already moved from Oxford and was living in London, taking classes at Chelsea School of Art with Henry More. Their parents were looking for a bigger house, so there was change at home too. The only university job to come up was at Royal Holloway College: the post of Demonstrator and Assistant Lecturer in Chemistry. Rosemary's application made much of her recent teaching experience, which, combined with research, she felt was 'an ideal combination'. At the interview in central London she found two other (male) candidates, Cambridge and London graduates respectively, but in this case she was not disadvantaged, because it was a women's college. When all three had been seen by the Board, the two men were sent away and Rosemary called in and offered the job at £150 per annum. It had been almost too easy – no challenging questions and no anxious wait for the results; in fact, no time to think it over before accepting.

'Well, well', she wrote in her diary, 'I am pleased but I hope that it is the right sort of job to have got with enough possibilities for research.' It was rather depressing to hear a few days later that Miss Orr-Ewing characterised Holloway as 'very schoollike & no chance of research.' Rosemary went down to see for herself on 14th June, the same day that she handed in her thesis. It must have been a shock to find the labs so small and badly equipped. Compared with the Dyson Perrins they were very overcrowded: 'I only have one bench … no desk or table'. She found the other chemists, Professor Moore and Dr Plant, rather dull, and was concerned about the latter's bossy attitude '…shall I find myself under her thumb?' Taylor was sympathetic when she told him that Moore had said she would have no time for research, and he admitted that Moore's subject was now out of fashion. It was not a promising scenario. 'How sad I am to be going', was Rosemary's private comment as she said good-bye to the other chemists, her Tutor, and Granny, and had a farewell supper with Ruth and Rosemary. But she still had one more experience to add to her Oxford years.

Rosemary loved travel, the more exotic the better, so she had been fascinated to hear about an expedition that students had organised to Iceland. Ursula Wykes, one of her year at LMH had taken part, and Rosemary jokingly suggested that she should go again with Rosemary as meteorologist. In the end they made plans to go to Lapland in the summer and Rosemary took on the role of ornithologist, for which she was well qualified. She first met the other 'Laplanders' at the end of May when they had tea in Ursula's room and discussed provisions and clothes. Rosemary took her role seriously, and once the thesis was finished spent much time studying bird books and learning about all those species likely to be seen in Lapland. It was an unofficial trip, but Ursula named it grandly, 'The University Women's Lappland Expedition', and put a notice in *The Times*. On July 2nd six girls sailed from Harwich to Goteborg: three zoologists, two botanists and Rosemary, who was going along primarily for the adventure rather than the science. They took crates of scientific instruments, food, tents, sleeping bags and suitcases. Rosemary had a very heavy rucksack. The train took them through wooded hills with frequent lakes and swamps to Abisko, above the fir tree line and on the southern shore of Lake Torne Träsk. They stayed at an observation post for meteorology for two nights and Rosemary immediately began recording the birds – redshanks, white wagtails, willow warblers and various gulls. The Lapps then transported

Rosemary sailing with Felicity, one of the 'Laplanders'.

the party across the lake and helped them to carry the luggage up to an isolated tourist hut, which they decided to use for cooking, sleeping in their two tents. The camp was surrounded by birch forest and wild flower meadows. Rosemary liked to walk uphill to lakes above the snow, on her own, through forests with no paths. There were views of distant snow-covered mountains and one day she saw a large herd of reindeer crossing. Sometimes she had an early morning bathe in the river. The zoologists trapped mice and chloroformed them, saving their parasites in alcohol and mounting the skins on card; the botanists picked flowers and pressed them, and Rosemary identified and recorded the birds – rough-legged buzzards and kestrels, snow bunting, a golden plover and a pair of skuas among others. She also examined buzzard pellets for evidence of the birds' diet and afterwards published a short paper in *British Birds*.[56] They were all plagued by 'pugnacious' mosquitos that found their way into every cranny. Rosemary described her outfit as 'skiing boots, puttees, breeches, wind-jacket, two pairs of gloves, straw hat and mosquito netting.[57]' There were several incursions of tourists, the strangest being an entirely naked young man who had rowed the twelve miles across the lake. Some of the girls were reduced to helpless embarrassed giggles. Rosemary looked on with scientific detachment.

Cadlington House, Horndean, after renovation in 2010.

Many family holidays and her experience as a Guide had prepared Rosemary for the spartan camping conditions, long walks and bathing in rivers and her scientific training made recording, tabulating and interpreting results second nature. It was just the sort of challenge that she loved. The women spent three weeks by the lake without any serious accidents or arguments and profited a lot from each other's scientific expertise. As Ursula reported, they had put together an integrated picture of their environment. It was the sort of expedition which would have been unthinkable for the previous generation, but post-war women were stretching the boundaries and proving that they could be as self-reliant as men.

Rosemary then had the strange experience of returning to a new home: the Murrays had moved the previous day to the imposing Cadlington House near Horndean. She was sorry to have missed that, but it was 'most exciting' to arrive there and realise that they owned this splendid property. Eight weeks of the vacation still stretched ahead before starting her first job.

– 5 –

Royal Holloway College and Sheffield University: the outbreak of war

CADLINGTON HOUSE WAS MORE than twice the size of 'Brookfield' and was set in grounds of six acres. Anxiety about the possibility of war had depressed the property market and enabled Arthur Murray to purchase it at auction for a knock-down price. It was constructed around 1850 in Regency style, with extensions forty years later, of flint and yellow brick, with a massive porch of Bath stone. At the back was a colonnade running most of the width of the house, and at right-angles to it a large conservatory with tall arched windows. It is now a listed building. There were numerous outbuildings, a cottage, a barn and a walled kitchen garden. Cadlington became a much-loved centre for the Murrays, their extended family and friends, and indeed for the whole neighbourhood, for they were generous in lending space for all sorts of activities. Ruth Spooner remembered arriving one evening and being told,

> 'You can't go into the study, for the tennis club are having a committee, and there is a lecture on Current Affairs in the diningroom and the Drama Group are rehearsing in the drawing-room and a lot of people are preparing refreshments in the kitchen.'[58]

On the day she returned from Lapland, Rosemary found only her parents in residence. Her father's study had been put in order, but there was 'a good deal of chaos' in the other rooms, offering plenty of scope for her love of organising. She was soon putting up curtains, sorting books, unpacking china and glass and painting the pantry. 'Marvellous to have such a lot of room', she thought. She was interrupted by curious visitors who had to be shown round. The other children drifted back from holidays, and all the talk was of the house and its lovely rooms. Ann was particularly thrilled, because she had been the one to spot the sale notice in *Country Life*. When Frances arrived back from music camp she found that she had been assigned a studio. Rosemary was in the 'dark blue room'.

Improving Cadlington took up a lot of time, but was not allowed to interfere with sailing. On her first day back Rosemary and her father raced *Kelpie* in the Emsworth regatta and won the race easily, out of twelve boats. The day ended with a party given by a retired naval Commander, Stephen King Hall, who was making a name for himself as an author and broadcaster. The weather for Itchenor Regatta, later in the month, was much less pleasant, squally with dark clouds and choppy water. Nevertheless, Rosemary and Richard were the winners of the Port to Port race. Local races and recreational sailing occupied them throughout the holidays. Visitors came and went – among them May Crum from Canterbury who had lodged at Polstead Road, and Arthur Murray's sister Barbara and sister- in-law Peggy (whose husband Michael had' tragically drowned very recently). John had started building a 14-foot dinghy at school, a most ambitious project which required the help of other members of the family, so there were many day trips to Winchester. John and his father did the heaviest work, while David and Rosemary, and occasionally Ann and Frances, sanded, painted and varnished and fitted various parts. On their drives they sometimes encountered army lorries hidden by the side of the road. The prospect of war must have seemed remote to all except Captain Murray, as they enjoyed an idyllic summer of sailing and tennis, walking and gardening, cycling and picnics. Rosemary had a short holiday with 'Odgers' at her home in Norfolk, bird-watching at Blakeney Point and sailing along the River Bure. She loved the landscape and the abundance of different birds. Here the signs of military activity were obvious: 'There are a large number of territorial camps, mostly searchlights and anti-aircraft,' she recorded without comment.

A personal deadline was looming for Rosemary. Her D.Phil. viva was fixed for 20th September in Oxford, so as soon as she returned after the Norfolk holiday she started to re-read her thesis very critically: 'Some of it is so badly written – why can I not write better?', she reflected. A few days before the exam she went to stay at Polstead Road and immersed herself in the stilbene research again. On the appointed day her diary records that she went with her usual 'trepidation' to the lab and 'rooted out TWJT' to discuss a possible paper arising from her work. Rather surprisingly, considering the close interest he had taken in Rosemary, he appeared to have forgotten when her viva was, and when told it was that afternoon said perhaps he should have been holding her hand. 'Dear me no', was Rosemary's reaction. She was never quite sure how to take his flirtatious remarks.

In retrospect she summed up her viva as 'pretty frightful'. The examiners were Drs Mills and Plant. Mills made 'dull but justified

Rosemary sailing with her father in 1938.

criticisms' and some suggestions; Plant asked tough questions that she couldn't answer, but it seems to have been a foregone conclusion that she would pass. Next day this was confirmed by Plant when she met him in the street; although it would not be official until the meeting of the Board of Faculties in November, a doctorate was assured. It was a relief, and most would have felt a triumphant end to her Oxford career. LMH had only produced about three scientists of this standing before. On the one hand Rosemary remembered reading up the regulations and thinking she would never be able to do it, but she was still troubled by her student record. 'If only I had got a 1st how much happier I should be, so near (apparently) and yet so far'.

Towards the end of September 1938 the threat of war finally broke into the idyll. The international situation was tense. News that Chamberlain had gone to Berchtesgaden for talks with Hitler held everyone in suspense. A stirring sermon by the new vicar of St Mary's Oxford, urged people to repent and seek God's will. A week later Rosemary and Frances went to Chichester Cathedral and heard the Bishop asking people to pray for peace, as war was too appalling to think about. But the Murrays were planning for the worst. In the event of war Frances decided that she would be a nurse, and her mother considered handing over Cadlington to be converted into a hospital and living in the cottage. Captain Murray was recalling men from leave to make preparations and Ellen was attending emergency meetings on arrangements for civilians, and was so distracted by the situation that one day she forgot to get off the train at Havant. This left Rosemary wondering what she could contribute: 'Chemistry, I suppose', she thought vaguely.

She still had a few things to tidy up in Oxford, writing up chemistry notes and finishing the work on the pellets she had brought from Lapland and handing over her bird notebook to a biologist studying nesting dates there. Finally she went to the Dyson Perrins Laboratory, where she had spent so much of the last six years of her life, and said goodbye to Dr Taylor, 'feeling very flat', even though he invited himself to tea at Royal Holloway. The personal and political situation combined to make it feel like the end of an era. 'The last link now seems to be severed', she wrote miserably. Only three days of the vacation were left: a final day's sailing in the Spinnaker Cup race with Frances and a friend crewing, her usual gardening and chauffeuring, and then a whole day spent packing her possessions in a very half-hearted way for the move to London. Suddenly, with the imminent threat of war, everything seemed impermanent and uncertain. There may even have been some wishful-thinking when she wrote, 'I may only be at Holloway for a few days and then will be I don't know where, doing war work'. Certainly she showed no enthusiasm for starting her first job, and could not rely on Cadlington as a safe retreat. A man came round asking how many rooms there were in the house, obviously with a view to requisitioning it. Writing to Aunt Rosemary from Royal Holloway, Rosemary summed up: 'How like the end of the world it was at the beginning of this week. Collecting my things for this place seemed so pointless'.[59]

Nevertheless, the Sunbeam was packed, and her mother and Frances went with her to the College. It had been purpose-built by a millionaire as a college for women and opened by Queen Victoria in 1886. Since 1900 it had been part of London University. The impressive Founder's Building, set in parkland, was modelled on the Renaissance style of the Chateau de Chambord with a double courtyard. A prime example of exuberant Victorian architecture, the red-brick structure was enlivened by outlines

The Chemistry Laboratory at Royal Holloway College in 1937.

of white marble and many fanciful turrets, towers and ornamental chimneys. It was probably much too elaborate for the Murrays' taste. Rosemary received a warm welcome, literally, because there was a fire in her room, also flowers and an ample tea, brought in by a maid. Before they left, Ellen and Puss transformed the room by completely re-arranging the furniture and unpacking the books. Dr Plant came to fetch Rosemary for supper in the great panelled dining hall, which dwarfed the few staff ensconced in the middle. Afterwards they all listened to the Prime Minister's broadcast, announcing that he was going to Germany again to negotiate peace. Three days later Rosemary happened to be on a Green Line bus which passed Chamberlain's cavalcade on the triumphant return from Munich. Crowds of people were waiting to see him, all the way through Chiswick and Hammersmith. Rosemary had a fine view of the cars and the police escort – as good as the King's entourage, she thought.

Rosemary quickly established a routine in College, very like the one in Oxford; lab work in the morning and recreation in the afternoon, exploring the Park around Royal Holloway, the poor shops in Egham and the better ones in Windsor. She was usually back in time for tea at 4p.m. or certainly for supper at 7.15 p.m. and then continued working or went to the cinema in Egham. She was thrown together with the other staff over meals, and tea and coffee in people's rooms, and she met the rather ineffectual Principal, Janet Bacon. There was much talk about Air Raid Precautions (ARP) – gas masks in the cellar and the designated shelter in a tunnel. Thousands of yards of blackout material were bought for the building's numerous windows. Rosemary found that the Maths lecturer kept an attaché case always by her, containing brandy, provisions and a torch. Proximity to London made them more acutely aware of danger than the inhabitants of Oxford or Havant. As there was really very little to do, Rosemary decided to take a long weekend before the start of term. Her father drove her to London to see Aunt Cath, who promised to lend etchings for her room. Frances helped her with clothes shopping, and father took her to the cinema and supper, followed by an exhilarating drive home at top speed in the Sunbeam. She had only been away for nine days, but how good it was to be back at Cadlington and to have practical tasks to do such as cleaning out the chickens – a very smelly job – and mending the door of their hutch, and also to have an afternoon's sailing with Pa and John. Granny was there, convalescing after an illness, and Ann had returned from Switzerland without a cure. Rosemary was most concerned to find her sister suffering a bad asthma attack, requiring continual injections of adrenaline and occasional shots of morphine: '… what is going to happen & when is her heart going to give out', she asked herself.

Back at Royal Holloway, Rosemary found to her dismay that she had missed a letter from Dr Taylor and that he had called on Saturday. What was worse, everyone from the Principal and Professor Moore downwards knew that the visitor had been 'irate' because she was not there. It was unfortunate, to say the least, that he had made his displeasure so widely known. Term started and Dr Plant approved Rosemary's lecture plan and Professor Moore told her the times when she was demonstrating. He advised her that there would not be much opportunity for research and she should only do it if she had a whole day free. She spent a morning with him interviewing the Freshers: all but two had done very little chemistry before, some were very shy and had 'Second Sch[ool] written all over them'. The prospect of teaching them was not stimulating. 'Am

I going to like being here?', she questioned herself. Soon homesickness for Oxford set in and she wished that Taylor would arrange another visit. Time dragged heavily in contrast to the packed days of research and entertainment in Oxford or physical work at Cadlington. She missed the constant stream of visitors which was a feature of the Murray and Spooner households, and easy access to the theatre and concerts. She was disappointed that she had to lecture at 9.00 a.m. on Saturdays, and so could only get home for a truncated weekend. To fill her spare time she devised activities, mostly solitary; practising the clarinet, walking in the Park and Windsor Forest, birdwatching and going for long rides on her bike. The reservoirs at Staines, two miles away, were a good spot for birdwatching, and later she obtained permission to go to Slough sewage farm. All the birds she identified were meticulously recorded in her notebook. College Chapel failed to inspire her and she complained about the rambling prayers and too much dull chanting, though still attending faithfully at 8a.m. before breakfast and on Sundays when in residence. At this time she seems to have adopted a 'rule', reading a chapter of the New Testament every morning and studying meditations in the evening.

Unlike the Oxford colleges, Royal Holloway was rather isolated and so the staff were heavily dependent on making their own entertainment in the evenings. Rosemary enjoyed the orchestra, despite conspicuous lack of success with the clarinet, and was quite a useful member of the choir, singing alto. There were plenty of small gatherings too, sometimes a 'bit sticky' but Rosemary found she liked some of her colleagues and could find topics of conversation. As term went on the teaching became more demanding and she worked hard to help the students to improve. Professor Moore occasionally came to see how she was getting on in the lab, and his wife invited her to tea, to get to know her better. They lived in 'rather a little villa of a house, cluttered up with ornaments. No nice pictures', said Rosemary, with a touch of cultural snobbery. Relations with Dr Plant deteriorated: she was always critical and lacking in tact, perhaps deliberately asserting her superior position over a colleague whom she found rather intimidating. Rosemary's diary mentions 'feeling very flat' and 'particularly gloomy' at times. Significantly, the two highlights of the term happened away from the College. Dr Taylor wrote, saying that he had been invited to read a paper to the Chemical Society in London. Since he wanted to present their joint paper about Rosemary's research on stilbenes, he apologised that he had to 'rush it off to the Publication

Committee pronto, and there wasn't time to get your OK about it'[60]. Rosemary seems to have overlooked this, and his comment, 'Will you come and help answer any questions. There won't be any', which she transmuted in her diary to 'come and listen'. In fact, when he read the paper she noticed a few *faux pas*, and there were some questions, though dull ones that he was able to answer himself. Before the meeting he entertained her in style. They met at his club, the Royal Societies, 'quite respectable enough for you', had a drink in Jermyn Street and then went to a 'terribly posh' French restaurant where they dined on soup, snails, chicken and morelles and salad, all chosen by the host. After some slight strain at first meeting, it was 'super'. She heard with interest about his forthcoming visit to the Galapagos Islands, to do tests on colouring matter in plants. Rosemary was flattered that he said he missed her at Oxford, having no-one to talk to when bored with demonstrating. She probably didn't admit that she missed him too.

The other exciting mail was the official notice of her D.Phil. She still marvelled at how far she had come since first contemplating it – she had achieved not only a degree, but a published paper. She took her degree as soon as she could arrange it, because she needed the status at RHC, signified by the D.Phil. hood. On November 18th she bought the gown and hood in Oxford and had lunch with Granny at Canterbury Road and tea with May Crum. Next day the Murray party – mother, father, Frances and Aunt Cath – all had lunch at LMH and walked from there to the Sheldonian Theatre for the ceremony, which Rosemary felt was 'rather badly done, bowing very vague etc.' She could hardly have foreseen that she would one day preside, with an equally critical eye, over many similar grand occasions. Lunching with the Taylors next day, she heard more details of their Galapagos trip, even examining the stores lists, while Georgie (Mrs Taylor) fell asleep in her chair. 'How I wish I was going on that expo[61]: it would be absolutely superb', she wrote. It was indeed a success, and next May, when they returned to the 'miserable climate' of England, 'Tommy' as she now thought of him, wrote to Rosemary:

'I have a good mind to renounce Oxford and all its works and go back to the Galapagos. You would like it; we could live happily on the local turtles, strawberries, bananas, paw-paws, pigs, asparagus, lobsters etc. and you don't need clothes, and get beautifully brown all over.'[62]

What Rosemary made of these frivolous remarks is, sadly, not recorded.

Encounters like this served only to emphasise the tedium of life at RHC and the irritation she increasingly felt with her colleague, Dr Plant. 'Oh what a place this is!' she exclaimed when most of the books she wanted for the library were vetoed. She dashed down to Cadlington, where all the Murrays were assembled for firework night, and visited John's gunnery training ship, HMS *Erebus*, stationed at Whale Island.[63] Dr Plant noticed her short absence and continued to make objections about Rosemary's equipment and her teaching proposals and even her use of the library. Rosemary's reaction was to get away as much as possible. In December she went to London two days running, to the Sadlers Wells Ballet and to a Downe House meeting about starting an Old Seniors Association. She was already one of their most successful old girls. The end of term exams were marked and reports written, and Rosemary was gratified when Professor Moore said she had done very well and had been a comfort to him when Dr Plant was ill. Miss Bacon congratulated her on her first term, adding 'We like you very much'. Rosemary couldn't wait to go home, and fretted that the forecast snow might prevent her leaving, but Frances and John drove over in the icy cold to fetch her. In a day or two snow came to Hampshire and all the Murray children, with the exception of invalid Ann, went out with skis and a home-made toboggan to have fun on the slopes. It was a return to carefree youth for Rosemary, who delighted in sharing these family activities, but she was reminded that childhood days were nearly over when David refused a Christmas stocking: 'Oh dear, how we all grow up', she thought.

After a delightful Christmas holiday, crowned by news of her father's promotion to Rear-Admiral, Rosemary left home 'with more sorrow than I have known for a long time'. Life at Royal Holloway went on much the same for the rest of the academic year, with Rosemary fulfilling all her duties in the labs, demonstrating, lecturing and teaching students in pairs. She still looked on a day in London as escaping, and lived for the weekends at Cadlington, where she launched into strenuous activities such as scything and sawing up immense branches. When war finally broke out in September 1939, the Murrays were again full of ideas about helping the war effort. Rosemary's father, who knew the Director of Scientific Research, made enquiries on her behalf about work in the Admiralty, without success. She would have been glad of a change, as she told the Taylors before returning for her second academic year in 'that bare and awful place' with the 'same old staff'. Taylor already had a job with the army, and his wife was joining the female equivalent, the Auxiliary Territorial Service (ATS). Cadlington was now being run as a smallholding and they were keeping goats, which Rosemary learned to milk. She helped John make a wooden cart which would enable them to save on petrol. They now had a farm helper, Diana Hoare, the daughter of friends, who lived as family for the duration of the War looking after the animals and doing quite heavy work like stoking the boiler[64]. Any able-bodied visitors were expected to join in whatever tasks were on hand. Horace Barlow, as a schoolboy, remembers arriving for lunch and being asked by Rosemary 'Can you scythe?'. 'No', he said. 'Then I'll show you', she replied, and indicated the area of the field she wanted cut.[65] Dr Taylor must have been surprised on his first (and only) visit to be asked to saw up a damson tree and get out the roots. He retired to the veranda: 'worn out?', wondered Rosemary, her own energy undiminished. She also records that Miss Blackwell, the only RHC colleague who visited, worked in the orchard in the hot sun and was 'laid out by it' and lay on a rug all afternoon.

During the phoney war period RHC stepped up its preparations; first a 'frightful' staff meeting about launching an economy campaign, led by Dr Plant who was very critical of the household staff, and then fire practices for students and teachers. Rosemary took the lead in organising First Aid lectures: she had passed the exams in Oxford but these lectures were directly relevant to war casualties, covering treatment for shock and various types of wounds. She also volunteered to learn ambulance driving with the ARP. Instruction started in February 1940. It involved a lot of waiting about, and driving in the dark without lights was risky, but Rosemary always enjoyed a challenge and it was good to have something to do that took her out of the College. Bombing caused disruption on the railways and Rosemary's chief anxiety was that passenger trains might cease to run regularly, so after some hesitation she decided to check whether she could get home by bike. In March she recorded a trial run that took four and a half hours against a strong wind and was very pleasant and unfatiguing. 'So now I know I can go home whatever happens to the railways', she wrote with relief. In the summer Ellen Murray was urging her to find some work more relevant to the war, and Frances agreed that Rosemary was wasted at RHC, but she had already decided to stay another year. 'Sometimes the thought appals me and sometimes it['s] not too bad'.

On June 9th 1940 Professor Moore received a letter from Professor Robert Robinson, Head of the Dyson Perrins Laboratory, saying that he would be pleased to have Rosemary there in the long vacation as there was a lot of (unpaid) work to be done. This idea may well have come from Taylor, who was doing associated research at the Experimental Station at Porton Down. Rosemary was happy to accept the post, hoping it might eventually lead to a real job. Also, since Italy had just entered the war and the Germans were closing in on Paris she probably felt obliged to do anything she could for the war effort. She had begun to feel rather guilty about enjoying herself playing tennis and birdwatching while 'awful things' such as Dunkirk were happening. Her father had been posted to the Red Sea, and she listened eagerly to news of Italian submarines being sunk in the Gulf of Aden. After a couple of weeks' holiday at Cadlington she set out for Oxford. When she said good-bye to 'Mom' she was overtaken by home-sickness, but quickly recovered once she visited the lab and felt needed there again. Robinson asked her to make chlorocyclohexanone for him to take to Porton, where they were developing modern nerve agents and (somewhat later) the means of defence against them. Chemical warfare was permitted under the 1930 Geneva Protocol only in retaliation, but the Germans were known to have such weapons. There is no record of Rosemary's lab work, which was of course secret, except that she also made pinacol hydrate, a white organic compound which is an irritant, and was asked to continue production in the laboratory at RHC. Prof. Moore, Dr Plant and Rosemary kept this up as a continuous process as part of their daily routine.

Meanwhile the war came to Cadlington too, as the army requisitioned most of the house to be a command centre for the area. Bombing raids on nearby Portsmouth had just begun. The Murrays were left with the servants' quarters, sitting room, breakfast room and kitchen. They already had nuns with a group of 80 children billeted on them, but these had to move out at short notice. On her first weekend off, in mid-July, Rosemary found a scene of hectic activity: soldiers putting up telegraph poles and converting the workshop into an exchange. Ellen Murray was in charge of the domestic side, organising the distribution of furniture very efficiently, and John, Frances, Ann and Diana were all helping. Furniture removers re-arranged their possessions and took van loads to storage, the contents listed by Rosemary. She also looked after the child evacuees, playing games with them and packing their blankets and beds into an army lorry so that they could go to a new home, 'pathetic sight, too like refugees'. After five exhausting days of clearing and cleaning rooms, re-routing electrics (John), and moving books and furniture, all were 'slightly jaded'. They perhaps did not guess how long the war would last. 'How little we realised that we were clearing up the Nursery for good and all'[66], wrote Ann in 1943. The military moved in, 'swarms of soldiers carrying chairs, tables, typewriters, cupboards etc. all over the house', and it was clear that the family was going to have an unpleasant time co-existing with them.

By summer 1940 Rosemary was on night duty for Civil Defence in Oxford, learning to reverse a lorry with a trailer, Frances was at a war hospital in Abbots Langley and John was passed for national service in July and called up in November. Ann had recovered sufficiently to take up her place as Exhibitioner at Lady Margaret Hall in Michaelmas 1939, though still much hampered by bouts of asthma. There, as at RHC, war preparations were evident: all windows were blacked out and a shelter had been created in a corridor, protected by sandbags and steel plates. The college was equipped with First Aid rooms and fire-fighting appliances and the hockey field was being cultivated as an allotment, while 'trousered members of the SCR may be seen slinking out of the Hall under cover of darkness for ARP duty.[67]' On a weekend at home, Rosemary had her first experience of a raid when she cycled over to supper with her relatives at Fittleworth – 'two maids to wait and grouse for dinner, war miles away' – but on the return journey there were many gun flashes and planes directly overhead and then searchlights all around. She was told of an invasion scare and church bells were rung to summon the Home Guard. Nevertheless, she found it exciting rather than terrifying.

Miss Bacon wrote to Rosemary asking if she would be returning to RHC for the Autumn Term, taking the opportunity to mention the re-arrangement of rooms consequent on air-raids, and warning that she might be asked to give up her study. Ellen Murray described the lack of organisation there as impossible and hopeless. On her way back, Rosemary saw a bomb crater at Weybridge and transport was disrupted. There was an air raid while she was on a bus, and gunfire in the evening. She immediately resumed ambulance driving, spending nights on duty or on call. For the first time she admits to feeling 'pretty frightened', when patrolling at 2 a.m. with waves of aeroplanes coming over, bangs and searchlights overhead. On November 15th there was a serious incident after a bomb fell in Egham High Street, trapping children in a cellar from which they could not be rescued. Sirens became the norm in the evenings, with call-outs at all hours. '15 mins from asleep to the post with ambulance', she recorded. It was not easy keeping up all the teaching and lab work after disturbed nights like this. RHC was never hit, but the lecturers' nerves became frayed and at one point the ARP Committee resigned in a body over some petty matter. Rosemary was an interested and critical observer of the Principal's handling of this situation. Birkbeck College was bombed and some of the salvaged lab equipment moved to RHC. In the New Year they heard the relays of German aircraft flying to attack cities in the Midlands.

By November the army had moved out of Cadlington, leaving behind a smell of stale tobacco. In their place the Murrays took in a stream of evacuees for the duration of the War. Rosemary was not able to get home every weekend, but helped when she could with the farm and repairs such as re-roofing the apple room to make it rat-proof. Cross country car journeys to Winchester, where David and Richard were at school, and to Oxford, were hazardous without lights and they sometimes met army convoys on the road. Raids on the South coast were a common occurrence and from Cadlington they could see a red glow in the sky as houses burned and hear the crunch of distant bombs. The countryside around Horndean was littered with wreckage of crashed planes. From her mother Rosemary heard a first-hand account of the effects of a major raid on Portsmouth on January 10th 1941: 'It was a Blitz indeed and Portsmouth is very hard hit ... Yesterday it was awful – all so disorganized – no water, no gas, no light, hardly any telephone ... I went about with people, messages etc. mostly & today mostly interviewed people ... and pretended I knew more than I did.[68]' Ann and David were roped in to help at the Cosham Emergency Centre, using their home-made cart for transporting loads.

The January term started badly, with an explosion on Rosemary's bench, showering glass all over the lab. 'Incredible I wasn't hit', she wrote. She was quite unsettled: 'sometimes the whole atmosphere makes me creep'. Tensions among the staff continued, and tired of trying to influence Dr Plant in private conversations, Rosemary had 'a proper stand up argument with her in the SCR' about the fire-watching system. 'Others much interested', she commented. In February Arthur Murray arrived back from the Red Sea posting and was briefly put in charge of the Signal School at Portsmouth which was doing top secret research on radar, which the British Navy had realised, rather late in the day, could be of crucial importance in wartime. Soon afterwards Rosemary made up her mind to quit Royal Holloway and take up an appointment there. It all seems to have been decided very suddenly in the last week of March, though as usual Rosemary agonised over whether she had made the right choice. She wrote to her mother, 'Even if the Signal School isn't so "*good*" a job I gather that it very much wants doing … though exactly what I couldn't make up[sic]' and 'I hope I've decided right[69]'. Once her duties concerning the scholarship interviews and practicals were over there was a round of farewell tea-parties, interspersed with packing up and tipping servants. 'Can't say I am overcome with sorrow', she remarked – a massive understatement – before getting on her bike for the long ride home.

Rosemary did not resign her lectureship, but secured leave of absence to undertake 'work of national importance'. Professor Moore was keen to have her back after the War, even if she had done no chemistry in the meantime. HMS *Signal School* was situated in Portsmouth Dockyard where it had started in 1904, specialising in communication by Morse code and semaphore. Research on radar began around 1935 when the government realised its potential for warning against air attack. A coastal chain of warning stations was developed in time to map the raids of 1940. The potential for naval radar had been noted as early as 1928, but not pursued. Arthur Murray was one of those who recognised the urgency, and when working there as a Captain in 1937 he told them they had been caught with their trousers down and it mustn't happen again! The Signal School speedily set to work to design equipment that could be fitted on ships, just in time to make a major contribution to the Battle of the Atlantic. On 10th March a very heavy raid caused severe destruction in Portsmouth, nevertheless the Signal School continued there for a while and Rosemary joined them as Temporary Experimental Officer in the Admiralty Scientific and Technical Pools in April. The job must have been rather a disappointment because it was designed for a physicist rather than a chemist and she was only the equivalent of a clerk. Had she stayed longer her merits might have been recognised, leading to promotion, but once again Professor (now Sir Robert) Robinson stepped in and influenced her career. On 20th May Aunt Rosemary sent a letter saying that she had seen Lady Robinson in the Bank, and she and her husband 'seem very 'upset' that you are not in Chemistry!'[70] Lady Robinson had telephoned later to say that Sir Robert would like to recommend Rosemary, if available, for the post of Assistant Lecturer at Sheffield University under Professor Howarth 'a very live wire'. There would be plenty of research work, related to the war effort and the post was guaranteed for the duration of the War as they would be releasing a man for the services. It was obviously attractive to Rosemary, who had always felt that chemistry was the best she had to offer in the service of her country, though she must have realised that it would be somewhat similar to the post she had just left in London; lecturing and demonstrating, but with more time for more applicable research. Robinson strongly recommended her to take the opportunity as it would be a very good launch pad after the war. Rosemary tried to hedge her bets, asking if RHC would consider this whole time war work from which she might return, but Professor Moore replied firmly, 'The position is the same as if you had asked to go direct from this College to another College – which would certainly not have been given'[71]. Her permission for leave of absence was only to work for the Admiralty or a Ministry of Supply laboratory. After a token interview when she was offered the job, Rosemary therefore had to resign from RHC and obtain a release from the Admiralty before taking up the post at Sheffield.

Rosemary moved North in September, and for the first term she lived in a boarding house, which Frances referred to as 'grim'. It was very inconvenient because, due to the lab work, she often missed the early supper that she had paid for. She was doing two and a half days of demonstrating per week and no lecturing at all until the second term, leaving plenty of time for research. She described herself as quite busy making compounds. There is no doubt that she was lonely, being too far away to get home to Cadlington or even Oxford during term. Things looked up when a Physics lecturer, Eva Widdowson, offered to let her share her house, further out of Sheffield but with buses and trams nearby, and Rosemary was soon putting up shelves, reorganising the kitchen and making the loft accessible with a rope ladder. Eva must have wondered what she had taken on. There were many distractions for someone so practical, and when they lost their cleaning lady they both spent half a day a week wielding the Goblin vacuum cleaner and cleaning the oven. Rosemary made a real effort to socialise, looking up friends and acquaintances of the family and joining a group to learn something about the intellectual achievements of Russia. Visits from the Hallé and London Philharmonic orchestras were a treat not to be missed. She continued as an ARP volunteer and was persuaded by a very flattering letter to help at the YWCA canteen. In leisure time she explored the surrounding countryside alone, by bus and on foot, despite ice and snow and biting winds. There are early hints that the job was not entirely satisfactory: after only a few months her father asked whether her research topic was promising, and said that if Sheffield was 'not what it seemed' he would try to get her a better job at the Signal School. At the beginning of 1942 he wrote, 'I saw Brundrett yesterday or so – and said you were in the saddle at Sheffield, & that you were not sure the horse suited you'[72]. Rosemary was discontented with her work, still feeling that she was not contributing anything useful to the war or society at large and that she was in a rather lowly position for someone with four years' post-doctoral experience.

A revealing letter from Frances reflects the confidences Rosemary had shared with her. 'Oh dear me it does sound so foul in Sheffield, everybody so snobbish and jealous and unfriendly ... I can't bear to think of you being wasted in that hateful place'[73]. She expresses the hope that the seven scientists have improved on acquaintance, and philosophises, 'Isn't it nearly *always* the better off levels of society that are so hypocritical & so mean & petty and unkind?' Were Rosemary's impressions again coloured by home-sickness, even at the age of 28? Having been brought up in such an homogenous upper-middle-class group, she could not adjust to a different world and reacted strongly against it. Rosemary was still very reserved with people she did not know well, and reserve may have been mistaken for arrogance. Indeed it bordered on arrogance, because looking back she described the period bitterly as one of 'subordination to stupidity'[74].

Weekends at home had made RHC bearable. Sheffield did not even have a Long Vac because there was an extra Summer Term. Rosemary was desperate to find opportunities to meet members of the family. In November 1941 she was back in Oxford to take her M.A., watched by her parents. It was an opportunity to see Ann and David too, both students, and to play music with Aunts Ruth and Rosemary. The long weekend was quickly over and she concluded, 'Am no forwarder in deciding whether to leave or not', so she was already unsettled. 'I long to see John', she wrote in October. He was serving on HMS *Birmingham*, stationed near Newcastle, and she twice made the eight-hour journey to spend a few hours with him. They walked and talked and looked over his ship. With uncharacteristic emotion she wrote, 'It was worth a year in Sheffield to have those two weekends'. Similarly, when her father was posted to Yarmouth in April 1942 she very quickly arranged to spend a weekend with him on her way home for Easter.

By this time, after only two terms, Rosemary had decided that Sheffield was not what she wanted. To her mother she wrote, 'I'm sure that I don't want to stay here & I think really the difficulty I'm having is to decide what to change to.[75]' Conscription of single women was brought in at the end of 1941, but did not apply to Rosemary as she was substituting for a man in a reserved occupation. Nevertheless, she soon began to consider the services seriously, in particular the WRNS, which she hoped might give opportunities for going to sea. Her father asked around and found that a fair number of harbour craft at Plymouth were manned by Wrens, but only a few had that sort of job: most Wrens were firmly shore based. He described the duties of the Wrens at Yarmouth: working in the 'degaussing range'; analysing records of instruments was fairly routine, plotting bearings was more interesting. Rosemary visited a WRNS interviewing officer in London, who suggested maintenance of wireless sets. Back in Sheffield she had similar replies from the WRNS and WAAF with the information that there was no guarantee of a particular area of work since vacancies were filled as they arose. 'It seems altogether a chancy affair', she thought. It is clear that Rosemary was initially looking for a commission, and in later life she used to say that she could have gone in as an officer, though this was perhaps through her father pulling strings. In the end she was proud that she started at the bottom, as a humble rating. She plucked up courage to tell Professor Howarth that she was leaving, and her father wrote, 'I hope Howarth will realise that those foul tho' complex compounds are not worth your serious study! And not be awkward.[76]' In May she finally sent off the WRNS application form, wracked by her usual indecision. 'I wish I could decide whether I am a fool to think I should be doing more good in the WRNS'. She was called to interview in Portsmouth, accepted as Grade I medically fit at the end of August, and awaited orders.

Rosemary (centre row, fourth from the right) as a Wren rating, 1943.

– 6 –

Life in the WRNS

ROSEMARY ENTERED THE WRNS on Trafalgar Day, October 21st, at a time when the service was expanding fast: by the end of 1942 there were 40,000 personnel, some of them conscripted under the National Service Act, which gave the government power to call up single women and childless widows between the ages of 19 and 30. Wrens had proved their competence in many different fields – catering, administration, and a variety of technical areas. The Admiralty was crying out for more Wrens and finding many ways of employing them to take the place of men fit for battle. Although closely linked to the Royal Navy, the WRNS was run by women at all levels, with a formidable and very effective Director, Vera Laughton Mathews. Recruits went first to a Training Depot, where they were given an introduction to service life and introduced to discipline. Those who did not make the grade were released after a fortnight; the rest were enrolled and received their uniforms and went on to more specialised work.

Rosemary was told to report to Mill Hill Central Training Depot in London for her probationary period. It had only been open since May, but already accommodated 900 recruits. It was 'a great bare barracks of a place'[77] as the Director admitted, and one of the tasks of probationers was to take a turn in getting up at 5 a.m. to scrub the nine storeys of stone staircases. The ratings were paid 1/9d per day. Rosemary was not there long, as she was moved to Westfield College, Hampstead, in November for the specialised training. Here there was also a lot of manual work, such as filling fire buckets with sand, and it was a long day, with breakfast at 7.00 a.m. and work starting half an hour later and continuing until supper at 6.15 p.m. with an hour off for lunch. The Wrens had to get used to their shore station being designated 'HMS' and described with all the naval terminology used on ships: cabins, bunks, galleys, mess and wardrooms. When they left the building they were 'going ashore' and morning parade was 'Divisions'. They attended lectures on badges and ranks, pay and allowances, security and ARP procedures. Rosemary's education and background was superior to that of the other ratings, so when asked what her civilian job had been she said she was a teacher, 'otherwise no-one would have talked to me'. A few weeks later Rosemary was sent to the Pay and Registry Office, working office hours. This was the section responsible for the allocation of Wrens' duties and messing arrangements. She found it very dull, 'mostly with nothing to do, just watching the wheels go round. But necessary I suppose.' She hoped she would soon be posted to another location, preferably Scotland or Portsmouth. Next she was sent to Supplies, the section organising the ordering and provision of stores such as clothing, and then back again to the Regulating Office for three months. John wrote that he was jealous of her learning all about messbooks and provision accounts, since he had been given the task of Victualling Officer for his ship, the destroyer HMS *Exmoor*. However, when she was still doing it in March he thought she should have been moved on: 'It would be such a waste for you to fill in Messbooks for the rest of your days'. Rosemary was not averse to doing routine work – she had always enjoyed listing and tabulating data – but she must have been relieved and excited to be chosen for the Officers' Training Course (OTC).

The course was held in the august setting of the Royal Naval College, Greenwich, one of the finest eighteenth-century buildings in the country, designed by Wren. Here the cadets were lectured on naval history, discipline and leadership by senior naval officers and the Director of WRNS herself. Rosemary took careful notes, but she must have been familiar with much of the material from her family's naval background. Rosemary described the programme of a typical day as divisions, squad drill, two lectures, lunch, one lecture, games – usually squash, which she enjoyed, another lecture or film, supper. She had been particularly interested in lectures on Sea Power and The Mediterranean, mainly recent history. Those on the service itself were very detailed, giving a complete overview of forces in the U.K. and the Wrens' varied occupations, more than 170 different classes of work, as well as everything an officer might need to know to run a WRNS unit[78]. The recruits were taught that the responsibilities of an officer were a thorough understanding of the disciplinary code and loyalty to it, teaching by example the thorough execution of orders and unquestioning obedience. Care of subordinates incorporated consideration of their health and welfare and an attitude of friendliness without familiarity. Rosemary had no problems about being in command. She had developed a natural authority since childhood, looking after her siblings, organising entertainments for local children, leading a devoted band of friends at school and running the Guide Troop. Nor did she object to discipline, having always been obedient to parents and teachers (quite frighteningly so, thought her sister Frances) and stifling her criticisms of superiors in a work setting. During the course an atmosphere of pride and privilege was created, partly from living in the impressive palace which belonged to naval history and also filtering down from the distinguished senior officers who participated. The recruits developed their own *esprit de corps*. Soon after her arrival, Rosemary and thirty others were chosen to be a guard of honour at Westminster Abbey for the celebration of the fourth anniversary of the re-formed WRNS. 1,500 Wrens marched past Buckingham Palace where Queen Elizabeth took the salute. It was a splendid recognition of their service and a boost to morale.

The recruits had some choice in the sections they would go on to work in. About half way through the OTC course Rosemary went to an Ordnance Board to learn about their duties, which were mainly abstracting and report writing, and decided this was not for her. Education or administration might be more her line, she felt. She wanted a job which was practical but also dealing with people. One can understand how the training developed Rosemary's character and brought out a latent ability to command. Frances remarked that Rosemary changed as soon as she put on a uniform: it gave her authority and a rôle which enabled her to overcome her shyness. The course concluded with an interview by the Promotion Board, chaired by Director Laughton Mathews, in whose office she was eventually destined to work. They were looking for intellectual qualities, practical common sense, and an interest in people which would aid responsibility and leadership. Rosemary could certainly offer all these attributes. She passed the Board and was commissioned as 3rd Officer on May 2nd 1943.

By the end of the OTC course Rosemary had decided that administration was to be her role, not education. She was not a natural lecturer, and when she had to give a presentation on the course was strangely nervous, despite all her previous experience. Administration would suit her business-like approach and give her contact with people, and it offered good career opportunities. Administrators required a thorough knowledge of the structure of the WRNS and all its paperwork. Hundreds of ships' forms were supplied by the Navy: pay, accounting, stores, discipline and personnel issues were all regulated and recorded in this way, and consolidated in weekly and monthly returns. In addition, the Wrens received weekly Admiralty Fleet Orders (AFOs), instructions designated by numbers with information that should be passed on to ratings and officers. Rosemary's natural tendency to bring things into order suited her to the tasks. A specialised course for administrators followed the OTC, after which she was posted to HMS *Ferret*, the shore base of the WRNS at Londonderry, Northern Ireland, from 12th May 1943. Londonderry, usually abbreviated to 'Derry' by the service personnel, was the most important base in the North West approaches, a depot for ship refuelling and taking on munitions. Thousands of men were stationed there; the base was shared with the Royal Canadian and US Navies, and there were some 600 Wrens doing all kinds of jobs: writers, coders, teleprinter operators, cooks, stewards and technicians. In retrospect Rosemary thought that they 'practically ran the base'.[79] At one time 140 escort ships were based on the River Foyle. It was always busy with boats going up to the stores to collect clothing and provisions. Ships came in for re-fitting, before sailing back to the Atlantic, one of the main theatres of war at that time. The Headquarters in Magee College was a communications centre of huge importance. Throughout the War the Battle of the Atlantic was unfolded on the great wall maps of the plot and operations room of Western Approaches Command, with Wrens working alongside officers of the Navy and Air Force. The whole base was buzzing with activity. Naturally it was heavily defended, but it was not bombed after 1941 and an almost surreal social life went on parallel to the constant war effort. The service personnel lived well, with few of the food shortages suffered in England. Provisions were brought in from America and also smuggled over the border from Southern Ireland.

Rosemary initially lived at Belmont, the Wrens Officers' quarters North East of the town, an easy bike ride downhill and along the wide river to the base. She admired the scenery with the gently sloping mountains in the background. Letters to her parents had a cheerful tone, with no hint of the former home-sickness she had suffered in London and Sheffield. The camaraderie of the services was a substitute for her own family network and the busy office and challenging circumstances suited her well. After three months in post she wrote: 'Wrens come pouring in, new homes to be opened and Navy weeks being organised. I don't have much to do with that, but it means that the First O[fficer] is out of the office most of the time, and the telephone rings almost continuously.'

The WRNS Director placed emphasis on running a 'happy ship': morale was certainly high in Ebrington Barracks where Rosemary worked. One of the girls wrote:

'You will find us always smiling
At our logging and our filing.
We will check and we will victual,
We will work so hard that it'll
Be the MO's occupation
To ensure recuperation.'[80]

Incidentally this verse tells us the sort of activity Rosemary was supervising: control of the masses of paperwork generated concerning feeding, housing and clothing so many women. She was constantly making decisions, based on the rules and regulations, about health and welfare, deployment and discharge of individuals. Her responsibilities grew as colleagues went on leave or were off sick. In August she reported that she was running out of accommodation: 'We shall soon be putting Wrens on the floor as we are absolutely full up; no beds anywhere'. No wonder John wrote, 'It just shows – you run the base by yourself after x months as a WRN… How many of your batch could have done that?' In what little spare time she had she loved to go on the river, or even to sea when the chance arose. Rowing in a whaler against the strong tide was very heavy work, especially when 'manned' by only four women, but it was always 'super'. For Navy Week 1943 Rosemary got together an officers' boat to race in the regatta, never having been in the boat before and with a cox who was taught to steer on the way. 'We are so inspired we are going again', she wrote, and they did. Long bike rides, solo or with her room mate Wren Officer Squirrell, around the scenic Londonderry countryside were a favourite recreation, whereas she skipped the endless parties and dances as often as possible. What she really enjoyed was a select dinner party featuring conversation and not too much drinking. She was horrified by the amount of alcohol people drank, as her parents were very abstemious. Nevertheless she picked up the habit of downing a stiff gin and French after work.

Occasional visits of Wren 'big bugs' kept the base on its toes. In September 1943 the visitor was the Deputy Director, Jocelyn Woollcombe, who had been consulted by Rosemary's father about her application to join up. By this time it was well known that Rosemary was Admiral Murray's daughter, because officers who had been his colleagues often passed through Londonderry. Rosemary had expected the visit to be an 'awful affair' and rather resented the time spent preparing for it, but since it resulted in the complement of administrative officers being increased, it was worthwhile. 'I think we shall be a happy trio in the office; and also be able to get out and round the base more', she said. Officers were also responsible for drilling the Wrens under their command, one of the subjects taught on the OTC course. Saturday morning started with half an hour's drill, which Wrens were supposed to attend every fortnight. There were usually about a hundred present. When they were performing well, Rosemary found it 'quite fun' to drill them. Parades through the city were not infrequent, for example for Navy Week 1943 Rosemary took twenty Wrens to march with sailors and the next day had a combined march to church with a very good army band. The Battle of Britain was celebrated in a similar way, but with combined services including Canadian and American forces.

Londonderry was for many Wrens an enjoyable place to be stationed, because they were greatly outnumbered by men and much in demand for dating. The Americans were particularly forward and were regarded as some kind of exotic species.[81] They gave out presents of nylons, chocolate and chewing gum; all practically unobtainable in the United Kingdom. Rosemary, as an officer, was sometimes invited to dinners aboard ship, a scenario with which she was quite familiar. She was soon writing home for her high-heeled shoes and pearls. Food was good and plentiful in Londonderry, and Rosemary, like others, sent parcels home. For Christmas 1943 she posted a turkey! This was the first Christmas Rosemary had spent away from the family since her stay in Neuchâtel in 1931. She thought of them making presents and running the usual popular children's parties: '... there were so many odd moments here when I wished I could be helping you.[82]' She was with three other officers at one of the smaller Wrens' quarters on the day. In a traditional reversal of rôles they served the women a classic Christmas dinner and then washed up: 'tin trays covered with grease seemed to be in all directions', she wrote. New Year was spent with the American Commodore, who had been at Pearl Harbour, and some of his staff. Rosemary was rather shocked by the way they talked about the Japanese as less than human. The Wren officers gave a small dinner party for eight, followed by a duty visit to a dance, and then went back to the American's house to listen to the bells ringing in the New Year. It had been good for Anglo-American relations, Rosemary reflected. There is just a hint that she was attracted to one of the party, because soon afterwards she wrote to her mother about a marvellous walk to Greencastle with '2 others' (it is unusual for her not to mention names), lunch in a hotel, and in the afternoon 'I and one went a walk up into the hills, up to the snow'… 'so nice to get quite away'[83].

In her letters Rosemary frequently refers to time flying. 'I have now been here 5 months it seems only a day'. She had expected to move on after about six months, but it seems likely she had become fairly indispensable. She was promoted to 2nd Officer at the end of January 1944, continuing the same work. There was 'such a lot doing' in the office that the days sped past. She mentions endless requests from Wrens to transfer or change their category, medical emergencies when girls had to be sent to sick bay or hospital, and in one case a fatality on the nearby railway line. She was handling pay, taking drill and ARP practices and doing statistical returns, working until seven or eight in the evening and snatching a sandwich at her desk. She did eventually get tired of the repetitive work and probably mentally tired as well. She particularly missed her brother John, hoping he might pass through the base and 'enliven the weary hours'. Suddenly an exciting opportunity came up when she received a letter from Georgie Taylor, wife of her Oxford supervisor T.W.J. Taylor, wondering whether she would like to go out to Ceylon to be Taylor's assistant at the Operational Research Division he was running.[84] At first Rosemary thought it was a marvellous idea, simply because she was ready for a change of scene and she always enjoyed travelling. Then she began to wonder if she wanted to leave Europe, and possibly also the WRNS, to return to a scientific post. 'I don't know that I want to go back to science – people are fundamentally more interesting tho' sometimes exasperating and boring'. Taylor confirmed that it was not worth coming for the sake of the job, only to see the world. He tried hard to give an impartial assessment, while obviously wanting very much to see Rosemary again. The idea was put aside when Rosemary was told by the WRNS Director, on a visit to the base in July, that she would soon be leaving. Rosemary found her 'so nice', but also determined. 'I think she makes up her mind as to what she wants and there isn't much option'. She had guessed that she would be posted to the WRNS Headquarters in London.

On taking up the appointment she was promoted to Acting 1st Officer,

Rosemary (far left) as an officer with Vera Laughton Mathews, Director WRNS, 1946.

reporting on 21st August 1944. From Wren rating to the immediate staff of the Director in less than two years was quite an achievement, though not unprecedented in wartime when accelerated promotion was fairly common. Vera Laughton Mathews had a habit of spotting talented women as she went round inspecting bases. In reports Rosemary was classified 'Character VG; Efficiency AA' throughout her career. The Director recommended her as an 'Officer of exceptional mentality and very attractive personality'[85].

The move from the tranquil and beautiful countryside of Northern Ireland to bomb-damaged London was quite a contrast, but on the whole Rosemary was pleased to be back in the capital. Frances was there, nursing, and other members of the family passed through, including her other sister, Ann, who was working in Cambridge. Cadlington was within range again. At Headquarters in Queen Anne's Mansions, a block of flats overlooking St James's Park which had been requisitioned by the Navy, she worked with intelligent, efficient women like Jocelyn Woollcombe, whom she respected. WRNS HQ had responsibility for all officers in the service. Rosemary was in the Officers' Appointments (OA) branch which dealt with promotions, appointments and releases. In this post she gained very useful experience of interviewing, which was later transferred to civilian life. One section called up candidates from a waiting list to the OTC, trying to forecast the numbers that would be required six to eight weeks ahead. Three WRNS First Officers dealt with appointments to various posts: administration, secretarial or communications. Two more organised the selection boards and officers' training. The Records section kept officers' papers up to date, filing confidential reports and maintaining several sequences of card indexes including a list of civilian qualifications, in case some particular talent were needed. Additions or reductions to the number of staff at an establishment had to be passed by the Director, who seems to have kept a close eye on promotions too, and was the final authority for releasing officers. Administration at this level was not just routine: often something unexpected turned up and the officers needed to use their initiative. Rosemary worked hard, seldom finishing before 8.30 p.m. in the evening. Meanwhile, although the Blitz was over, London was suffering the attacks of the V1 unmanned planes, the Doodlebugs, and in September 1944 the V2 rockets.

Rosemary must have joined in the relief and euphoria of VE Day on 8th May 1945, celebrating the end of five years of conflict in Europe. There were plenty of Wrens partying in London, singing and dancing in the streets. She would have been thankful that her immediate relatives in the Navy were safe, although tragedy had touched the family: she had lost two cousins, both in the RAF; 'Young Bill' Spooner, Uncle William's only son, killed on his first bombing raid, and Aunt Kitty Inge's youngest son, Richard, a flying instructor who died in an air accident. Her father, a Rear Admiral since 1939, had spent the early years of the War patrolling in the Indian Ocean, and then endured a hard and unpleasant time based in Aden, keeping control of the Red Sea and evacuating refugees from Eritrea. As a result of this posting he contracted typhoid, and was invalided out with the rank of Vice Admiral in December 1942. The disease necessitated a long period of convalescence and shortened his life.

Just before Christmas 1945 Rosemary received the news that she had been posted to Donibristle Air Station outside Edinburgh, one of the first establishments to employ Wrens working on naval aircraft. These were the air mechanics, engineers, electricians, gunnery and airframe technicians and the rather superior specialised radio mechanics.

Rosemary's train journey to Scotland was miserable; freezing cold with a very leaky window and door, so that in tunnels the smoke came pouring in through the cracks, but her status meant that she was met by car at Edinburgh, given time to wash and brush up in a hotel and driven to the base. Donibristle was set in lovely countryside with views across the Forth towards the city, and the Pentland Hills to the South. It was rather like being back in Londonderry, except that the accommodation was palatial by service standards. She had two rooms in a hut, each provided with a stove, and a bathroom to herself: 'with the longest bath I ever met, when lying against the top end the feet don't touch the bottom. [Quarters] Suitable for 3 at least but I haven't yet asked anyone to share.' Rosemary was on the staff of the Flag Officer, Flying Training and was initially vague about her duties: 'I hope that light may dawn as to what I am to do', she wrote. In fact she was ordered to visit air stations all over the country to report on conditions and look after the welfare of the Wrens stationed at them. Rosemary's first inspection, in Wiltshire, and her very first flight are described in a letter to Ann.

> 'It was a very windy day and it took 3 hrs to get there against a head wind and was quite bumpy, in fact it seems to have been quite a bad trip, but as it was my first I couldn't tell. It is super flying and seems quite natural. You bump along the ground with a great noise, then the noise and bumps decrease and you see the earth getting further below & looking just like a chess board, or like the view from a mountain. Rivers meandering between brown fields and woods & baby trains & little houses & towns just like sand tray models.'[86]

She was able to stay at Cadlington for two nights, visit the base at Hensbridge and go on to one at Zeals, back to Cadlington for Sunday and then returned to Scotland via Lee on Monday. This kind of packed schedule continued, but she did get a little time at home, and on other trips she was able to stop off in Oxford, sleeping on the sofa at Polstead Road. Life was returning to normal there. Rosemary heard the cathedral choir 'singing quite marvellously', and a concert of the London Philharmonic. The Taylors were back in their house at Iffley. When at Donibristle she worked in the office writing up reports until 6.00 p.m., and had free time in the evenings for reading and letter-writing (she commonly wrote three or four per day). Altogether Rosemary visited ten bases during January and February 1946, taking notes covering everything from accommodation and messing to firing ranges[87]. Unlike her predecessor, she began to make comments on individual officers: 'bright little thing', 'dull and not much personality', 'mouselike but quite agreeable'. This ability to sum people up in a few words was shared with her grandfather Spooner. In general, Rosemary was very sympathetic to the needs of the Wrens, feeding back useful practical suggestions (although most of the bases had begun to release Wrens and some were due to close completely so the suggestions may not have been carried out). As one might expect, her inspections were very thorough, right down to the comfort and decoration of the recreation rooms and the condition of coal and vegetable stores. She always commented on the cleanliness or otherwise of individual facilities. Rosemary clearly enjoyed this period of service: the continual activity, flights, observation and listing, and probably also the status were all very congenial, so much so that she emphasised this post when talking to journalists about her career, giving the impression that it had lasted much longer than three months[88]. She also liked to recount a frightening incident in the air when a mistaken reading of instruments at the station directing their descent nearly plunged the plane into the sea. The pilot managed to pull out just in time.

Once her inspections were completed, Rosemary was moved back to more standard administration. By mid-March 1946 she was at Chatham Royal Naval Barracks, where on 1st April she was promoted to Chief Officer, equivalent to a Commander in the Navy, with the title Drafting Officer, Nore Command. She was one of only 40 Chief Officers in the WRNS, and her task was supervising the demobilisation of the 1,400 service women at Chatham. A large new department had been set up to cope with the Government's release scheme. Some whole categories of Wrens were declared redundant and other sections were being run down. Each Wren was allotted a release number and knew when to expect demobilisation. There was a period of two months' paid leave before finally quitting the service. It was not just a matter of keeping records (complicated by the number of women who had married and changed their name since joining up) but taking in uniforms, handing out a grant for civilian clothing and coupons, a ration book and an identity card. Final pay was issued, together with a gratuity based on length of service and a railway warrant for the journey home. Clearly this was a massive operation at all the home ports and a challenge for administrators like Rosemary, but she relished the opportunity of managing a significant part of it. The Director WRNS considered the operation 'a major administrative triumph'.

The demobilisation process at Chatham took about six months, and Rosemary was discharged on 16th October 1946, almost four years to the day since she became a Pro-Wren at Mill Hill. Her rapid promotion and exemplary record throughout must have been a source of pride and self-esteem, qualities which had been so lacking in her pre-War days. As a Chief Officer she received from the Director a hand-written commendation, which could be used as a testimonial.

> 'This officer has a clear and constructive brain and exceptional ability. Her integrity is of the highest order & she is extremely efficient and hard-working ... I recommend her with confidence for a position of responsibility.'[89]

Dame Vera's speeches to the Wrens acknowledged what a life-changing experience war service would be for many women:

> 'Our lives are going to be wider and deeper because of what we have learned in the Service. And when peace comes you will take your place in civilian life to such good purpose that people will say, "Well, you see, she was a Wren".[90]'

This was quite prophetic in Rosemary's case. She may not have realised it, but service life had driven out the latent snobbery that caused her to look down on people outside the charmed circle in which her family operated. She now valued the qualities of different types and classes who all had something to contribute to society. A natural tendency in her to take command had been developed and tested in arduous circumstances. She was able to draw on it again when once more in charge of a major project. Rosemary admitted, 'One feels slightly guilty about saying one enjoyed one's war. But I got a lot out of it, because it broadened my horizons'. She kept in touch with the WRNS throughout her life, attending the reunions and dinners of their Association and chairing the Cambridge and District Branch from 1979 for 25 years.

– 7 –

The Girton years

Rosemary's post-war plans were vague: she was due to be demobbed in September, but had not decided what kind of work she would look for. In May, quite unexpectedly, she received a letter from Professor Alexander Todd, the Head of the Chemistry Laboratory in Cambridge, asking if she would like to apply for the post of Demonstrator, combined with a College Lectureship at Girton[91]. Although she had no great enthusiasm for returning to academic life, it seemed an obvious course, so she went over to Cambridge for a few days at the end of the month. We have a snapshot of Rosemary's appearance in 1946 in a letter from Ann, recounting the impressions of a friend of the family who had seen her after a long gap. '…she thought you were so beautiful – just like Mama must have been – voice exactly alike and such lovely hair! And height and figure.' Rosemary had blossomed in the WRNS, not only in character but appearance. She had a neat, short hair-cut and went to the hairdresser regularly for a perm and she applied a dab of face powder. Consequently when Alex Todd took her round the Chemistry Labs, in uniform because she had nothing else smart to wear, many heads were turned and it was more like one of her naval inspections than an interview.

Alex Todd was an imposing figure, a tall handsome Scotsman with a gruff, no-nonsense manner. He had been brought in from the University of Manchester to reorganise and revivify the moribund Chemistry Department. Rosemary guessed that he was 'sweeping away a good many cobwebs' and was shown masses of new apparatus that had been recently purchased. Aged 38 when they met in Cambridge, Todd had already had a distinguished career, becoming an FRS in 1942, and he continued his upward trajectory, winning a Nobel Prize in 1957 and being elevated to the peerage as Lord Todd of Trumpington in 1962[92]. Rosemary liked him at once, and he, with his wide experience and astute judgement of character, wanted Rosemary in his Department. After the visit to the labs she was undecided. She went on to dinner in Girton, followed by an informal interview with the Mistress, Miss Butler, whom she compared unfavourably with Miss Grier of LMH in her diary. They talked mostly about education in the Forces. Curiously, Rosemary had supplied references from Oxford (Grier and Taylor) dating from 1938, not from RHC and Sheffield, probably because she could not guarantee that the later ones would be so glowing. The next day, at 6 p.m., Rosemary had her Final Appointments Board interview, one of several candidates, all head-hunted without the post being advertised. Writing to Mama directly afterwards she announced, 'Well, they have offered it to me – so what now?', and then, by the end of the letter, 'I think I shall have to accept, tho' the "comfortableness" of Girton rather appals me'[93]. After the excitement of the WRNS, Rosemary would have preferred something more ambitious. It was indeed a very tame option, as the post was lower ranking than the one she had held in Sheffield, albeit in prestigious Cambridge University. Girton were probably lucky to find such a well-qualified female chemist, especially as the package they offered was not particularly generous.[94] It was College policy not to offer a Fellowship for the first three years of an appointment, but Rosemary would have been pleased to find that they gave a £100 allowance in lieu. The starting salary was £250 a year with board and lodging and a probationary period of three years. She must have felt that she had stepped down from a high pinnacle to start again near the bottom. Arrangements for dining made this very clear: on busy evenings Rosemary was asked to sit on a lower table and leave High Table to the Fellows and their guests. It was a very hierarchical society.

Girton College was founded in 1869 as a 'recognised institution'. It was proud of its history as the first Cambridge foundation for women. The original buildings were of red brick with high gables and solid chimney stacks, about as plain as RHC was fanciful. Inside, long arched corridors, floored in red tiles, and punctuated with heavy wooden doors, stretched round square courts modelled on those of the men's colleges. Girton had deliberately been placed two and a half miles out of the city to discourage fraternization between the female students and male undergraduates, a distance which was a serious inconvenience to staff like Rosemary who had teaching responsibilities in the University. The Chemistry labs were in Pembroke Street at the time. There was only one other foundation for women in Cambridge, Newnham College, two years younger than Girton. A Fellow of Newnham, Dorothy Garrod, was the first woman to hold a professorial chair in Cambridge, in 1938, and when Rosemary arrived in 1946 there were only two female professors and twenty lecturers in the whole University. The post-war years were soon to bring about profound

THE GIRTON YEARS

Four pioneering women who influenced Rosemary

Olive Willis, Headmistress of Downe House School.

Lynda Grier, Principal of Lady Margaret Hall.

Dame Myra Curtis, Principal of Newnham College.

Helen McMorran, Vice Mistress of Girton College.

changes in which she became one of the prime movers. During her summer leave, Rosemary began to revise chemistry. There had, after all, been a gap of four years since teaching at Sheffield and she must have felt a little nervous about resuming. While at Cadlington she took up sailing again; *Kelpie* and John's boat *Calliope* coming out of their long period of disuse. The Murrays once more participated in the regattas along their stretch of the coast – Emsworth, Itchenor, Bosham, Langstone and the Spinaker Cup – usually picking up prizes, and the family also went out just for fun, no doubt delighting in the freedom to explore the coastline once more. Rosemary was finally discharged from the WRNS on 16th October, by which time she had already started at Girton. It cannot have been difficult to slip back into the rhythm of an Oxbridge term, albeit as teacher rather than student. At the beginning of the academic year there were meetings with the Freshers and other students to arrange their courses of study and their college teaching. It had been agreed that Rosemary would have a reduced load during the first year of her appointment in order to catch up: she did 5-7 hours of supervising per week instead of the maximum of 10. New Fellows were ceremonially admitted and the Commemoration of Benefactors celebrated with a Chapel service and dinner. Rosemary was invited to drinks parties with individual Fellows and an 'At Home' with the Mistress, opportunities to get to know her colleagues. Some of them, like herself, were fresh from war service. Alison Duke, a classicist, had been a relief worker in Egypt and Alison Fairlie, a Modern Linguist, had been in the Foreign Office. Robin Hammond, (English) had worked for the Board of Trade from 1941-3. Despite this shared experience, the prevailing atmosphere was probably just as formal and serious as it had been before the War.

The college was full to capacity with over 300 students, an unprecedented number, due to the extra places for ex-service personnel allowed by the government, and staffing problems were acute. Although the blackouts had been removed and garden vegetable plots, created in the 'Dig for Victory' campaign, returned to flower beds, rationing was still in force, so ration books had to be handed over to the Junior Bursar and small weekly portions of fat, sugar and tea issued. High Table members were allowed one scuttle of coal per day for the open fires in their rooms. In 1947 Rosemary became an early member of the Pig Club, a government initiative which encouraged groups to raise pigs for their own consumption and to sell the surplus meat through the Ministry of

Food. She had become quite knowledgeable in farming matters through her experience at Cadlington, and would have been a well-informed committee person. More than twenty pigs were kept in three sties at Girton and fed on swill from the kitchens. M.C. Bradbrook, in a prize-winning entry to a College Song competition, celebrated the success of the Pig Club in supplementing meagre rations:

'The Girton pigs are bonny
When fattening in the sty
But bonnier is the bacon
That on our plates will lie.'

The first verse concluded:

'An it were not for the Pig Club
We'd simply fade away.'[95]

It must have been clear to Rosemary from the start that Girton was a very closed environment. Staff were expected to be in residence five nights a week during Full Term and during parts of the vacation as required. Students and some of the junior staff had to be in by 9.00 p.m. and there were strict rules about male visitors, who had to leave before dinner. Consequently it was very quiet in the evenings except when the community made its own entertainment. There was a choir, an orchestra (which Rosemary seems to have decided was too good for her standard of clarinet playing), a Research Club, where Fellows read academic papers to each other and the students, and occasional dramatic performances, many of them written in house. Rosemary was to be stage manager for two ambitious opera productions.[96] As Janet Harker, former Fellow, recalled, 'everybody went, because that was all there was to do anyway'. She particularly remembered a performance of Haydn's Toy Symphony in which Rosemary played the rattle and other Fellows cuckoo and nightingale pipes and a triangle: 'it was really a very important occasion. We all were rehearsed terribly solemnly'. The Girton Ball was one of the annual events that Fellows were expected to attend, sitting in a line on the dais in the Hall. 'And there were comfortable chairs there, and we sat there solemnly, all dressed up in evening dresses and occasionally some very bold young man would come and invite somebody to dance'.[97]

Staff of the University of Cambridge Chemistry Laboratory, 1950s.

Rosemary left no account, but it would certainly have been her worst nightmare.

The Fellow and Director of Studies in Natural Sciences was Helen Megaw, who had been a student and Research Fellow at Girton 1926-36. She returned at the same time that Rosemary started, after a period of teaching and working in industry as a crystallographer. Older than Rosemary by nine years and very self-assured, she was not likely to have much time for someone who was new to Cambridge and the College. What is more, she was appointed as a Fellow directly, as a result of her previous experience, and there is some evidence that Rosemary had expected to be Director of Studies. Rosemary seems to have kept a low profile in the early years while readjusting to university and civilian life, and it was not until she became a Fellow in 1948 (a year earlier than expected) that she became more prominent in College. With the loss of her officer status and uniform, Rosemary reverted to her former shyness and slight paranoia, often preferring to stop for a poached egg at a café on her way home rather than join the dining circle. She even felt out of place among the (predominantly male) chemists. 'Do the bodies look down their noses at you in the Tea Club still?' enquired Richard, responding to a letter. However she wasted no time in taking advantage of the city and university activities. She was a regular attender at the Music Society (CUMS) choir on a Friday Night and always on the lookout for concerts, plays and lectures. She soon found that the Scott Polar Research Institute had interesting talks (such as 'RAF polar research') and discovered Pevsner's popular lectures on Art History. She also joined the Antiquarian Society and the Cambridge Philosophical Society, of broader scope than its name suggests, 'philosophy' being an older term for science. From the outset she offered her services to the WEA, despite being very nervous about the undertaking, and lectured on scientific subjects in the local villages. Attendance at Girton College Chapel led to her soon being put on the Chapel Committee, and in addition she went to hear sermons at Great St Mary's, the University church. Beyond Cambridge she was attending meetings of the British Federation of University Women at the historic Crosby Hall in Chelsea, the WRNS Association, and Downe House Seniors Association, in London and at the school, when she could get to them.

Rosemary's first winter at Girton was bitterly cold, with snow on the ground from December until March. College heating proved quite inadequate and biking up and down the icy Huntingdon Road to the laboratory left her very chilled. She wrote about a hazardous journey:

> 'One day I went to supper with Prof. Todd ... off the Trumpington Road [i.e. South of the city]. It was a cold night with a thick, thick, fog, cars nearly at a standstill. I bicycled back to Girton to teach at 5.30 & then set off at 7.00 again ... I nearly lost the way in Sidney Sussex Street. Luckily I had been once in the day to another house in the same road & so by following the curb arrived O.K.[98]'

'It must be <u>killing</u> living so far away', commented John.

That same winter there were floods in Cambridge, and in March a mighty gale blew down a dozen fine trees in Girton grounds. It was not a good introduction for a newcomer, but Cambridge had its compensations. Rosemary's sister, Ann, was living there, in Jesus Lane, during the first term and she must have been sorry when Ann and Diana Hoare departed for a lengthy stay in Southern Rhodesia in April 1947, in the hope that the warm climate would alleviate Ann's asthma. It was quite feasible to keep up with friends and relatives passing through London and the Proby family near Peterborough were within easy reach. Rosemary went over to stay at Elton Hall occasionally. Richard, who had started at New College, came over for a weekend and Rosemary sometimes went to Oxford on the direct train line which then existed.

Rosemary relished the generous University vacations which enabled her to get back to her pre-War pattern of holidays. In January 1947 she was in Sedrun in the Swiss Oberalp for a fortnight, attending the ski school. Her brothers, now in their twenties, still liked to go with her. In the Easter vacation she had a week on the Norfolk Broads with her parents, and Richard and John each spent a few days with them. Richard had become extremely keen on sailing and wrote to Rosemary almost exclusively on the topic of joint sailing projects, new equipment they might buy and ultimately a new boat. The summer that year was fine and warm and Rosemary had more free time than for many years. She had the great pleasure of expeditions with her mother and all three boys in two boats. '... day after day of fine weather, gentle N'ly breeze, generally changing to S'ly sea breeze around lunchtime.' We can picture her in her aertex blouse and white cotton sun hat, scanning birds through John's binoculars. One afternoon they took out *Calliope*, heavily laden with food, water, sleeping gear and a primus stove. They ate supper by moonlight and bedded down on the shore under blankets and sails. '... and so to sleep with stars and birds calling and a fire far away on the Downs flickering, dying down and starting up again'. It is unusual for Rosemary to write so lyrically. More characteristic was her summing up of the night outdoors as 'a super expo'. She and John also had a joint project, surveying the many channels to the South of Thorney Island. When John was at home they went sailing most days. 'The surveying was most systematic, navigating officer's notebook & continual bearings & transits taken with the prismatic compass'. The operation of measuring and recording was entirely to Rosemary's taste.

Rosemary returned to Cambridge for a Michaelmas Term that was to usher in significant changes for women in the University. When she first arrived at Girton in 1946 she must have found it strange that the students she was teaching were not allowed to take degrees. Women at Oxford had won this battle in 1920, when a Statute admitting women to degrees and consequently to University government was passed by the Congregation without opposition. In the same year in Cambridge it had been rejected by a vote for the second time, and with outbursts of violence. However, without formal consultation with the women's colleges, a Memorial led by two male Cambridge dons was presented to the Council of the Senate in September 1946, with 140 signatories, requesting that a Syndicate be appointed to consider the wider question of the numbers and the position of women in the University.[99] The report of this Syndicate proposed to admit women to membership on the same terms as men, while reserving the right to limit their numbers. Opinions had altered radically since the 1920s because of social change engendered by the War. The essential work performed by the WRNS and the WAAF and civilian women in men's jobs demonstrated that women could work as equals: Rosemary was one of many examples. Consequently, at the debate on the Report, only one man opposed the motion and the Grace admitting women to full membership went through on the nod, on 6th December 1947. Rosemary's diary contains no reference to this momentous event, which was to have such an impact on her future career. Her entry, 'Sherry 5.30-7.00' might indicate that this was the way Girton immediately celebrated the fact that it was to become a College within the University. Significantly the Syndicate's Report stated that the University would have the power to recognise other institutions for women as 'approved foundations', while limiting, through Ordinances, the numbers admitted. This was the route later followed by New Hall. Another crucial change influencing Rosemary's long-term future was that women became eligible for membership of the Council of the Senate. The possibility of the Head of a women's college becoming Vice-Chancellor was mentioned by Canon Raven, the current VC, in his speech at the luncheon following the admission of the Queen to the degree of Doctor of Laws: 'only the most elderly among us', he guessed, 'would feel it inappropriate if Cambridge were to follow the example of London (whose Vice-Chancellor, Dr Lillian Penson, is happily with us today) and elect a woman into the office I now hold.' The point was picked up by the Mistress of Girton in her reply, and the distinguished Fellow historian, Helen Cam, spoke of 'the dream of Emily Davis' to have the institution she founded received into the University of Cambridge, and its Mistress, and the Principal of Newnham, ranked with the Heads of male colleges in eligibility for the highest office in the University. It would take nearly three decades before a woman became Vice-Chancellor, and it would be the Head, not of one of the two nineteenth-century foundations, but of a 'Third Foundation for Women' who would be elected into that office.

For 21st October 1948 Rosemary simply wrote 'Queen' in her diary, but she can hardly have escaped the excitement in the preceding weeks, for Girton had the honour of providing afternoon tea for the royal party. Discussions were held with the Palace officials and alternative plans for dry and wet weather drawn up. Red carpets were laid in corridors on the route, lavish flower decorations placed at strategic points and banks of potted chrysanthemums massed at the college entrance. In the morning most Girtonians went to watch the royal procession through the city, and, if entitled, the degree ceremony in the Senate House. The Queen lunched in Christ's and visited Newnham before driving up the Huntingdon Road. As her car swept into the drive, her royal standard was hoisted in place of Girton's flag. She was greeted by the Mistress and taken on a short tour of the college, meeting groups as she went. Rosemary would have been in the group of Junior Fellows and members of High Table who were presented in the Fellows' Dining Room. The culmination of this celebration was the announcement that the Queen would become Girton's Visitor, a largely honorary office, though with an occasional advisory or disciplinary rôle.

Rosemary became a Fellow in June 1948 and in November was appointed to Girton's Special Purposes Committee, quite a commitment because it met every two weeks in Term to discuss a miscellany of college matters. Girton had a powerful Bursar who was an economist[100], but all Fellows were expected to examine the accounts and had a 'sort of tutorial' in advance of the audit meeting: 'we went through the whole lot and considered every figure and talked about it, so that we were trained up...'[101] Rosemary took this seriously, and it was certainly useful experience for a future College head. In 1949 she was elected to the College Council, the executive body, giving her a voice in major decisions; two years later she was re-elected. Clearly Rosemary's good judgement and capacity for hard work were gradually being recognised. She became Director of Studies for Chemistry and even directed the smaller subjects Agriculture and Architecture at various times. Supervising Girton students, usually in pairs, was mostly done in the afternoon and early evening. After the initial reduction, Rosemary's hours went up to eight or nine a week, which with preparation and marking time was equivalent to two full days. She also liked to attend some of the lectures the students were hearing, to understand how the subjects were presented. Invigilating and marking examinations were annual tasks in the Summer Term. It is not surprising, in view of all these responsibilities and her chemistry research and demonstrating duties, that when she was offered a Tutorship in 1950 she sensibly asked for a trial period of one year to make sure she could fit everything in. Her salary had risen from £350 p.a. plus board and lodging in 1946 to £385 plus residence and a Fellowship Dividend in 1950, not a huge increase, although the value of residence was deemed to have doubled. There exist a few sheets of notes in Rosemary's hand, outlining the many areas a Tutor had to cover.[102] She saw her quota of students individually at the beginning and end of Term, registered them for exams, and dealt with disciplinary matters, health problems and general welfare. Cambridge colleges were still acting *in loco parentis* and gate rules were in force, with strong restrictions at Girton on entertaining any male visitors who managed to make their way to the outer fringe of Cambridge. Rosemary found she could cope with the workload and remained a Tutor for the rest of her time in Girton. She was a popular Tutor who was committed to getting the best from individual students. Many years later a former Girton pupil wrote: 'It was an exceptional privilege for me to enjoy the tutoring of someone so dedicated to helping each student to achieve their goals, and to live by the principles they value ... there was warmth and friendship and also an atmosphere that contributed to a search for knowledge'.[103]

Rosemary not only found time to be a Tutor, but took on an important external responsibility. Towards the end of her time at Girton, Lady Adrian, wife of the Chancellor of the University, proposed Rosemary as a Justice of the Peace and she was appointed, much to the annoyance of the Mistress, Mary Cartwright, who was obliged to give her time off to attend court. Ellen Murray was a J.P., and Rosemary was keen to follow her mother's lead. Colleagues were probably non-plussed: involvement in the City was unusual for a woman already busy in the University, and the Tutors' Office was impressed when the Cambridge Evening News wanted to interview her, putting the message into verse:

'Congratulations Miss J.P.!
(How good we now will have to be!)...'[104]

By the time she was trained, she was at New Hall, which was more conveniently placed for the Magistrates' Court.

Alex Todd had made a point of introducing Rosemary to the Tea Club, which was simply an informal gathering in the Department for tea in the afternoon. It was a useful place for people to get to know each other and to discuss their work. Many important collaborations have started over tea in the scientific departments of Cambridge. Rosemary made an effort to attend, but was still shy in the presence of new people. No doubt she was right in thinking that they were all looking at her, because she was the only female Demonstrator in the Organic Chemistry Laboratory. Rosemary spent two afternoons a week demonstrating, i.e. supervising groups of students doing practical work. The great majority, probably 90%, were men, and in the early years many of them were older than the usual school-leavers, having served in the War. Former students remember her as charming, patient and efficient as she went round advising groups doing analysis and the preparation of chemical compounds and answering questions. They liked her and found her warm and approachable. At the same time she was dignified and highly professional, neat and tidy in appearance, described by a former student as 'a well put-together person'[105]. Her teaching schedule did not leave much time for research during Term, and she had no topics that she urgently wanted to pursue. Looking back, she would say modestly 'I wasn't a very good chemist', but given the right topic she might have flourished. In a reference Dr Taylor said that she had a distinct flair in the laboratory and quick and neat fingers. Organic synthesis is subject to many failures and frustrations. It requires determination and perseverance, which Rosemary certainly had in plenty, and also the time to set up one experiment after another, which she did not always have. However, she collaborated with Herchel Smith, a researcher from a younger generation, in an area he was developing, the synthesis of polycyclic systems. Smith went on to make discoveries which led to the contraceptive pill. In 1951 they published, together with A.J.Birch, *Reduction by dissolving metals. Part IX. Some hydronapthalene derivatives*,[106] five pages in which numerous complex experiments are described. At the same time she and Birch published a short paper, *The Constitution of Lanceol*[107]. These were to be Rosemary's only two papers written while at the University Chemical Laboratory. Chemistry was changing in the 1950s, as knowledge of electrons opened up a new way of understanding chemical reactions. Those who had trained before the war had to make a big adjustment or be seen as old-fashioned. Rosemary was one of those who was left behind, though she continued demonstrating into the 1960s. She was moving in a new direction which was ultimately more rewarding.

– 8 –

The Third Foundation for Women

Sharing in the excitement of progress, but realising that there was much more to be done to improve women's educational chances, gave Rosemary a renewed interest in the British Federation of University Women (BFUW). She had taken out life membership in 1940, while at Royal Holloway College. It was convenient at that time to attend the meetings in Crosby Hall, a beautiful fifteenth-century house in Cheyne Walk, Chelsea. In 1949 she started going again a few times a year and soon joined the local Cambridge branch of the BFUW. The organisation, founded in 1907, was a useful support group for women graduates, lobbying on such issues as the attempt by Liverpool University to impose a marriage bar in the 1930s. The status of women university teachers was not high and they were very much a minority (around 13% of the total number of teachers country-wide). Women were mainly on the lower grades, with lower pay and difficulty in obtaining promotion. Rosemary was not only personally affected by the restrictions on women which still permeated British society; she also had an insight at all levels, from schooling to University teaching. She was made a governor of Downe House in 1949, and so came into contact with the National Union of Women Teachers (NUWT), who were seeking equal rights with men. Through involvement in admissions and examining at Girton she was well aware of the paucity of places for girl students, Cambridge having the lowest proportion of any British university. As Girton's representative on the University Women's Appointments Board she had evidence that the job market for women was rather limited and she knew only too well the difficult position of women academics in the Oxbridge colleges and other universities.

It was in the immediate post-war period that a group of academic women and wives of Cambridge academics began to agitate for more places for women undergraduates in Cambridge. Mrs Margareta (Greta) Burkill, wife of the eminent mathematics lecturer J.C. Burkill, was one of the prime movers. A tiny, energetic Austrian/Russian Jew, she had fostered two children from Europe during the war, alongside her own three, and with her husband helped to settle hundreds of Kindertransport children arriving from Germany. Greta, a Newnham graduate, had immense sympathy with the under-privileged, and next turned her attention to the position of women in the University. In 1948, with Mrs Winifred Parsons, a Girton graduate, she had a meeting with the Vice-Chancellor to discuss the provision of additional places for women. Canon Raven was quite encouraging, as he had been in his speech before the Queen. A group was set up to investigate, but it was three years before the Council of the Senate reported on the matter. Meanwhile the two women convened a meeting of interested parties, on 13th January 1949, held in the drawing room of Lady Whitby, wife of the Master of Downing and a strong supporter of the cause. (She became the first Chair of the Council of New Hall.) Those invited comprised Newnham and Girton dons and married Cambridge graduates, forty-four in all. Later in life Rosemary was irritated that she had missed such a landmark meeting because she was skiing in Hochsolden at the time. Seven Girtonians were present, but the Mistress, Dr Cartwright, sent her apologies with a note that she doubted there was a sufficient supply of women mathematics candidates to fill more places. Dame Myra Curtis, Principal of Newnham, did attend. Greta Burkill's record of the meeting states that 'discussions became acrimonious, and indeed insulting'[108]. Some women wanted to maintain the exclusivity of Newnham and Girton; the scientists were worried that their laboratories could not accommodate an increase in numbers, and some thought that it would be better to expand the number of women research students: Dame Myra Curtis had already proposed a new college for graduate women students, but the idea had been turned down. Those in favour of expansion pointed out that a large number of intelligent women candidates had to be turned away from Cambridge and there were job vacancies in the professions for women graduates. There was also a difference of opinion between members of an existing Dining Group, who were interested in promoting a College for people like themselves, resident MAs already teaching students, and those belonging to the group led by Mrs Burkill and Mrs Parsons whose focus was on admitting more women students. The latter envisaged a small institution run by a minimal number of academic staff which could be self-funded by the students' fees. 'Notes concerning a possible third women's college', written by Mrs Parsons in May 1949, foresaw a foundation very similar to the future New Hall. She explained that the advantage of starting small was that the foundation could get up and running quickly and develop according to the available finance. She emphasised that the independence of the founding group would free them to take decisions. Their aim was to raise money from donations without calling on the University for support – after all, it seemed in no hurry to decide the matter of 'additional provision'. In conclusion she wrote:

> 'We should like to see a meeting called to appoint a committee to consider ways and means for a Third College, and to start collecting money for its endowment ... We consider that gradual growth from a small beginning is better for the College's own sake.'[109]

It was, however, some time before a formal committee was set up, largely because of lack of co-ordination between the various factions and also because the report of the Council of the Senate was expected soon. In the event it did not appear until June 1952. Mrs Burkill's group met informally and tried to make progress on practical matters. On her initiative Lady Nora Barlow and Sir Charles Darwin were consulted about their property, 'The Orchard', on Huntingdon Road as a possible site for a new College. She also proposed naming the college after Queen Elizabeth, but Dame Myra Curtis would not allow her to pursue an introduction, fearing that the name would have a greater appeal than Newnham or Girton. Meanwhile the Dining Group continued to promote their model of a college to the Vice-Chancellor and Council of the Senate. It was not until 30th July 1952, after the publication of the Council's Report, approving additional provision for women, with some limitations, that the groups came together to form the 'Association to Promote a Third Foundation for Women in the University of Cambridge'. Rosemary does not seem to have taken much part in the early meetings, and although she was one of the 70 women invited to consider setting up an Association, again missed a historic occasion because she was on holiday. The Murrays were having an ambitious 'expo', sailing off the coast of France. Consequently she was not available for election to the Committee formed at this meeting. With Mrs Parsons in the chair, it was authorised by those present to draw up a scheme for an appeal, explore the question of accommodation and take legal advice on setting up the Foundation. All those who had been invited to the meeting were eligible to join the Association, on payment of a £1 subscription. The Committee reported back to its members on 22nd November 1952, and it was at this stage that Rosemary finally became involved. She was one of 42 members who attended and approved the co-option of male Senior Members of the University to the Committee and the invitation (by letter) to all Senior Members to join the Association. In a couple of months membership rose rapidly to around 260 and 120 were present at the next important meeting in February, called to elect a new Committee. Rosemary was one of the fifteen members elected at a ballot in the Arts School. Dame Myra Curtis became the Chairman. She was a former Civil Servant, very well qualified to direct this enterprise, having a clear strategy and expertise in managing committees. Her ambitious target was to open the new institution for Michaelmas Term 1954, less than two years away. She immediately set up five sub-committees, with considerable overlap in the membership, to work on different aspects. Rosemary was assigned to both Accommodation and Admissions. The other areas were Appeals, Finance and Constitution. As envisaged in 1949, the Committee was aiming for a small establishment in a reasonably central house. After inspecting many properties, they settled on 'The Hermitage' in Silver Street, owned by St John's College but rented at that time for use as a guest house. Although it was a smaller building than they ideally wanted, it was in a good position, close to Newnham, Queens' and other colleges, the laboratories and Arts lecture rooms. After some negotiation the price for the remainder of the lease became affordable. The Accommodation Sub-committee also followed through on Mrs Burkill's contact with the Darwin family regarding 'The Orchard', which was leased to Byron House School at the time. The generous gift of the freehold of the house and land was received from the owners, Nora Barlow and Ida Rees Thomas, in October 1953, assuring a future site on which to build a College.

The Admissions Sub-Committee was chiefly occupied with the method of selection of candidates. Rosemary was keen to cut some of the red tape, and also give opportunities to girls who had not been well prepared by their schools for the entrance examinations. Perhaps she had in mind her own schooling, which gave her a breadth of experience, good for character-building but not for passing academic exams. The blueprint for the famous New Hall entrance paper 'designed to test logical thought and power of expression' was drawn up at this time, with the decision that candidates would sit it in October and be interviewed in November, ahead of the other women's colleges. It was a shrewd move, because many girls offered a place at New Hall did not bother to take exams for the other colleges. It was too late to put this into operation for 1954, so Girton and Newnham allowed their applicants to be contacted and informed of the opportunity to apply to New Hall. Members of the Headmistresses' Association were also invited to put forward special recommendations. As a result there were over 100 applicants, of which half were interviewed and 16 admitted, two by special recommendation. The University Report had set a limit of 100 on the number in residence, which could only be reached when larger premises were available.

The Constitution Committee also had to follow the requirements of the Report that the new institution should be recognised under Statute H III of the University.

> 'It would need to be founded and maintained without financial assistance from the University, and it is possible that in the course of time it might apply for recognition as an Approved Foundation of the University; but any such development would depend on the fortunes of the new institution and the extent to which it was fulfilling the purpose for which it had been established.'[110]

This guarded statement, with its qualifying clauses, shows a lack of confidence in the success of the project and the reluctance of the University to have any involvement until it was proved viable. Fortunately there were many supportive individuals in the men's colleges ready to give practical help, for example the Revd Dr J.S. Boys Smith (St John's), G.Kitson Clark (Trinity), C.W.Crawley (Trinity Hall), F.R.Salter (Magdalene), D. Thomson (Sidney Sussex) and L.P.Wilkinson (King's), all members of the Third Foundation Association Committee in 1953. Of these men, John Boys Smith was to be the most important influence on Rosemary. He was a Professor of Divinity who had been head-hunted by St John's College to be Bursar. Outstanding personal and administrative qualities led to his election as Master in 1959 and Vice-Chancellor of the University in 1963, but meanwhile he found time to serve on New Hall's Council, becoming the first (and only) male Chairman in 1964. Rosemary acknowledged how much she gained from his handling of committees and ability to progress business.[111] From him she learned to aim for consensus in committees – a vote was no good if some members were unhappy– to give everyone a chance to express their views, and to prepare thoroughly. The institution was to start as a company not for profit and limited by guarantee, as Newnham and Girton had done. The Constitution Sub-Committee drafted a Memorandum and Articles of Association which outlined the governance and objects of the new Foundation, in which it was made absolutely clear that the aim was to promote its development into a college of the University. These were duly recognised by the Council of the Senate, thus allowing the Foundation to matriculate students and present them for degrees. The articles also had to be approved by the Board of Trade, and for that purpose the Association Committee rather urgently needed to register a name. There was no shortage of suggestions; people even wrote to the newspapers with their ideas, among them St Etheldreda's, Chesterton, Huntingdon, Buckingham (subject to ribald jokes in the men's colleges), and Darwin (disallowed by Sir Charles Darwin). Eventually 'New Hall' was chosen in a ballot as a provisional name, leaving an opportunity for a donor to change it.[112]

The main committee set up an Appointments Committee, of which Rosemary was initially a member, together with Dame Myra and Mrs Horton. Its first task was to select a Tutor-in-Charge to head the foundation. This person was to handle all the practical details of setting up and running the future college, until such a time as it was appropriate to appoint an 'eminent woman' as President. The post was not advertised: applicants were found by networking with women's higher education bodies. Shortly after the search began, Delia Agar, the forceful chemistry don at Newnham who had become a friend of Rosemary's, said to her, "Wouldn't you like to apply?" and Rosemary replied, "I suppose I ought to". The words indicate her reluctance. Rosemary did not like change and still sometimes lacked confidence. Indeed, it was a difficult decision to give up her tenured post at Girton and strike out on a new and uncertain venture with only a five-year contract. She was encouraged by the Head of her Department, Professor Todd. Looking back, she saw the decision as a watershed: 'my whole career altered, partly through the advice of an individual'[113]. At the next committee meeting (4th December 1953) it was reported that Miss Murray had stepped down from the Appointments Committee because she was a candidate. She was replaced by Mrs Benians, wife of the Master of St John's College. Five candidates were shortlisted and on 6th December interviews were held in Newnham College, resulting in two of them being ruled out. By this time Rosemary's competitive spirit had been aroused, though she was not holding out much hope, as the remaining candidates were strong: one of them had been head of a women's college in London. The Appointments

Committee was unable to decide between her and Rosemary and the decision was referred to the full committee, who arranged a vote on 14th December. The result was 10 votes for Rosemary and 4 abstentions, a clear endorsement. Rosemary's appointment must have been the chief topic at the Third Foundation Association's Christmas party two days later, an important occasion used to publicise the plans for a new college to representatives of business and the professions. Dame Myra likened the long process to the ascent of Everest (which had been accomplished earlier in the year). They were now on one of the lower peaks and gathering breath to climb higher. The Senior Tutor of King's made a rather unfortunate analogy with the Cinderella story, referring to Newnham and Girton as 'elder' rather than 'ugly' sisters who had allowed her to go to the ball. He was, of course, complimenting them on their support. The press commented on the amount of bureaucracy the Association had surmounted, the inordinately long time it had taken the University to act, and its past history of misogyny. *The Guardian* reporter wrote: 'In making the College a success, Cambridge can atone a little for its past man-made shortcomings in the treatment of womankind.'[114]

An announcement of the appointment of the Tutor-in-Charge appeared in *The Times* and was picked up by other newspapers, quickly spreading the news to Rosemary's colleagues, friends and acquaintances. Letters of congratulation flooded in, commending her suitability for the job. Mrs Benians wrote of 'moral courage & integrity & willingness to pull your weight – all with the good temper and sense of humour that will be a boon to your colleagues and undergraduates…' The Secretary of the local WEA mentioned her 'warmth and a great breadth of interest in people as people'. Kate Bertram, soon to be Secretary of the New Hall Association, admired her energy and enterprise. The WRNS Director Vera Laughton Mathews commented, 'I think I can judge as well as anyone how well fitted you are for such responsibility'. Olive Willis, her old headmistress, sent £10 from the 'Heather Fund' and some advice. '…what an opportunity – you start with no tradition except the best one of intellectual activity & you are going to make a real community – where there shall be no cliques and barriers of age or interest. Make people mix & don't let them get into their small exclusive societies!' Rosemary Syfret, a former Fellow of Girton, wrote perceptively: '…your life's work is now clear before you. What does it feel like to be Emily Davies?'[115]

New Hall was registered as a Limited Company on 20th April 1954 and the Association was dissolved the next day, handing over all its assets, some £38,000, to New Hall. (The rumour that New Hall started with one penny relates to the penny stamp on the legal document.) Rosemary's official appointment was changed to this date so that she could become an *ex officio* member of New Hall's Council as Head of the institution, but her residence and salary did not begin until 1st October. She formally applied to Girton for permission to work during the summer on preparing The Hermitage for opening, and the College Council agreed. In practice, of course, she began planning as soon as she accepted the job. University recognition was received in May, with a Grace approving the 'Report on the Recognition of New Hall', recommending that it should become a Recognised Institution for Women. Members of the old Association were invited to become members of the New Hall Association. At its first annual meeting in June, a new Council was elected under the Articles of Association, with Lady Whitby, in whose house the stormy 1949 meeting had been held, as Chairman and Delia Agar as Secretary. Dame Myra retired, and Rosemary was probably not sorry to lose her, because there had been a clash of personalities when she had tried to step in and organise The Hermitage, which Rosemary rightly felt was her prerogative. However, the Foundation was deeply indebted to her for her excellent management of the project.

Meanwhile the search was on to find a Tutor, as the second-in-command to Rosemary was to be called. Rosemary Syfret, whom she had known at Girton, was approached, but did not want to leave her current post at Somerville College, Oxford. However, she in turn recommended her friend Robin (Hope) Hammond, another Girtonian, who had left the Fellowship in 1949 to take up the post of Lecturer in English at Queen Mary College, London. Robin was attracted by the idea of starting a new foundation and doing something about the deplorable ratio of men to women students in Cambridge, which stood at 11:1, and Rosemary was keen for her to apply. Robin's references highlighted exactly the qualities that the committee was seeking. 'She works very harmoniously with other members of the High Table and shows to a marked degree an understanding of student problems and personalities'[116]. M.C. Bradbrook commended her teaching and 'her friendly competence and willing co-operation'. Robin also had experience of being in charge of 16 students in 'The Grange', a house in the Girton College grounds. 'Her management of it has been admirable in every way', wrote the Mistress, K.T. Butler[117].

Rosemary Murray and Robin Hammond in Rosemary's sitting room at The Hermitage, 1954.

As Tutor-in-charge, Rosemary must have had a considerable 'say' in the selection process, and when Robin was successful, wrote the most exuberant letter of welcome beginning, 'Hurray, hourah, hurrah, hoorah, how does one spell the word – any way you know what I mean. I am so thrilled that you will be coming'[118]. Rosemary hoped that Robin would visit in the summer, but she preferred to arrive on 1st October, avoiding some of the 'tiresomenesses' predicted in the letter. Rosemary went on to say that she was relieved to have found a nice, elderly, Scottish cook-housekeeper. This was Miss Dufton, who proved a thrifty, reliable and long-serving member of staff. Her broad Scots accent was very memorable. The Accommodation Committee had turned into a House Committee with Miss Vera James, Mrs Parsons and Mrs White helping Rosemary. They confirmed the rental of The Hermitage and the hand-over was effected on 1st May, together with much of the furniture and a cellar full of chamber-pots. Soon Coulson's the builders were doing remedial work on the building.

Rosemary still had the term to finish out at Girton, with supervisions and tutorials, exam marking and meetings, committees and Council. In addition she was learning her new duties as a Justice of the Peace. A Fellows' farewell party was held for leavers, incorporating the tradition of

Girton poems. The author, probably modern linguist Alison Fairlie, gave a masterly summary of Rosemary's character:

> 'Calm, kindness, common-sense, clear-mindedness
> Made meetings meaningful, quite clarified
> Tutorial tangles trippingly untied
> And gently murdered muddle-mindedness.
>   ***
> Firmness forthright the difficult defied
> (And what is more she understood accounts).
> Direst Dame Myra did not her depress ...'[119]

The *Girton Review* offered a salute to the new Foundation and a glowing tribute to Rosemary as Fellow and Tutor. '...she has played so important a part in College affairs that we cannot express in words how much we shall miss her.'[120]

The Fellows had not seen Rosemary in leadership mode, but early in 1954, while they were both in residence, Janet Harker witnessed it at first hand. Rosemary rang her very early one morning with news of the flooding disaster on the East Coast. She had heard on the radio that a severe gale in the North Sea, combined with a high spring tide, had caused extensive damage, with hundreds of people made homeless and many fatalities. "We must go and help," said Rosemary, commandeering Janet and her car. When they arrived at one of the emergency centres, they found it in chaos, with no plan of action. Rosemary immediately took charge, arranging an appeal for clothing, food and medical supplies. People were calmed, and by the end of the day the centre was operating smoothly, as Janet admiringly recounted. It was a foretaste of Rosemary's organising skills at New Hall.

Rosemary had learned a great deal during her eight years at Girton: tutorial duties and committee membership in particular had given her a useful training for the future. She had no intention of making New Hall a carbon copy but it provided a baseline for all the procedures required in setting up a college. She must have been pleased that Girton was proud of her achievement but sorry to lose her; a combination of 'glory mixed with grievousness' as the poet put it.[121]

During the Summer the House Committee appointed further staff, notably the stalwart Mary Boothman, a strong woman of the Fens who was maid-of-all-work and kitchen helper. She was immensely loyal to Rosemary and shared her 'can do' attitude. There was much practical work to tackle at The Hermitage: existing furniture to be sorted, adapted or sold, and new furniture selected, carpets purchased and curtains made. On Rosemary's shopping list were pillowcases and tea towels, a rake and a broom – and prayer books[122]. The impression has been given that Rosemary did all the preparation herself, but in her book she gives credit to all members of the Committee and especially Miss James, who 'furnished the house with taste and discrimination'[123] and the minimum of expense. She roped in her friend Janet Harker to scrub the floors with her on Sundays and transport furniture in her car, and called on her brother John and his fiancée Lilias for help in the garden. An appeal, organised by Miss Whetham, was made for books, and the great and good of Cambridge contributed plentifully, though not always appropriately, to the first Library. Despite the tight deadline for having everything ready, Rosemary was not prepared to give up her annual sailing holiday, and spent a fortnight in August in the Western isles, starting from Ardrichaig and calling at Iona, Muck, Eigg, Oronsay, Malaig, Coll and Colonsay. On her return she threw herself into the practical tasks with her usual vigour, putting up curtain rails, coat hooks and light fittings, distempering, hanging pictures and gardening. She had frequent meetings with Mrs White, who had taken on the management of the New Hall finances, and other supporters, and kept Lady Whitby informed of progress. There was also a lot of administration, corresponding with students, setting up systems for records and accounts, sorting and cataloguing books for the library and finding supervisors in the fourteen subjects to be studied. Mrs Benians kindly introduced her to the University circle she would be joining in a series of dinner parties. Despite the Murrays' social status, this was where Rosemary was most unsure of herself, so it was a great help to have the advice of an experienced Master's wife.

By October they were just about ready for the first intake of students. The Hermitage was now adequately furnished, with Rosemary installed in a large room on the first floor given character by an attractive semi-circular bay, overlooking the garden and a bend in the river. She worked at an antique knee-hole desk. A large sofa dominated the room: many interviewees had cause to remember it. Long floral curtains hung at the windows and paintings by Ann and Frances decorated the walls. A celadon bowl was prominently displayed. Directly below was the JCR and part of

Rosemary's leaving party at Girton College. In the centre is the Mistress, Mary Cartwright, flanked by Rosemary (left) and Helen McMorran (right). Janet Harker is second from the right in the front row.

the Library: the remainder was in an outhouse. The room next to it was the kitchen, with a hatch through to the dining room which extended along the frontage. It had green Lincrusta wallpaper and was dominated by a convex mirror. There were two long tables for the students, and at right angles a very small High Table for the two Tutors. Student accommodation was very varied, as the rooms were all different sizes, and had various advantages and disadvantages, such as access to the roof for sunbathing, or proximity to the noisy crossroads. The staff office, for the Accountant, Secretary and Housekeeper, was one very cramped room next to the kitchen. But whatever the shortcomings, morale was high: there was a sense of achievement and the beginning of a great adventure.

THE THIRD FOUNDATION FOR WOMEN

The Hermitage in 1954.

The front door.

The first dinner at New Hall, October 1954.

The first year at New Hall with Rosemary and Robin.

– 9 –

New Hall: early days as a Limited Company

THE FIRST NEW HALL STUDENTS started to arrive on October 4th. They were from such varied social backgrounds that to some The Hermitage looked like a mansion and to others a very ordinary nineteenth-century house. The entrance was marked by a stone portico with sturdy columns flanked by railings. In common with the other colleges there was no nameplate, but in response to a request from Mrs Darwin[124] next door, who had been bothered by the newcomers, an index card bearing the handwritten name NEW HALL was pinned above the letter-box. It all looked very provisional. To avoid complaints about the allocation of the rooms, spread over three floors, each student was asked to draw a rolled slip of paper on arrival, and inside was her room number. Mary Boothman was on hand to carry the trunks upstairs.

On Wednesday 6th October the first formal dinner was held in the dining room, the girls smartly dressed and wearing their gowns and Rosemary and Robin sitting at the small High Table, graced with flowers and silver candlesticks for the occasion. To make sure the historic event was properly recorded, a professional photographer, Antony Barrington Brown, had been commissioned to produce an image of all those present. Another important gathering was the election of a President of the JCR by a vote of students who had hardly had time to get to know one another. They chose Annabel Balfour, a tall girl with an air of authority, and toasted her with non-matching glasses. The young women felt special, and as pioneers were prepared to suffer inadequacies and lend a hand. Rosemary encouraged them to help in the garden, picking pears from the prolific tree by the river, sweeping leaves and mowing the grass. The students must have been surprised to find that their Tutor was also general handyman, and might appear at any time with her canvas toolbag to fix plumbing, electricity or woodwork. This added to the general air of informality. There were not many rules but a certain standard of behaviour was expected. On the first morning several girls came down to breakfast in their dressing-gowns with hair in rollers. According to one, Rosemary walked in and gave them a 'basilisk stare' and it didn't happen again.[125] Gate hours were universal in the colleges: initially the door of

First year students Dinah Burford, Annabel Balfour, Alison Wright and Audrey Durno on the way to lectures.

New Hall was locked at 10.00 p.m. and anyone arriving late had to ring the bell. Because they had no porter, either Rosemary or Robin had to be available every evening to open the door. According to Robin, Rosemary was 'anti-institutional', hoping to avoid having a lot of regulations and rely on common sense and community spirit to make the society run smoothly. She was, however, most anxious about appearances, because she knew that New Hall would be under a great deal of scrutiny from the University and the press, and any scandal could jeopardise the whole project.

   A number of articles appeared anticipating the opening of the college, picking up on the speeches made at the Third Foundation Party. A Guardian editorial commented: 'Outsiders will watch with interest to see whether, through this new movement, so largely inspired by women, Cambridge can evolve a college of a new type, both in constitution and spirit'[126]. *The Times Educational Supplement* reminded its readers: 'Oxford has five colleges for women and about 1,000 women students; New Hall will bring up Cambridge's score to three and may soon increase the number of women students at the University, which is now about 700[127]'. In a broadcast in early October, Mrs Kay Baxter, secretary of the Cambridge University Women's Appointments Board, described the origin of the new foundation and stressed the value of higher education for women.[128]

Once the students arrived, Rosemary arranged a press tea-party, where they were interviewed and photographed. She took the opportunity to repeat the aims of the institution, to grow and to become a full college, and the need for further funding. Photos and quotes were widely distributed and the journalists continued to look for stories throughout the first year. The JCR President was invited on to a TV programme hosted by Malcolm Muggeridge, who argued against the education of women and hardly allowed Annabel to get a word in. The next story reported was about the students' exploits on Poppy Day (the predecessor of RAG). The New Hall women dressed up as St Trinian's schoolgirls and set up

Rosemary with two students, 1954.

Jenny Stanesby, one of the first year students, cycling past Queens' College, 1954.

a road block in Silver Street, shaking their collecting tins. They offered a prize to any young man who could collect all their signatures at a penny a time, while making sure no-one won it. The result was that they raised more money per head than any other college and won a firkin of ale. All this offered good photo opportunities, and Edward Malindine, who had been an official War photographer, was sent over to Cambridge to do a feature for the national Illustrated Magazine. He produced a brilliant set of prints recording the daily life of the New Hall girl; setting off for lectures wearing gowns, having supervisions, studying in their rooms, holding tea parties, attending dances and drinking beer with male students outside 'The Mill'. A photo of Jenny Stanesby cycling past Queens' with her gown fluttering has become the iconic image of the lively emancipated woman student of the 1950s.

The women were keen to join in University societies – musical, theatrical and sporting, including rowing. They were upset to find that the debating society, the Cambridge Union, did not admit women, and so became front-runners in starting a Women's Union.[129] Invitations to the whole cohort, to parties and dances in the men's colleges, came flooding in. Most of the girls acquired boyfriends and some challenged the college gate hours by climbing in through a downstairs window. In this era there was definitely a desire to gain a husband as well as a degree. Rosemary, concerned about the reputation of the college, would not countenance any public display of affection. One of the first girls to get engaged was told that she and her fiancé must not hold hands in the street.

Robin and Rosemary were quite confident in the success of their project. Looking back, Rosemary described New Hall as 'one big challenge', but Robin considered it 'all great fun – not hard work at all'[130]. She felt she had a relaxing influence on Rosemary, and this is apparent in some of the photos taken in Rosemary's room where they are almost giggling together. Robin persuaded her not to have unrealistically high standards, or to expect others to be quite as virtuous as she was. The two had their time at Girton in common, but otherwise were very different in character and experience. Rosemary was serious and shy, and devoted, like her Spooner relatives, to a Christian ideal of service. Robin considered that she had led a sheltered life, despite her time in the WRNS. Robin had spent two years in Paris, at the Sorbonne, before the War and had acquired more worldly wisdom and a smoking habit. (The Murrays frowned on women smoking.) Robin was stylish, Rosemary was conventionally dressed and had reverted to a spinsterish hairstyle. Rosemary drove a Ford saloon and Robin a sporty two-seater Jaguar. Robin was a town person, while Rosemary loved the countryside, especially the coast: she would drag Robin out on picnics at weekends. Somehow they contrived to work most amicably together because they complemented each other and both had the success of the institution at heart. Frances recalled a marked change in Rosemary: she became more outgoing and cheerful under Robin's influence and would spend visits to Oxford chatting about their life at New Hall. She had reason to be cheerful, because she realised that she had found her ideal job. It was challenging but manageable, and she had the stamina, determination and good judgement to succeed in it.

Individual students who came into contact with Rosemary found her warm and caring. Stories from alumnae abound of her offering lifts, giving sound advice and even gently persuading them to obey the rules. To one girl who was convinced she would fail her finals she suggested planning what she would do afterwards in that case, and probably as a result of a positive attitude, she passed. To others Rosemary's reserve was a barrier and it was Robin who supplied the ready ear and the perceptive comment. She would offer her tutees a cigarette or a gin and tonic before discussing their essays. If they came to her with a problem, she helped them put it in perspective. She and Rosemary talked through all the decisions together and Rosemary's rather severe judgements were often toned down. Robin also went through the speeches Rosemary gave to schools and other organisations and helped her to improve them. Pat Houghton (NH 1955) observed that Robin was very influential in setting the whole tone and ethos of the College right from the beginning.[131] Many felt that she did not get enough credit for her contribution, but Rosemary always acknowledged that she could not have managed without her, calling her 'my ideal Number Two'. Fortunately Robin had no wish to be in charge, and when Rosemary was on holiday for a fortnight in 1955, climbing in the Dolomites with David, she wrote somewhat tongue-in-cheek that it was 'insuperably difficult' keeping up with everything[132]. The tone of her letters is affectionate, humorous and sometimes teasing, suggesting a very harmonious relationship.

At the second AGM of the New Hall Association, Rosemary was able to report a very successful first year. A deficit had been expected, so members were agreeably surprised to find £45,000 in assets, thanks to the 'careful spending' of the Tutor and Housekeeper[133]. Further donations and subscriptions of nearly £3,000 had been received together with rent of £225 p.a. for 'The Orchard'. No students had dropped out and supervisions in other colleges – St John's, Queens', Peterhouse and Downing as well as the women's colleges – had been satisfactorily arranged. The students had taken part in many extracurricular activities. Members of New Hall had been made to feel welcome in the University and had received the warmest encouragement. This general acceptance of the new institution was in part the result of Rosemary's promotion of its aims and ideals. She was indefatigable in writing and speaking about New Hall and in making contacts across the University and in the Old Schools, battling against shyness which meant she had to nerve herself to pick up the telephone to speak to the Registrary, a top official. She was included with Heads of Houses on the Colleges' Committee and was invited to dinner in the men's colleges, where she would usually have been the only woman present. In fact in Magdalene, a male bastion, she was told by the butler that no woman had ever handled the silver coffee pot before. Rosemary also kept in contact with the influential women in the Association and the BFUW and with members of the Dining Group. It was characteristic of her that she never abandoned adversaries, but sought to maintain a persuasive dialogue. Kate Bertram and Anna Bidder, both members of the Dining Group, were on the early Councils of New Hall. Entertaining took up quite a lot of Rosemary's time: eminent people were invited to dinner and there were frequent tea-parties for local supporters. Lynda Grier from LMH called in and told them that there had been people who had reservations about starting a new college, but when they heard that Miss Murray was to do it they knew it would be all right. During the vacations the Tutors could accommodate overnight visitors: the Principal of St Anne's College, Oxford, wrote to thank them for a 'delightful stay' which cemented the alliance they had just made as sister colleges. Rosemary's mother came in October 1955 and was full of praise. 'There's such a nice atmosphere of friendliness about it all – smiling staff as well as smiling students - & the very nice rooms also, especially yours, which must be enjoyed by the girls in their tutorials'[134]. In Wren parlance, New Hall was a 'happy ship'.

The First Year were indeed very positive and happy, being treated like celebrities and having all the rights of students at the established colleges. Annabel Rathbone (Balfour) has written 'The New Hall experience was mind-blowing on all sorts of levels: horizons were broadened to such an extent that one hardly knew which way to look'[135]. The results of the first year exams suggested that they had spent rather too much time socialising: there were nine Thirds and a 'Special' (the lowest grade). Roma Gill, a talented English student who became an academic, just scraped a 2/1. The poor results have often been blamed on the lack of older girls as role models. In the end they did all receive degrees, and it was a great day for Rosemary when she led them in procession to the Senate House for General Admissions in 1957.

The First Year were scarcely settled in before it was time for the next batch of applicants to sit the first New Hall 3-hour entrance paper. This too had considerable press coverage, because it appeared quite a startling innovation to test logical thought and ability to write rather than formal learning. The attempt to level the playing field for candidates was commended. The paper was published in full in *The Times* and other commentators called it 'stimulating' and 'very fair'[136]. Some fun was had by columnists giving their own answers to the questions. Meanwhile

Rosemary and Robin pored over 110 scripts, called 75 candidates for an interview with each of them and eventually offered places to twelve (finally increased to fifteen, two of them from abroad). This gives some idea of the competition women faced at the time, although a few may have subsequently been accepted by the other colleges. What the interviewees did not realise was that Rosemary was as nervous as they were. She often broke the ice by asking them to plump up the cushions on the sofa, perhaps a homely touch intended to ease the formality? Then she would enquire about their journey and what they had been reading on the train. One girl who answered 'Pilgrim's Progress' found that Rosemary knew a lot more about it than she did. There was a well-read copy at home, given to her parents as a wedding present. Nowadays interviewers are warned not to put too much weight on common interests and opinions, but Rosemary was certainly influenced in favour of those who could chat about sailing or birdwatching. She did not favour girls who did nothing but work, or those who wore too much make-up, nail varnish being a particular abhorrence. In a speech on 'Selection', Rosemary said that New Hall was looking for 'enterprising girls of character and ability who have other interests besides their work and do not come to the University exhausted by cramming.'[137] She told the students that they were all people she thought could particularly benefit from going to Cambridge.[138] Interviews with Robin were more relaxed and friendly, even prefaced by the offer of a cigarette, and at best gave a taster of stimulating discussions ahead. She was a shrewd judge of character.

When the 1955 cohort moved in, the first sixteen students were found accommodation in licensed digs, some of which were rather distant and unsatisfactory. The new Freshers were somewhat envious of their predecessors because they had attracted so much attention, but were more focussed on their work. They all had meals in The Hermitage dining room, and by the time a third set of undergraduates arrived it was full to capacity. Rosemary remembered that the legs of her chair were in the fireplace. In 1956 the first hostel, Bredon House in Selwyn Gardens, was acquired, housing twelve, and the next year St Chad's in Grange Road added twenty places and the Old Granary close to The Hermitage another five. In 1960 the lease with Byron House fell in and New Hall was able to occupy 'The Orchard', a charming Arts and Crafts house which still had the servants' bells in the kitchen. It was set in an extensive garden that had been carefully designed and planted by Ida and Horace Darwin, and Rosemary remembered staying there once as a little girl. By this time New Hall had a few more Senior Members, who were housed as the Resident MAs in these outposts to satisfy University regulations. There was a great deal of practical work in setting all this up, and Rosemary insisted on doing most of it herself, despite an increasingly packed appointment diary. She could no longer afford to take generous vacations at Cadlington. 'We never see you these busy days', wrote her mother in spring 1957.

Only a year after the opening, a *Guardian* journalist had noticed a 'different' atmosphere at New Hall compared with other colleges. 'There was an adultness, a determination, and a wit amongst the undergraduates of New Hall which is often noticeably lacking among the undergraduates of older foundations'[139]. By the time the 'fifties drew to a close New Hall had developed its own ethos, summed up by Sheila Coates (NH 1959) as 'a combination of elegance and simplicity, pragmatism, friendliness and individuality'[140]. It had avoided controversy and turned a blind eye to any signs of prejudice. 'its character has been one of quiet dignity and skilful economic management, wrote David Thomson.[141] Inevitably there had been some difficult problems to confront and Rosemary was grateful to have Robin at her side, urging a humane and tolerant approach. In 1957 one of the second intake found that she was pregnant, which in those days was a social disaster. The Tutors agonised about whether to send the student down. She writes 'I myself was aware that our fledgling college could not but be affected … I made my decision to leave, and with much sympathy it was accepted'. They would certainly have considered allowing her back to complete her degree had she wished. Students were strongly advised not to marry during their studies, but some did and were allowed to live out. Rosemary was not averse to offering a place to a married research student. Colleges at this time were *in loco parentis* to students under the age of 21. When the age of majority was lowered to 18 in 1970, rules were relaxed considerably, but in the 'fifties Rosemary clearly felt a weight of responsibility on her shoulders. A letter from Alice Bacon[142], the MP and educationalist, indicates that Rosemary wrote to her for advice after surprising a couple in bed after dinner, asking how she should proceed. The reply recommended asking the girl if she had considered the risk of a baby and stressing the 'selfishness of bringing a child into the world to be illegitimate'; secondly advising that emotional involvement would affect her work. She states that Tutors have a right to enforce a standard of behaviour in a residential college, and if the girl were quite unrepentant she would send her down. Robin would not have gone along with this hard line, and it may have been at her suggestion that Rosemary instituted talks for students on sex education by an outside speaker. A student who arrived in 1964, Jenny Gartland, writes, 'The oddest part of our initiation into New Hall was the talk on our bodies being like an instrument [played upon by men]. One contemporary turned to me and quoted, "I took my harp to a party, but nobody asked me to play".'[143]

In an article published in the *Cambridge Review*[144] entitled 'The First Year of New Hall', in which Robin's style can be detected, Rosemary had rehearsed again the aims to have a 'collegiate character from the start', taking the best from Newnham and Girton and adapting it to their own needs but within the traditional structures. The article concluded, 'What New Hall needs now is a benefactor'. The New Hall Council had already set up an Appeal Committee, chaired by Lady Whitby and employing a paid secretary to operate in both Cambridge and London. The appeal was launched in London by the Chancellor of the Exchequer, 'Rab' Butler, with a lunch in the Apothecaries' Hall. Letters and leaflets were sent out to 15,000 Foundations, women's groups and individual professional women, but funds were slow to come in. False hope was given in 1956 when the businessman Sir Charles Colston offered to donate £500,000 from a Trust Fund. Preparations went ahead to re-name New Hall 'Colston College' in accordance with the original assumption that it would be named after a benefactor, but the disposal of the trust money was contested and delayed for years. New Hall eventually received a welcome, but not transformational, £55,000 in 1968. Nevertheless, Rosemary and the New Hall Council pressed on with the building project so as to be ready when they had sufficient funds. Realising that 'The Orchard's four-acre site was rather limited, they attempted to buy 'The Grove' next door. It was an elegant early nineteenth-century house that had been bought by Emma Darwin after the death of her husband, Charles Darwin. Negotiations went on for some time but it became clear that the Association could not afford it. Recognising the strategic importance of the land, in 1957 the University stepped in and purchased it with money from the University Grants Committee, giving three acres to New Hall and the rest, including the house, to Fitzwilliam College.

The next step was to decide on architects. The Professor of Architecture, Sir Leslie Martin, had just been appointed Head of

Department, and 'he became the driving force behind up-and-coming architects receiving commissions in Cambridge'[145]. When consulted, he produced the names of a number of practices thought to be in the forefront of modern architectural design. After talking to four of them and seeing their suggestions for developing the site, the Council appointed Messrs Chamberlin, Powell and Bon (CPB), a group of lecturers who had only recently gone into business after winning a contract for The Barbican. They were much influenced by Modernists such as Le Corbusier and keen to try out new techniques in building with concrete. It was only because of expense that grey fair-faced limestone bricks were substituted for most of the walls and the interior left unplastered. The ceilings in the public rooms were of 'bush-hammered' concrete, a very labour-intensive process designed to give an interesting texture. The donation of £100,000 by the Wolfson Foundation in 1960 enabled the Council to commission plans, and Rosemary was closely involved from the start. The original architects' brief was merely an outline of requirements, which needed much supplementary work as time went on. There is no doubt that Rosemary came to know every detail as well as the architects themselves, looking at successive drawings with the closest attention and sometimes suggesting improvements, such as the widening of the internal Walkway from the crossing to the Library. CPB were keen to co-operate with Denys Lasdun, who was designing Fitzwilliam College at the same time, and worked up a scheme where New Hall, Fitzwilliam and Churchill Colleges would be integrated on one big campus. Unfortunately Lasdun rejected this and CPB had to quickly prepare new plans, which it was rumoured (but never confirmed), led to the re-use of a proposal for an institution in the Near East, complete with an Arabian style Fountain Court.[146] It is quite surprising that Rosemary was happy with such an innovative design, but she had no great feeling for architecture and was a believer in leaving experts to do their job. Memories of Miss Nickel's stark white buildings at Downe House may also have influenced her taste for a 'monastic' style. She said later that she had never felt enthusiastic about the Dome.

Building was begun in autumn 1962, and from then on a Building Committee met regularly with the architects, who occasionally also made presentations to Council. Robin recalled Peter Chamberlin, a tall, professional man with a superior air, arriving from London and spreading out his plans in the Dining Room. He listened to his clients, but was very persuasive about carrying through his own ideas. There was also an Associate Architect on site, Peter Honer, who died young and was succeeded by his brother John. The latter was hugely impressed by Rosemary, with whom he had frequent informal meetings, calling her the best client they ever had. She was often to be found on site in gumboots. He would no doubt have reported back to her about the frequent site meetings between the architects and the contractors, W & C French, which became increasingly acrimonious. It was not long before Phase I, the Library, Dining Hall, Fellows' Rooms and Fountain Court, ran into difficulties because of severe weather. It was a winter when the River Cam froze over, and soon frost and snow damaged the brickwork of the footings of the new building and the damp-proof membrane was breached. Ground slabs were forced up by the frost, cracking the drains below. In an effort to preserve the brickwork the contractors put down salt, but it had the opposite effect, damaging the limestone bricks beyond repair. The base of the Library had to be broken up and started again, the architects insisting that the remedial costs were the contractor's responsibility. CPB also complained constantly about the quality of the ready-mix concrete, saying that it was inadequately compacted. In March and April 1963 there was a shortage of bricklayers and they were reduced to four working on site: the contractors eventually managed to find seven

A section of the Dome arriving at Huntingdon Road.

The Dome under construction, 1963.

more and had them working nine hours a day, six days a week to catch up. A tower crane arrived in April to erect the sectional roofs of the Dome and Library. In one Building Committee meeting Rosemary spotted a lorry transporting the concrete 'petals' of the Dome along the Backs, and let out an excited whoop! The Dome was a very innovative structure: the pre-cast sections, only four inches thick, overlapped, with glass panels between. They had to be lowered into place with the greatest precision and bolted onto a ring beam, itself formed of sections tensioned together by steel cables and delicately poised on slender columns. The Library barrel vault was also sectional and similarly tensioned together. These were all very challenging operations for the builders.

In 1962 New Hall had about half a million pounds in its building fund, which was insufficient to complete the planned residential court. A second Appeal Committee, under the Chairmanship of Sir Hugh Beaver, launched a drive to raise money from industry and also suggested that Rosemary should visit the United States in a part investigative, part fund-raising role. Council warmly supported the idea that she should tour the 'Seven Sisters' women's colleges over five weeks and then meet representatives of foundations in New York. Although it was an official visit, she did not mention it in her history of the College, perhaps because it failed to bring in any money and she was concerned by the expense. The visit took place in the Michaelmas Term, consequently Robin was left in charge at a busy time of year with new students settling in. The institution was stretched for accommodation and continued to house students in 'The Orchard' in the midst of the building site. Rosemary and Robin wrote to each other every few days. At first all was calm, and Rosemary must have been gratified to hear that she was missed: 'Whenever I mention you being in the States to any of the undergraduates (who all seem to know) their faces fall into a sort of melancholy cast...'[147] Attending the Colleges' Committee in Rosemary's place, Robin found it 'as good as a play'. 'All those Historian Heads of Houses are so splendidly eloquent and telling once they've got warmed up'[148]. Rosemary answered: 'it's a meeting like that that makes one feel so inadequate as an administrator or anything else'[149]. But only a week later Robin had to pass on two items of bad news: a girl starting her third year had just found that she was pregnant, and a member of the College Council had raised a serious point jeopardising New Hall's Phase II building plans. Rosemary replied calmly, and even quipped, 'Poor Robin ... you will soon have to be student advisor for premarital babies'[150], but then praised her for coping admirably and made suggestions about allowing the girl to continue. She could do nothing about the building question except shelve it. Rosemary had a useful ability to put worries aside until they could be tackled. In America she was spending 12-hour days on the campuses of Vassar, Smith, Radcliffe, Wellesley, Bryn Mawr, Mount Holyoake and Swarthmore, meeting VIPs and being treated as one herself, collected by chauffeurs and accommodated in University guest houses with modern conveniences she was certainly not accustomed to at home. She met presidents, deans, admissions and accommodation officers. She toured dormitories, libraries and chemistry laboratories, rather as she had inspected Wrens' quarters, and sat in on student lectures. She was quite often critical: one college was 'too superior for words'; the students at another shocked her with their 'tight shorts to 5 ins above the knee ... and untidy football sweaters'. The Head of Radcliffe was 'revolutionising' by relaxing rules and allowing real student government (a demand Rosemary had to meet herself in the 1970s). Rosemary was often called on to talk for a few minutes to schoolchildren or University audiences, and since the topic was New Hall or Cambridge it was not difficult, though she was annoyed to be identified immediately as a 'Britisher'. The big doctor's bag she had bought specially was ideal for the maps, booklets and admissions material that she was constantly being given. Her schedule was so full that she admitted to feeling fatigued and from the beginning was counting down the days until her return.

Rosemary enjoyed seeing something of the American countryside and observing how people lived, in everything from plantation houses with verandas to vast apartments, but she was not keen on the big cities. First impressions of New York were: 'Too many dashing cars, hooting wailing of fire engine sirens, rude taxi cab drivers and shop assistants, ostentation, noise, beastly food...' On further exploration she did find things to like; the Museum of Metropolitan Art, the Natural History Museum, the view from the Empire State Building, an 'inspiring' guided tour of the United Nations and the night-time view across the Hudson from the Staten Island Ferry. However, she was dreading the two days of visiting Foundations, bringing out her youthful cliché 'much trepidation' to describe her mood. George Cadbury, a member of the Appeal Committee who accompanied her to the meetings, was good at saying the right thing at the right time, but the ground had not been prepared and through modern eyes it seems a very amateur effort at fund-raising. Ford Motors would not give for buildings, nor would the Bollingen Foundation, although they sent books for New Hall Library for many years; Rockefeller had already given a grant to Churchill College; one unnamed official was frankly anti-women. Rosemary was secretly thankful when it was over. She swiftly moved on to Barnard and other women's colleges. One of the highlights of the trip was a Lieder recital in the Carnegie Hall, by Elizabeth Schwarzkopf. Their paths were to cross again when the singer received an honorary degree at Cambridge. Returning via friends in Montreal, Rosemary finally arrived back on 4th December, to be met at Heathrow by the faithful Robin. At a Council meeting a few days later she reported that she had visited 15 women's colleges and universities and made a number of useful contacts. She had also met the officials of six foundations. Privately she thought the trip had been interesting for her but of little relevance to New Hall. 'Someone in your position has to have been there, I reckon, these days', Robin consoled her[151].

Meanwhile a substantial donation of £120,000 was given by the Elizabeth Nuffield Foundation specifically for graduate accommodation, and very unexpectedly, money from the University Grants Committee was transferred to New Hall from the University because it had to defer a major project. The hitch found by R.E.Macpherson was that Chamberlin's plans did not meet the UGC's standards of economy. He was accused of having misled the Council and deluded himself, and the architects had to quickly change the design. One thing they did was to introduce some two-tier shared rooms to reduce the space per student. Another UGC condition was that the residential buildings must be started in 1964, consequently Phase II of the buildings began before Phase I was completed. 'The Orchard' had to be demolished in summer 1963 and alternative homes found for the undergraduates expecting to live there.

In 1961 Rosemary's uncle, William Spooner (only son of Warden Spooner) decided to set up a Charitable Trust, and New Hall soon became the beneficiary of large cheques. Unlike his father, he was a practical man, a trained engineer who in mid-life became an inventor and made a great deal of money from a factory manufacturing drying machines. Rosemary never felt particularly close to him, but he admired her energy and industry in getting the College going. In fact he remarked in a letter that if she had only been a boy she would have been a wonderful assistant in his business! One can imagine Rosemary's irritation at this gender stereotyping. Nevertheless, she was grateful for the benefaction, naming the Spooner Building after him. In 1960 he offered to pay for her portrait in oils, by his chosen artist, Patrick Phillips, former Head of the Byam Shaw School of Art. He wrote, 'A good portrait will be fitting for future generations to see, & I hope add distinction to your hall. So don't say "no" '[152]. Rosemary agreed, for the sake of College record, but was not very satisfied with the result because it made her look older than her forty-seven years. Nevertheless it is a fine portrait which hangs in the College today. She disliked a later one by a different artist even more, because it made her look cold and forbidding, not at all how she wished to be remembered, and in Churchillian fashion, she asked the Keeper of Pictures to destroy it.[153] A third portrait, by David Tindle, was never finished because of the artist's ill health.

By 1962 four more College Lecturers, and a Research Fellow, the classicist Elizabeth Rawson, funded by the Leverhulme Trust, had been taken on to the staff of New Hall and external Directors of Studies appointed in the larger subjects where there was no resident senior member. The Council decided to call the lecturers Fellows, and the following year appointed Rosemary as the first President, in preparation for applying for collegiate status. She must have been very gratified that they did not consider any other candidates. The original plan had been to appoint an 'eminent woman' after a start-up period. In 1959 the University had agreed to an increase in numbers up to 300 and this was to be the target once the new buildings were available. In anticipation of the move, the Council allowed 102 places for 1964, and gave up some of the hostels, so they became increasingly concerned as the building work fell behind schedule and it became clear that it would not be finished in September. There was really no option but to move into the parts of the building that were habitable, so Rosemary took over her small flat in Fountain Court and with the Steward and Housekeeper prepared the rooms for eleven students which had been created by partitioning the basement of the Library. Upstairs, 20,000 books were being sorted and arranged by New Hall's first Librarian, Sarah Newman. Fitzwilliam and Churchill Colleges offered some hospitality while the kitchens were being finished. Meals were then served on trestle tables in the Fellows' dining and drawing rooms for the rest of term. In the New Year the full glory of the Dome and its unusual rising servery was revealed. An undergraduate of that year recalled, 'Throughout all this Miss Murray was a calm, sympathetic & inspiring presence, whose leadership enabled us youngsters to get on happily with university life…'[154] Another writes of 'a spirit of adventure for all of us involved in taking over a new building and turning it into a community'[155]. Around the building was a sea of mud, with construction work continuing in a feverish race to keep to the scheduled opening by the Queen Mother on June 6th 1965.

The Queen Mother inspecting a model of the new buildings with Rosemary, 1965.

– 10 –

New Hall: from Approved Foundation to College

ROSEMARY WAS HUGELY EXERCISED in making arrangements for the royal visit, confessing later that it was a 'low point' for her. Not only was she extremely nervous, she was faced by the situation of a half-built college, with a tower crane still in place, many unsightly areas and no proper entrance. Nevertheless, invitations were sent out to various categories of people: Heads of Houses, Fellows, members of the New Hall Association and alumnae, the architects and contractors, VIPs and benefactors. After much negotiation with the tenant, the drive of 'The Grove' was diverted to provide a route, with a hastily laid turf border, to a temporary staircase at the end of the Walkway, where the Queen Mother was met by Rosemary and the recently elected Chairman of Council, Revd Dr J.S. Boys Smith. Unluckily, June 6th was a very wet, cold day, but the programme went ahead as planned, with speeches by Rosemary, Boys Smith and the Queen Mother on the Walkway, which at that time was unglazed and open to Fountain Court. Their voices were almost drowned by the noise of the water-spouts channelling the pouring rain into the pool below. The party then made a tour of the finished buildings where groups, from kitchen staff to distinguished visitors, were waiting in all the public rooms to be presented. The Queen Mother took tea with a few undergraduates and then signed a Visitors' Book in the Library. Inwardly Rosemary was apprehensive, but she managed to give the impression that she was enjoying the occasion. Her proud Mama, who was among the guests, said, 'You really seemed to be as much yourself as the Queen herself!' In a letter to her other daughters, Ellen reported that Rosemary did her part perfectly, 'so natural and just there, but never obtrusive or fussed – and looking particularly beautiful as everyone agreed'. In a photograph of President and guest inspecting a model of the buildings Rosemary appears every bit as aristocratic as the Queen.

Another milestone in 1965 was the recognition of New Hall as an Approved Foundation. The application was scrutinised by the Council of the Senate, who produced a Report describing how the 'Recognised Institution' had grown since 1954 to over 100 students, most of whom could be accommodated in its new buildings. They recommended

The Queen Mother arriving at New Hall, escorted by Rosemary and Dr Boys Smith, to open the new buildings, 1965.

The Queen Mother walking past the assembled guests on the Walkway.

approval, and the change of status was finally confirmed in November. Rosemary must have been gratified that New Hall was now well on the way to becoming a full college of the University, but the next decade was to be, if anything, more difficult than the first.

As sections of the new buildings were completed, the rented hostels were given up and there was a phased move of undergraduates and Fellows to Huntingdon Road. In January 1966 Robin Hammond moved into a first floor flat in Orchard Court and before long a narrow ladder had been rigged up to her window so that the cat, Smokey, could come and go. By this time the 42 graduate students were occupying the accommodation built with money from the Elizabeth Nuffield Foundation, including a small Graduate Dining Room and MCR. From 1967 some of the students were studying for the new one-year B.Ed., which allowed those who had completed three years at a College of Education to obtain a degree. Rosemary was a great supporter of this scheme, having been much involved with the Teachers' Training College, Keswick Hall, which later became part of the University of East Anglia. She was a Governor from 1958, as representative of the Diocese of Ely, and attended the Standing Conference of the Church Colleges of Education three years running, 1968-70. The more extensive premises and growth in numbers meant that Rosemary could no longer manage every aspect of the College as she had done in Silver Street. For the first time porters were employed, and a maintenance man, Tony Norman, who served New Hall loyally until he retired in the 1990s. More secretarial and kitchen staff were recruited. The first professional Librarian, Sarah Newman, and the first full-time Tutorial Secretary, Margaret Wright, were both appointed in 1964. The volume of the President's administrative work increased, but she kept a tight control over all the departments and continued practical tasks such as controlling the keys. She would always personally change the lock if a student lost her room key, and this thoroughness paid off in the era of the Cambridge Rapist, who was found to have a number of New Hall keys in his possession at the time of his arrest.

Rosemary had a very settled routine, eating breakfast at 7.30 in her flat, while the cleaner started work, and moving to a combined sitting room and office, overlooking the garden, at 8.30. Her secretary had a separate office and would come through at 9.30 with her shorthand book to take dictation. As well as correspondence there would be all the College committee minutes, written by Rosemary, to type. The rest of the day

The pristine white Dome in 1966.

would be full of meetings, especially during the period as Vice-Chancellor, but she would cycle back up the hill for lunch, sitting in her appointed place on high table, whenever possible. The magistrate's assignments often came through at quite short notice. In the evenings she returned to the flat after dinner to continue working, or sometimes to watch TV. She enjoyed football, Wimbledon and snooker and became a devotee of the soap opera 'Coronation Street', with its insights into the life of the working classes. Even then she was not idle but had some knitting on the go. Her secretary described her as a workaholic, and her flat reflected her life: there was no getting away from the job. With the staff she was quietly firm and very formal, calling them by their surnames in service style until the mid-seventies. The only one she fell out with was the gardener, who resented her interference.

If one asks any alumna of this period about Rosemary, she will inevitably mention that she 'did the garden'. From a muddy building site Rosemary created a Fellows' garden, with a particularly fine herbaceous border at the end of the Library, a 'Servants' Garden' (her own outmoded terminology), and flower beds around Orchard Court. She was a familiar figure in her wellingtons and old clothes, but not always recognised. Some students felt it was rather demeaning for a President to dig the garden and sweep out the moat, but Rosemary found the physical activity invigorating and relaxing, as she had done at Cadlington. On a Sunday morning a resident Fellow might find her knocking on the door at 8.30 a.m. with the smiling request, 'Weeding?'

The move to Huntingdon Road also brought considerably higher expenses, not all of which had been anticipated. Running costs for utilities and telephones were much higher than before. There were more people on the payroll, and as most of them were women, the Equal Pay Act of 1970 made it necessary to increase their salaries. Despite Rosemary's economies, such as using low wattage light bulbs and turning down the heating, so that Fellows sat on the carpets to make the most of the under floor warmth, expenditure exceeded income. New Hall was still dependant on the trickle of donations coming in and donations in kind, such as gifts of books, silver and pictures. Among the books were bequests from J.B.Leishman, an Oxford don and friend of Rosemary Syfret, and Inez Macdonald, a Newnham Fellow in Spanish who had been an early supporter of the New Hall Association. The Bullough family gave most of their library, which included 2,000 books that had belonged to the actress, Eleonora Duse[156], and a valuable collection of books on women came from the NUWT when they dissolved their association. When Lady Sibyl Thorpe gave £2,000 for 'some distinct purpose', Rosemary decided to spend it on the garden. Most of the money collected by the appeals had financed the construction, consequently New Hall had only a small endowment, not producing much income. Compared to the older established colleges it was poor, and as it continued to grow (to 253 undergraduates in 1972) it became set in a mode of making do and mending which, after the initial pioneering phase, was bad for morale.

There were problems too with the new buildings. The rising servery in the Dome was prone to flooding from water seeping through from the ground, the 'petals' of the Dome leaked and there was damp in the Library basement. Rosemary became so irritated with the architects that she invited a member of the University Estates Management team to her next meeting with them. He recalled that Chamberlin (noted for his persuasive powers) took a superior line, thinking that he could talk down this woman, but Rosemary proved to have done her homework, having read the British Standards and knowing the plans intimately, and was more than a match for him. Without raising her voice she used phrases such as 'I'd like to correct…' and 'I don't think that's quite right'. Further meetings followed about the contractual obligations and some snags were fixed. The architects took the easy way out, blaming the contractors, but many of the defects were clearly design faults. Impractical elements in Chamberlin Powell and Bon's plans soon became obvious to the inhabitants. The under floor heating in the dining room was inadequate in the colder months, partly because of draughts from the four staircases and partly because the insulation of the Dome was under-specified. Thick curtains at the entrances did little to alleviate the problem and college members took to wearing their warmest clothes to dine. The open walkways past the Library and on two levels in front of Fellows' rooms along Fountain Court were usually freezing and made the surrounding accommodation hard to heat. It was many years before they were glazed. The upper walkways, which the architects had visualised as a route from the Library to the Dining Hall, were inconsistent with library security, as were the garden doors to Fountain Court. The top floor of the Library had just one concrete retaining beam to protect those on the narrow gallery from falling to their deaths. The Librarian complained that there was no lift that would take a trolley and was told by the architects that once the books were in place they probably wouldn't be moved very often! On one occasion the moat overflowed, and Rosemary found that neither she nor the equally strong Mary Boothman could shift the large wheels that opened the sluice. Reluctantly she had to call in 'a man'. For the clean-up operation she co-opted anyone who was around. Zara Steiner remembers being telephoned at 8 a.m. and asked to come at once because papers on the floor of her ground floor room were threatened. Rosemary thrust a broom into her hand and told her to sweep the water from the passage into the moat.

 Despite the difficulties, the students were proud of their gleaming white, *avant garde* buildings, and it seemed like a violation when some male undergraduates from Magdalene College climbed on to the roof at three o'clock in the morning and painted black footprints on the side of the Dome. Fortunately Robin Hammond heard them before they could carry out the rest of their plan, which was to continue down the far side and across the Library barrel vault. She phoned the porters, who 'arrested' them, and Rosemary locked them in a room while she phoned the police, but to her great annoyance they escaped through the window and were never caught. It was a particularly stupid prank, because they used an extremely tough enamel paint, and in the process of removing it the fibre glass surface of the Dome was irreparably damaged.

Attempting to clean black footprints off the Dome.

Dealing with all these practicalities, which might well have completely preoccupied a less competent person, was just a small aspect of Rosemary's life. As Tutor-in-Charge Rosemary had immediately begun to forge links with girls' schools across the country, many of them members of the Girls' Public Day School Trust (GPDST)[157]. The aim of the GPDST was to provide a high standard of academic education for talented girls, with bursaries for those who could not afford the fees, consequently they became a major provider of good candidates for New Hall and the other women's colleges. In a typical year, 1956, Rosemary made speeches, often at prize-givings, at nine schools, some local, some as far away as Dame Alleyn's School, Newcastle. Although she hated speech-making and usually had the full text in front of her, vetted by Robin, she saw it as an important part of the job. Robin insisted that she did not write the speeches, only corrected them and tried to make them less stilted. Rosemary became Chair of the Committee of St Felix School, Southwold in 1956 and a member of Wycombe Abbey Council and Governor of Norwich Training College in 1958. Her old school, Downe House, was glad to have her on the Board of Governors to deal with two difficult episodes, an inadequate Head, whom Rosemary persuaded tactfully to resign, and a tiresome master who had to be confronted and ejected. In both cases she was praised for her sureness of touch in handling the problems. She was soon on the committee of the GPDST and joined the National Council in 1969. Letters of appreciation when she resigned or retired from these organisations show how much her good sense and practical advice was valued, especially by headmistresses. This was just the beginning of many outside interests which benefitted the College and satisfied Rosemary's wish to have a life outside Cambridge.

Remarkably, in the early 1960s she was still demonstrating ten hours a week and teaching, while beginning to be recognised in the University and appointed to committees. In addition she had a significant workload as a J.P. Her reputation was also spreading beyond Cambridge and into government circles. She was invited in 1963 to become a member of the Lockwood Committee, which was set up to consider the foundation of a second university for Northern Ireland, as part of the plans for the expansion of higher education in the U.K. As well as her academic credentials, Rosemary had the advantage of having lived in Londonderry during the War, and she was the only woman, apart from the Assistant Secretary. The Committee met at Stormont in Belfast, so it was no light undertaking for Rosemary to accept the appointment, but of course she rose to the challenge. At the first meeting, a full discussion of teacher training, and whether it should be part of their remit, was probably instigated by Rosemary. The committee went to see Belfast University, and in April 1964, in a solo, packed 2-day tour, Rosemary visited schools and colleges in Northern Ireland and reported back. Later in the year the Lockwood Report was published with the recommendation to found the New University of Ulster in Coleraine and close Magee College in Londonderry. This threatened closure provoked so much opposition that Magee was incorporated as the location for Continuing Education (one of Rosemary's strong interests, so perhaps we can see her hand in this). The Irish did not forget Rosemary: she received her first honorary degree from the University of Ulster in 1972. Her proposer described her as 'familiar with this terrain' and one who had come to love it.[158]. Rosemary spoke of her vision of university education: the variety required to cater for individual students' needs and abilities and the importance of encouraging their curiosity, leading to the excitement and satisfaction

The Lockwood Committee.

of discovery. In her opinion, 'True education in a university must lead to the acquiring of discrimination and judgement' and she questioned whether some universities had 'perhaps sought to concentrate too much on technical or vocational training at the expense of true education'[159]. She returned in 1979 to give the Convocation Lecture on the future for universities.

Two more government appointments were to take her to London and further afield. In 1968 she accepted an invitation to serve on the Wages Councils. These had been set up to protect the pay of workers in the inelegantly named 'sweated trades', with the laudable aim of eliminating poverty. One can see that this would appeal to Rosemary's sense of social justice. The low paid industries included 'Flax and Hemp', 'Sack and bag' and 'Ostrich and Fancy Feather and Artificial Flower'. Rosemary was assigned to the 'Rope, Net and Twine' Wages Council and also served briefly on the Shirtmakers and Bread and Flour Confectionery Trade Councils. Each Council had a number of workers' and employers' representatives and an odd number of independent members, usually three. Minimum rates of pay were laid down and regulations relating to hours, holiday entitlement and working conditions were discussed, with the independents encouraging and facilitating negotiation. These topics, which some would have thought dull, Rosemary found absorbing. As in her J.P. rôle, she was looking for a fair outcome and was a keen observer of human interactions. She remained on the Wages Councils for 25 years until they were abolished, all through the busiest period of her University career and well into retirement.

Even more time-consuming was membership of the Armed Forces Pay Review Board (AFPRB) for ten years, starting in 1971[160]. It was a most prestigious appointment, since the Board reported directly to the Prime Minister. The terms of reference set out in Edward Heath's letter to Rosemary were 'to advise the Prime Minister on the pay and allowances of members of the Naval, Military and Air Forces of the Crown, and of any women's service administered by the Defence Council'. The committee of six men had been meeting for a few months before it belatedly recognised the importance of having a woman member. Later they were joined for a short time by Baroness Edith Summerskill, but otherwise Rosemary was the sole representative of the women's views. Two to three meetings a month in London was a considerable commitment, and she made clear that she would not be able to attend them all. She managed about two-thirds. There were also reviews of bases in England and abroad, sometimes in groups and sometimes singly. The Secretariat would write to members to invite them to indicate the service units they would like to visit and the programme was arranged by the Ministry of Defence. Rosemary's inspection of WRNS units at the end of the War was highly relevant. The experience she had gained then of quickly assessing staff and facilities made the AFPRB assignments a fairly simple matter. She enjoyed being back in a military environment where her itinerary was set out to the minute and she was whisked around by chauffeur driven cars or occasionally by planes or helicopters. Her first visit was in 1972, to the WRAC base at Larkhill, Wiltshire, with the Director of the Royal Army Corps, and from then on she did a review every year – more than was expected from committee members. In 1973 she was in Germany, visiting army bases at Gutersloh and Bielefeld; in 1974 she was guest of the WRNS at HMS *Heron*, Yeovilton. In 1975 came a trip to Malta which her companion, Jean Orr, a civil servant, labelled 'our great visit to the Navy'. They enjoyed cocktails and dinner with the Commander, British Forces and stayed on for a short holiday in the sun, bathing and having picnics. The next year Rosemary was close to Cambridge at RAF Brampton and in 1977 was on home ground, visiting the Navy at Portsmouth, specifically to see HMS *Herald*, a hydrographic survey ship. It was felt that the pay of these sailors should be increased because of the unfavourable conditions of service and limited promotion prospects. Other assignments were Colchester barracks, the SAS in Hereford and Queen Elizabeth Hospital Woolwich for discussions with disaffected army medical officers. All the time Rosemary was taking notes, showing a particular concern for wives and families in married quarters, recording the condition and size of houses, kitchen equipment, distance to local shops and schools, as well as listening to the men's complaints. She chatted very naturally to service men and women about their work, showing a sympathetic understanding of their problems.

Despite all her activities, Rosemary managed to block out time for holidays at Easter and in the summer, though giving up the Christmas skiing parties. In 1955 she was in Burgundy in the spring and had two and a half weeks in the Dolomites with her brother David during the Long Vacation. Here she did a different climb every day, keeping notes on the distances and heights of mountains, sometimes walking as far as 16 miles and climbing between 2,000 and 4,000 feet. Her stamina was impressive for a woman in her mid-forties. In 1956 it was the Lake District at Easter and climbing in Italy in July; in 1957 Southwold and Mont Blanc with David, her chief climbing companion. There were only brief visits to Cadlington, where much had changed. Admiral Murray had been invalided out of the Navy with tuberculosis, and after a long period of convalescence occupied himself running the smallholding as a commercial venture with crops of potatoes and apples and a variety of animals. Ann, unfit for regular work, looked after the flower garden when well enough, but she was slowly weakened by the problem with her lungs and died in 1957, a cause of great sadness to the whole family. She had a long and brave struggle against the illness which began in her teens, achieving a 2:1 at LMH and working when she could as a commercial artist. She and Rosemary shared a love of nature, especially birdwatching, and Ann, always stylish, did her best to improve Rosemary's fashion sense. Arthur Murray, keen to do something useful in enforced retirement, founded the Horndean Community Association in 1946 'to encourage social, moral and intellectual development and recreation,' persuading the locals to buy an old country house and equip it as a social centre, where a dozen clubs were soon advertised on flyers hand-printed by the Admiral. Cadlington also became a venue for rehearsals and events. Arthur Murray died in

1959 but Ellen continued to live there, finding it increasingly difficult to manage the estate. Rosemary was deeply attached to her father, who was a formative influence on her, and she must have missed him greatly. Her brother John had joined the Royal Navy as a Special Entry Cadet in 1938 and worked his way up to the rank of Commander in 1960, becoming Chief of Staff of the Flag Officer Scotland and Northern Ireland stationed at Rosyth. In 1963 he was promoted to Captain and worked for the Weapons Department of the Admiralty at Bath[161]. After retirement from the Navy he became Bursar of the Cambridge Technical College and settled in Newnham with his family. David and Richard both avoided call-up by volunteering for the Navy and quickly became officers in the RNVR. David served mainly ashore in the Far East and Richard trained as a Fighter Direction Officer in the Home Fleet, and then was posted to the East Indies. Both were demobbed in 1946, David later returning to the Navy as a Scientific Civil Servant at the Admiralty Signals Establishment at Portsmouth, where both his father and Rosemary had worked, while Richard became an academic.

Frances married Ian Crombie, an Oxford don, in 1946 and by 1957 had five children. Rosemary visited from time to time and did her best to help them with useful gifts, such as a washing machine. The lives of the two sisters could not have been more different: Frances immersed in domesticity and child-rearing, Rosemary now clearly destined to be a spinster academic and administrator. The question is often asked, why did she never marry? Many men found her attractive, and she got on well with them, both in a working environment and socially. Rosemary once said, "If I had married during the War, I wouldn't have been able to do all this", i.e. make a career in Cambridge and beyond[162]. This comment suggests that she did receive a proposal, or at least had a serious relationship with a man while she was in the WRNS. No diaries are preserved from 1942-5, and her letters were written with a wide family readership in mind, so the evidence is lacking, apart from the hint that she enjoyed the company of the American Commodore and his retinue, the Chief of Staff, ADC and Naval Officer in Command in Londonderry.

Rosemary also forged strong relationships with women, just occasionally verging on the passionate. She adored Marjorie Verney at school, praising her artistic and musical talents and was gently warned against such 'pashes'. At Royal Holloway she observed one or two female 'couples' with distaste. People have wondered whether Rosemary and

Robin had a lesbian relationship, but this is unlikely. There was initially a spark of attraction between them as Rosemary learned from Robin to take life less seriously and she may have been in danger of idolising her, but Robin was already in a close relationship with Rosemary Syfret, her life-long partner. Their letters reveal that there was a little group of unmarried Girton women who socialised regularly and looked out for each other, among them Henriette Bibas ('Henry') and Alison Fairlie. Henriette's sister drew a very good charcoal portrait of Rosemary in 1961.[163] In 1964, amid her many other tasks, Rosemary arranged care for Henriette when she had what sounds like a stroke. However, undoubtedly the special friend from Girton days was Helen McMorran, Fellow and Librarian since 1930 and when Rosemary arrived, just taking up her appointment as Vice-Mistress. Rosemary first met her at a sherry party in October 1946, at which time the gulf between them of status would have been considerable. There was also an age gap of 15 years. Helen perhaps became a rôle model, especially as that rôle was not primarily academic, despite a background in Slavonic Studies, but professional and administrative. She was a very vigorous person, upright and dignified and is remembered sitting at the end of the breakfast table dispensing tea to the other resident Fellows. She had studied Modern Languages at Girton in 1916-19 and then trained as a Librarian, returning to Girton to manage the new library, an anonymous gift of her father. Gradually she took on College duties such as editing the *Girton Review*. In 1947 she became Registrar of the Roll, the record of Girton's alumnae. Rosemary, with her obsession for lists, soon started helping her collect material. They had much in common, membership of the BFUW and GPDST, high professional standards, Scottish connections and a love of gardening and birdwatching. Muriel Bradbrook could be describing Rosemary when she wrote in Helen's obituary of 'combining great dignity with great modesty'. Helen's high standards as Librarian were legendary, so she was the obvious person to turn to when Rosemary was setting up the embryonic New Hall Library, accessioning, cataloguing and classifying all followed Girton's pattern. Rosemary's elevation to Tutor-in-Charge brought her to the same level as Helen the Vice-Mistress, and, together with the observation of Robin's relationship with Rosemary Syfret, may have given her the confidence to express her feelings towards Helen, to whom she sent a touchingly affectionate Valentine in the form of an alphabet of attributes.

'I love my love with an
A because she's Anonymous'

And so on throughout the alphabet. Some of the interesting lines are:

'G because of the GPDST...
N she's North British...
O because she's an Ornithologist
P because she's Perfect
Q à cause de son je-ne-sais Quoi'...
'X because she's eXtremely difficult to please
Y because she's WISE
Z because she's the pearl of Zenana'.[164]

The final reference is to apartments in the Mughal palaces reserved for royal women. Helen was born in India, the daughter of an East India merchant, and spent a year travelling there in the 1920s.

How much should we read into this declaration of love? It was not uncommon for Victorian women to send Valentines to each other, and Rosemary's Spooner grandmother had kept up the tradition, sending specially composed verses to her grand-daughters. Robin helped her with the composition, which is cerebral rather than emotional, a clever and innocent *jeu d'esprit*. Rosemary was a serious person, but Robin brought out her lighter side.[165] Helen, perhaps anxious that it might be misconstrued, acknowledged the alphabet of love as a secret between the two of them:

'HEART-felt thanks
For a Valentine that
Cannot be shown or shared. 14.ii.57'[166]

The exchange initiated a close friendship, and there were plenty of opportunities to meet. Helen would have attended many of the same events as Rosemary. She was a founder member of the New Hall Association and went to the BFUW and GPDST meetings, while Rosemary frequently had the opportunity to socialise at Girton as she had been given dining rights as a member of High Table when she left. Occasional lunches and suppers together, usually at weekends, are noted in Rosemary's diary, but the most time they had in each other's company was on holiday. The first documented holiday was in Central Italy in 1959, visiting Assisi, Spoleto, Urbino and Ravenna. It appears in a list of holidays that Rosemary made, annotated 'HIM 1st'. In September 1960 they returned to Italy for a three-week tour, this time with a focus on seeing Palladian villas in Vicenza, Mantua, and Todi. In Verona they met up with Ellen Murray, who was en route to a cycling trip with Ruth and Rosemary Spooner, and she wrote afterwards, 'I enjoyed every moment … & for your driving & guiding my admiration is as great as Helen's'. As these sight-seeing tours by car were untypical for Rosemary, who usually preferred adventure holidays, they must have been designed to suit Helen. There were other similar trips to Italy in the 1960s and at least one to France, in 1964, when they looked at Romanesque architecture – Vézelay, Autun, Cluny – before Rosemary drove all the way to Geneva, over 1,000 miles in ten days as she carefully noted. Helen retired as Vice-Mistress in 1962 and was made a Life Fellow of Girton. A very successful portrait was commissioned from Patrick Phillips who had painted Rosemary three years earlier[167]. She continued to live in Girton until at least 1968, editing the *Girton Review* until 1966 and retiring as Keeper of the Roll in 1969. Rosemary kept another Valentine dating from 1976 or 1977, a simple cut-out red heart inscribed 'A VALENTINE FOR A VICE CHANCELLOR[168]', most probably in Helen's writing, suggesting that their relationship was long-lasting. Helen's health deteriorated until in 1978 she entered a local nursing home. She died in 1985. Many of her books, distinguished by a book label decorated with a woodcut of St Jerome, were given to New Hall's Library, and it is thanks to her example that Rosemary decided to appoint a professional Librarian.

Rosemary also went to Italy on her own. After the devastating Florence floods of November 1966 there was an appeal by the Biblioteca Nazionale for librarians and bookbinders to come and help salvage and conserve the damaged books. Rosemary, who had learned bookbinding at the local Technical College[169], determined to do this and spent three weeks in August 1967 tackling some of the thousands of volumes covered in mud. She described to Aunt Rosemary how the books had all been dried and 'are now being opened, mud partially removed dry, books taken to pieces ('pulled') and washed page by page. They will then be mended and eventually rebound … very tricky not to tear the pages especially when they are crumpled as well as stuck together with mud'[170]. It was an overwhelming experience for all those who took part. The Library, located alongside the River Arno, had been flooded to a depth of 12 feet and more than a million books were affected. New methods of conservation had to be devised, workers trained and a reading room turned into a massive repair room. Rosemary had the privilege of learning from two of the finest English bookbinders of the period, Antony Cains and Christopher Clarkson. No wonder she went at least three more times in the next few years and brought home a packet of Florentine mud as a souvenir!

***

The next period of New Hall's development was from 1965, when Approved Foundation status was achieved, to 1972. The Council set their sights on the goal of becoming a full college of the University and worked purposefully towards it. They had established a Constitution Committee in 1963, and it now became a forum for Fellows to consider the eventual structure and governance of the College: its Council and Governing Body, College Officers, regulations for employment and admissions, preparatory to drafting Statutes. Undoubtedly the most controversial issue was whether New Hall should become co-educational. By the end of the 1960s some of the men's colleges were considering becoming mixed; Churchill and Clare voted to admit women in a few years' time. King's College produced a report in 1969 suggesting that more good women candidates would apply to Cambridge if there were to be co-residence. They suggested that the College should open some of its external Research Fellowships to women, and in due course all the internal Fellowships as well. Rosemary annotated her copy 'very attractive'[171]. However there was little doubt that an increase in the number of Fellowships open to women would reduce the field for the women's colleges, 'since few women would be likely to accept a Fellowship in a women's college in preference to one in a mixed college'[172]. The same argument applied to junior members. In 1969 there were 1819 applicants to the women's colleges, of whom 444 were accepted. It was doubtful whether applications would rise sufficiently to serve all the male colleges who wanted to go mixed as well as maintain the numbers in the women's colleges. The Third Foundation Association had been set up to give more opportunities to women in the University, so New Hall could hardly argue against the opening of men's colleges to women, an eventuality which had not been considered in 1954.

Nevertheless, there was a conflict of interest that must have exercised Rosemary. She constantly argued for a phased approach to co-residence to give more time for recruiting good women candidates. Her considered position on New Hall was that the College should stay true to the ideals of the founders. They had subscribed and donated and volunteered to create a women's college: no-one knew better than Rosemary how much dedication and unpaid work had gone into this cause, and she would not deviate from their vision, arguing '...it would not be in accord with this [object] for men in *statu pupillari* to be admitted immediately upon achieving the status of a College. It would be possible at a later date to seek amendment of Statute if at any time New Hall wished to change its membership'[173]. Rosemary was very persuasive and had plenty of support from her colleagues. She was prepared to compromise on having a mixed Fellowship; after all, many of New Hall's supervisors had been men, and in certain subjects it would have been difficult to find suitable women. In 1971 New Hall appointed a Bursar, George Levack, who became the first male Fellow. There was some opposition, led by Prof. Anscombe, an eminent philosopher, who felt that the appointment was depriving women of career opportunities, but it was not long before a male teaching Fellow in Medicine, Chris Huang, joined him on the Fellowship.

Rosemary still kept in touch with Lady Margaret Hall by attending alumni events and must have been agreeably surprised when, in 1967, her old College saw fit to elect her as an Honorary Member. Sir Harry Verney thought it was long overdue: 'At long last LMH have recognised you and about time too'. Rosemary Syfret expressed her delight that the college had decided 'to readopt you in so exalted a capacity'. 'I bet you'll end up as a Dame', she wrote presciently.

For her book, *New Hall, 1954-1972: The Making of a College*, Rosemary chose a photograph of the Council of New Hall in 1969[174]. These were the people who led the final push for collegiate status. The six women in the front row were Fellows of New Hall: Rosemary and Robin, Helen Clover, the first History Fellow, Vivien Stewart, the part-time Bursar and Lecturer in Land Economy, Yvette Spencer-Booth, a Zoologist, and Esther Welbourn, Director of Studies in Medicine since 1964. They are flanking the Chairman, the Revd Dr John Boys Smith, Master of St John's College. He had been a member of the Council of the Senate Committee, set up in 1952 to give guidance to the Third Foundation and was a member of the early Councils of New Hall. Rosemary was grateful

The New Hall Council in 1969. Rosemary next to Dr Boys Smith, Chairman, and Robin Hammond on the left of the front row.

for his continuous support and sound advice. The woman in the back row is Miss Duff, retired Principal of Keswick Hall, who was co-opted on Rosemary's recommendation and did much useful work as a volunteer. Of the men in the back row, Dr Kitson Clark of Trinity College was a great supporter of women's rights who corresponded helpfully with Rosemary on many subjects, notably on the prospect of Trinity 'going mixed'[175]; R.E. Macpherson, an Eton and King's man who later became University Registrary, efficiently prepared documents relating to the recognition of New Hall as a College for the Council of the Senate to discuss and approve; Trevor Thomas, Bursar of St John's, drafted the Statutes and prepared the Charter and Petition for submission first to the Council of the Senate and then to the Privy Council for the Royal Assent. There was no objection from the Council and the recommendation to add New Hall to the list of colleges went through on 20th March 1971. Since Rosemary was a member of Council she was able to sign the document. An unexpected hitch occurred when the Privy Council, in response to suggestions from the National Union of Students, recommended student representation on the New Hall Council and the formation of a students' union. Rosemary wrote to Kitson Clark, 'We are in the unenviable position of being the first college of Oxford or Cambridge to be faced with this problem, and what we decide to do could set a precedent.[176]' In the event neither request proved an obstacle, though the amendments caused a year's delay. The Charter of Incorporation was granted on 28th June 1972. Thanks to a donation in 1967 the College already had a Coat of Arms.[177] It only remained for the New Hall Association to wind up the Company and hand over its assets to the College. Rosemary felt a huge sense of satisfaction at having fulfilled the obligations she had taken on in 1954 and completed the work begun by the Third Foundation Association twenty years earlier. Diplomatic as ever, she said that she considered the Association of New Hall to be the Founder of the College.[178]

Rosemary in the new library, c.1965.

Four men who influenced Rosemary's career as Chemist and administrator

Dr T.W.J. Taylor.

Sir Robert Robinson.

Alexander Robertus Todd, Baron Todd.

Revd Dr John Sandwith Boys Smith.

– 11 –

University responsibilities

ROSEMARY WAS ALWAYS a University as well as a College person. When she arrived at Girton she realised that there were considerable differences in the way the Universities of Oxford and Cambridge operated, and she read *The Reporter* assiduously to discover more about the Cambridge system and its unique jargon. Once appointed as Tutor-in-Charge at New Hall she gained a real insider's view at the Heads of Houses Committee. Her good judgement and capacity for hard work were noticed, and towards the end of the 1960s she began to play a part in University affairs. In 1968 the Vice-Chancellor, Sir Eric Ashby, invited her to be a member of a consultative committee revising the edicts relating to students, proctorial duties and the functions of the Court of Discipline. He wrote: '...of course it will be uphill work, requiring a very equable disposition, to overhaul our antiquated system of rules and discipline[179]'. Echoes of the student protest movement in California, Paris and elsewhere had reached Cambridge, and there were demands to revise some of the more old-fashioned conventions and to have student participation in the governance of the University. On the recommendation of the working party, sensible concessions were made, but further demands from students arose over the next few years for representation on University bodies. Rosemary was appointed to the Discipline Committee and Statutes Committee, resulting in a number of Reports that led to changes. It may have been on Rosemary's suggestion that the Vice-Chancellor appointed an additional female pro-Proctor in 1969.[180]

In New Hall rules were being relaxed: the wearing of gowns for Formal Hall ceased to be compulsory in 1965, and gate hours were extended to 2 a.m. Rosemary was persuaded that it was safer to have male visitors signed in and out than to have them staying illegally and climbing out of windows. As for pre-marital sex, her attitude appears to have become more liberal and she thought it was a matter for individual decision. In her talks to Freshers at the beginning of the year she urged them to become well informed about the consequences of men and women working in close proximity and to be selective about their men friends.[181] She also gently cautioned them against demanding change – 'ask what the change is leading to'. However, the JCR lobbied for student representation on the College Council, which at the time was not possible under the terms of the Articles of the Association of New Hall. Instead Rosemary set up a Liaison Committee to which students could bring their concerns, and involved them in discussion of the draft statutes. Student representatives were included on some of the main committees – Finance, Estates and Library – and on several occasions were allowed to put their case at Council meetings. Some may have expected Rosemary to be more authoritarian, but she realised that society was changing and the College would have to change with it. At an impressionable age she had been subject to Olive Willis's idea of a community where there was a good deal of consultation and participation, steered with a light hand by the Principal. She also favoured a delaying technique when changes were mooted, allowing time for consideration and for the hot-heads to cool down. Some of the messages sent to Rosemary by members of the JCR were quite disrespectful, and unrealistic in expecting her to be available at short notice to meet them, but she kept calm and always replied politely giving explanations. She has been described by an alumna as 'incredibly accessible ... always interested and friendly'[182]. Her approach to negotiations, treating the students as adults, always trying to reach a compromise, and showing that she really cared, avoided any major upsets, although there was a sticky period in 1973 when some New Hall students held a rent strike in support of NUS demands concerning grants. It was an anxious time for the College, because finances were very stretched. As the 1970s drew on, inflation rose to 20%. The University had to cut its expenditure and in New Hall a Working Party on Economies was set up in 1974, leading to a reduction in heating and laundry and sparing use of telephones and stationery. It was typical of Rosemary that she brought the New Hall Union into this discussion. These were lean years, with repeated references in the Governing Body minutes to lack of funds. In 1969 the architect, 'Joe' Chamberlin, visited and tried to persuade the College to build Phase 3 of the original plans, comprising further accommodation, a porters' lodge and a chapel. Despite the impressive visualisations he exhibited, the Fellowship were not convinced that a chapel was needed. It was a different, more secular age than the 1950s, when the plans were first mooted. The College did need more accommodation, but instead of a Library Court they opted for two modest blocks designed by a local architect, eventually named Hammond and Clover after two of the Fellows[183]. The Vivien Stewart Lecture Room, opening off the Walkway, was built in the hope of more conference trade, which was a source of much-needed income. It is unlikely that CPB approved of this intrusion into their Orchard Court.

The 1970s were also the time of a second wave of feminism in Britain, concentrating on gender equality in the social and political arena and demanding childcare facilities which would enable mothers to pursue their careers. The movement reached the college in 1977 when a New Hall Feminists' Group was set up by the students. They met every week for films and discussions and added feminist books to the Women's Collection in the college library. Rosemary had little sympathy with protest movements and was rather dismissive of the 'libbers' as she called them, but she did not make an issue of it. She felt that there were plenty of jobs open to women (only they did not always apply for them) and that there was little gender discrimination. What always concerned her was how women could cope with a career while bringing up children:

'I can quite see why a woman wants both careers. And I think it's sad when some libbers concentrate wholly on career. I feel sure it must be bad for the children to be parked at a nursery always. That's why I hope we can make it possible for women to come back [to their first career].'[184]

Rosemary's work on University committees led to her election to the Council of the Senate in 1969. At that time she was the only woman member. It was an accolade for New Hall as well as for Rosemary personally. No-one could doubt that the young institution was now on track to become a college. Rosemary was appointed to the Lodging Houses Syndicate, the Education Board and the Women's Appointments Board; she had experience relevant to all three, but particularly to Education because of her contacts with schools and training colleges and membership of the Council of the GPDST. The University's Council is a constitutional and procedural body dealing with a great deal of routine business, as well as important policy making: for example, approving changes to the syllabus, appointments, nominations to committees, remuneration and pensions, and changes to College statutes. The major concerns during Rosemary's first term on Council were financial. Quinquennial planning did not work well in a time of high inflation, and the situation was complicated by uncertainty about government policy. The Robbins Report of 1963 had recommended a rapid increase in the number of university students, but it was not clear how they would be financed or accommodated. The Council's Joint Standing Committee on Student Numbers, of which Rosemary was a member, met between 1970 and 1974 to investigate the views of the colleges.

Rosemary, growing in confidence, was a success as a member of the Council, and had plenty of admirers amongst the predominantly male establishment. She felt strongly about issues and was not afraid to say what she thought. Her tone was never shrill or demanding: she put her ideas across with firmness and clarity and was not easily deterred. Her leadership and drive at New Hall were much admired. When the Vice-Chancellor, Owen Chadwick, welcomed New Hall to full collegiate status in October 1971, he 'congratulated that society on arriving so quickly'[185]. It was therefore not surprising that Council were prepared to consider her for nomination to the Vice-Chancellorship as soon as she became eligible. Selection was made more than two years in advance, to enable the chosen Head of House to sort out the delegation of his college duties and external commitments. Rosemary was not technically eligible to stand in 1971 for the period 1973-5 because New Hall was not yet a college, nevertheless the Registrary included her name in the list and she was asked by Owen Chadwick to withdraw from meetings when the matter was discussed.[186] This was the first indication Rosemary had that she would be a serious candidate in the future. Many years later she admitted that she had been 'absolutely staggered' to be nominated, but she didn't say no[187]. The indisputable mark of approval was a great affirmation, proving that she was not just being included on committees as a kind gesture, as she had modestly thought. A female VC was more of a landmark than it seems today; there had only been one previously, Dame Lillian Penson at London University (1948-51). In the event another chemist, Jack Linnett, the new Master of Sidney Sussex, was chosen for 1973-5 with Rosemary in second place, which, following custom, meant that she was next in line. Rosemary's period on Council came to an end in December 1972 and the next selection of a Vice-Chancellor took place a month later. The procedure was that a list of Heads of Houses was scrutinised and narrowed down to about six candidates by taking out those who had already been VC, those who did not want to stand and those considered over-age. After further discussion two names were put forward for the election and at a special meeting in the Syndicate Room of the Old Schools the voting papers, with nominations in Latin, were 'pricked' by members of Council, an ancient method of preserving the anonymity of the voters. The ceremony was witnessed by the Proctors, Esquire Bedells and the Registrary. The Senior Proctor announced 'Ego … electam a vobis pronuntio Doctorem Murray in Procancellarium huius Academiae in annum sequentem'[188]. Rosemary was successful: the other candidate, Alan Cottrell, the Master of Jesus College, was to become her successor. The election of the first woman VC was a breakthrough, but not completely unexpected since the possibility had been mooted in 1949 when Girton and Newnham became full colleges. For Rosemary it was a great honour, because Council had made a personal choice: it would have been possible to elect a Head of Girton or Newnham at any time after that date, yet none had been selected.

Well over one hundred letters of congratulation arrived when the announcement was displayed on the Senate House noticeboard and appeared in *The Times* and other newspapers. Characteristically Rosemary made a list, surely with a hint of pride[189]. She had, by this time, built up an extensive circle of friends and acquaintances: former and current staff and students of Girton and New Hall, Senior Members throughout the University, teachers and contemporaries at Downe House, former Wrens, GPDST and AFPRB committee members and many more, including the Bishop of Ely, the local MP and contacts in America. She was obviously well-liked by those who worked for her: her gyp[190] at Girton, hairdresser and Miss Dufton the former Housekeeper of New Hall took the trouble to write. She would have been pleased to receive Sir Harry Verney's note, 'But how glorious. If we ever meet, how could I grovel enough'. Ellen Murray realised that Rosemary's appointment was all the more impressive because she had not sought it.

> 'I feel I must write you a word – its all so exciting & the more one thinks of it, bigger it grows … apart from everything its so very nice to know that the opportunity to use all your great talents is now there! – and all come with less than no push – and no ambition either I would guess!'[191]

The New Hall JCR sent flowers, the Fellows arranged drinks in her honour, but not everyone in College was delighted, as a letter signed by all the assistant staff reveals.

'The staff at New Hall would like to make clear that on no account do they wish to be associated with any adverse feelings that may be expressed within the College either personally or otherwise.

We are very pleased for you in respect of your recent appointment and proud to be associated with the College.'[192]

No doubt there was disquiet among the Fellows because some thought that Rosemary's College duties would be side-lined for two years and that the VC post would bring New Hall fresh expenses for entertaining. Robin Hammond, by this time Senior Tutor and the obvious person to cover for the President, soon decided that she did not want to take on increased responsibility and announced that she would retire in 1974. Others realised that the College would gain in reflected glory. Charles Crawley wrote, 'The nomination is a big feather in your cap and also in that of New Hall'.[193] Rosemary was interviewed by the daily newspapers and *Varsity*. She was invited on to Anglia TV, probably her first television appearance, and gave sensible answers to a very crass interviewer, 'putting him to rights in no mean manner', as the bookseller Reuben Heffer wrote to her.

Nomination as the first woman Vice-Chancellor was such an outstanding achievement that it brought further honours from institutions. Girton made Rosemary an Honorary Fellow in 1975. As Muriel Bradbrook wrote in a personal letter, this was long overdue: 'Of course it is we who gain the honour'[194]. Oxford University conferred an honorary D.C.L. on her the following year and Sheffield, where she had spent such an unsatisfactory year, an LLD in 1977. Sheffield sent apologies because their degree certificate referred to Rosemary as 'he'. She replied with the witty rejoinder, '… my principle has always been that 'he' should include (embrace) 'she' where appropriate'[195].

Rosemary joined the Council of the Senate for the second time in October 1973, as Deputy Vice-Chancellor for two years, a useful and customary period of preparation for the main rôle[196]. There were two other women members, Phyllis Deane, Fellow of Newnham and Reader in Economic History, and Kate Bertram of Lucy Cavendish College, who had been Secretary of the New Hall Association, both immensely resolute characters. Another member, Peter Avery of King's, said he was confident that Rosemary would succeed as VC: he could see the Admiral's peaked cap sticking out of her handbag![197] Council was preoccupied by two matters, the fall-out from a student sit-in in 1972 when there had been serious damage to property on the Sidgwick site, and continued anxiety about finance. Also in the background was the Government's Green Paper on Equal Opportunities which proposed action against discrimination in employment and education and therefore might oblige the University to consider the number and position of women at all levels of the organisation. At the first meeting, Rosemary suggested that the matter of the pay of the Secretary of the Lodging Houses Syndicate should be reconsidered. She brought with her a list of the salaries paid by 27 other universities and carried the day. It was a small victory, but it proved that she would prepare thoroughly and argue persuasively, hallmarks of Rosemary's success throughout this period.

Lord Devlin, High Steward of the University, had been commissioned to write a report surveying existing measures for student participation in University governance[198]. His proposal for student representation on University bodies was a matter on which Council was bound to act. They set up a Joint Committee on the subject, of which Rosemary was a member, which produced its First Report in March 1973. After much discussion it was agreed in November that any Faculty Board that wished to do so might include students as full members. The Committee's recommendation that there should be four student observers on Council was even less agreeable to many Council members, who responded with delaying tactics, but a militant students' union kept up the pressure. It was two years before Council agreed, after a vote, to report to the University proposing the admission to meetings of Council of three student observers, one of whom was to be a graduate student. Consequently it was on Rosemary's watch as Vice-Chancellor that student observers were present for the first time, on 2nd February 1976. Possibly due to her courteous handling of the situation – the 'equable disposition' that Eric Ashby had mentioned – there was little further trouble apart from an attempt to move from observing to participating and a request to see reserved business.

In October 1973, a letter from the UGC, indicating that government funding beyond the next twelve months was uncertain, had caused the Council much disquiet, because they were used to planning five years ahead. Only a month later the UGC asked the University to prepare simple growth plans, suggesting an increase of 11% in the number of students between 1976/7 and 1981/2 (later revised downwards). In response to this a Committee on Long Term Development was set up. Then in January 1974 the UGC took the unprecedented step of withdrawing the Supplementation Grant for 1974-5, an extra £800,000 that had been negotiated. It was small consolation to Rosemary that she knew the Chairman, Fred Dainton, a former chemist.[199] Careful arrangements were made long in advance for the visitation of the UGC auditors in April 1974; when it came, the University representatives were chiefly concerned to explain the financial constraints they were under. They would have pointed out that they had just implemented a 50% reduction in lighting and the restriction of heating to a maximum of 63 degrees in University buildings.

Council were aware that legislation for equal opportunities would profoundly affect the University and they discussed the Government Green Paper as soon as it came out. Rosemary became Chair of the Women's Appointment Board in 1973, and took the opportunity to highlight the national discussions in the Annual Report, suggesting that there was still much to be done in the world of work. It was no coincidence that Catherine Belsey and Helen Clover, Fellows of New Hall, were also members of the Board: Rosemary was always keen to bring on younger women colleagues. In its opinion,

> 'The right kind of legislation might encourage a climate of opinion which would enable women to develop satisfying careers without feeling that they were in any way unusual or had to fight excessively hard for opportunities'[200].

Rosemary became a member of The Colleges Committee Working Party on Co-Residence, set up in 1973, and its Standing sub-Committee on the Admission of Women, chaired by the Principal of Newnham, Jean Floud. A year later she was appointed to the Standing Consultative Committee on Equal Opportunities for Men and Women. Equal opportunity raised the vexed question of what the number of women in Cambridge should be, and was complicated by the fact that several men's colleges were taking women students: King's, Churchill and Clare admitted their first women in 1972. Although between 1968 and 1973 the number of women in the University had increased by 50%, Cambridge still had a lower proportion of women (17%) than other Universities. The average across the country was 36%. There was anxiety at University level that more women would mean more arts students, whereas they actually wanted to increase the number of scientists. With so many discussions going on in different fora, Rosemary decided in February 1974 to set out her personal view in a confidential paper entitled 'Admission of Women'[201]. It was probably circulated to Heads of Houses. In a clear and simple exposition of the subject she got to the heart of the problems and set out ideas which became very influential. Rosemary calculated that to reach the number of undergraduates quoted in UGC planning, 10,000 by 1980, while at the same time increasing the percentage of women to 30%, would mean doubling the present number (1,500) over five years.

> 'Such a very rapid increase with the collegiate structure of the University would inevitably lead to problems and could well not be to the advantage of women in the long run. I should, therefore, like to see a much slower rate of change in the proportion, in order that the admission of women by individual colleges could be co-ordinated, and problems such as admissions, applications, balance of subjects in the University, and so on could be properly considered.'

Rosemary was concerned that there might not be enough good women candidates to go round if more men's colleges opened their doors, because the number of applicants over three years had remained constant, despite the availability of more places. New Hall was now filling about half its places from the 'pool'. 'We consider that the girls to whom we have offered places are deserving of them, but I think we would have had difficulty if we had had more places to offer'. She cites the large number of women candidates graded 'F' in the Cambridge Joint Entrance examination as evidence. In particular, the women's colleges would have difficulty in finding enough applicants in the Sciences and Maths. There was a likelihood of five more men's colleges admitting women, increasing numbers by about 800 if each college filled one third of its places with women. 'If applications from women to Cambridge do not increase it would be quite possible that the women's colleges would not be able to fill their places.' In fact Rosemary had previously written to R.D. Gray of her anxiety that 'we might be forced to admit men'[202].

Rosemary did not believe that more places were needed for women postgraduates, because New Hall already had places unfilled, and if mixed colleges started to take them the women's colleges would be in difficulty. For once she was wrong: there was a steady increase in women graduate students in the University as a result of more women undergraduates and foreign students. Considering Senior Members, she pointed out that the proportion of University posts held by women was only 7%, amounting to 104 women on whom the women's colleges could draw for teaching, hence there was considerable nervousness about the men's colleges appointing some of them as Fellows. More non-University Teaching posts in the mixed colleges would be desirable, producing an increased number of jobs for women in Cambridge, so long as the other colleges did not pay salaries that the women's colleges could not afford to match. Only half the teaching Fellows at New Hall had University posts: the rest were dependent on a stipend from the college. Rosemary was well aware that the salaries of non-UTOs were inadequate as she was constantly lobbied by Catherine Belsey and others at New Hall on the subject. She anticipated that under the Equal Pay Act salaries would have to rise: 'It seems likely that a very substantial proportion of our endowment income will go to subsidising salaries', and she concluded, 'I reckon that the greatest help any men's college could give towards improving the position of academic women in the University, of whom a large number are the senior members of the women's colleges, is to contribute towards the endowment of these colleges so that salaries can be raised.' The First Report of the Sub-Committee of the Colleges Committee on the Admission of Women and of the Co-Residence Joint Working Party, both of which had Rosemary as a member, came to the Council of the Senate in October 1974. The former echoed her argument for a carefully controlled increase in women's admissions, so as not to damage the women's colleges. The latter agreed on the gradual increase in mixed colleges, but was much more upbeat about finding suitable women candidates for both undergraduate and postgraduate places than Rosemary had been. They anticipated a 50:50 gender balance in the University, and in the long term their prediction proved correct. Picking up another of Rosemary's points, they suggested that colleges going mixed should not have less than 25% women, mainly for social reasons. Much more effort should be made to publicise the increased opportunities for women, they felt.

In New Hall anxiety was growing about the drop in the number of applicants, and the question of co-residence continued to be debated as more colleges went mixed. A paper from the Publicity Committee to the College Council in June 1975 on the effect of co-residence on the admission of women, described the outlook for women's colleges as 'alarming' and concluded, 'There is something ironic about a situation in which Cambridge colleges are being dissuaded from co-education to protect the women's colleges, which were originally founded in the belief that Cambridge ought to be co-ed. The time may have come to take that belief to its logical conclusion.'[203] Rosemary, and a number of Fellows who had been pioneers in women's education, could not agree. Around the same time, a paper from a Philosophy Fellow, Jenny Teichman, was circulated.[204] She favoured 'twinning' with a men's college, preferably St John's, which was always thought of as an 'elder brother' to New Hall because its senior members had been so supportive. Like Professor Anscombe, Teichman was anxious to preserve teaching posts for women, especially for non-UTOs, suggesting an agreement with the men's colleges to protect them. She came up with the splendid statement, 'It is not for men to jib at quotas: Oxbridge has had quotas on women for 100 years.' In June Rosemary produced a paper for College Council on 'Long Term Alternatives'[205], basically going over old ground, toning down the conclusions of the Publicity Committee and outlining four possible scenarios in what appears to be her order of preference. No.1 is 'Stick it out': remain as now until at least 1977 when the effect of four more colleges taking women would be known. No.2 was similar, suggesting that if applications fell they could accept fewer students and fill any surplus accommodation with 'lodgers' from other colleges. A third possibility was an alliance with a men's college, but 'How would an alliance rather than a take-over be maintained?' She saw a danger that men would displace women at both senior and junior levels. Lastly there was the opportunity to 'go mixed' but they would lose New Hall's special character. Council opted to explore twinning, and after a meeting with Fellows to consider New Hall's requirements, unofficial meetings were arranged between Rosemary and senior members of at least four men's colleges; Peter Swinnerton-Dyer, Master of St Catherine's, Edward Miller, Master of Fitzwilliam, a senior Fellow of Christ's and John Hall of St John's. This last seems to have been the most productive as they went into some detail. Teaching would involve joint appointments and exchange of supervisors, residence could allow some 2nd year men to live in New Hall and admissions would still be handled separately. In November a Council paper on Future Policy[206] summed up the position, which was for the College to retain its independence in governance and finances while having an interchange of teaching, exchange of dining rights and possibly co-residence for students on both campuses. Council authorised 'serious negotiations' with St John's, but they came to nothing and were dropped within a year, perhaps to Rosemary's relief.

Amid all the hard work, Rosemary received indications that she was becoming a VIP. She found herself in the *World Who's Who of Women* for 1973 and in a magazine article about high-flying women. In 1975 she received the honorary degree of Doctor of Science from the University of Leeds. As none of her family could attend she took two young New Hall Fellows as her guests. Kate Pretty remembers Rosemary driving hell for leather to Leeds and then adopting her calm official persona. Prof. Greenwood, who presented her, was quite pertinent in his remarks. Concerning New Hall, he said,

> Her practical approach to getting things done, in a community of scholars who are still at times depressingly skilful at avoiding uncomfortable decisions, proved to be the crucial factor in giving physical reality to the imaginative scheme ... it is salutary to see how much can be achieved by discreet and sensible action, albeit resolute'.[207]

Deputising for the Vice-Chancellor brought another honour. Rosemary must have been delighted when Sir Eric Ashby asked her to represent Cambridge at the Penn University Bicentennial on May 18th 1975. It was an opportunity to visit America again and to network with senior colleagues, the Presidents of Radcliffe, Princeton, Columbia, Brown and Rutgers Universities. Among the participants were several Vice-Chancellors, from Trinity College Dublin, Scottish Universities and Sir John Habbakkuk from Oxford; all people she would later meet on national committees. It was arranged that she would receive an honorary degree (which presumably would otherwise have gone to Sir Eric) as one of the distinguished guests. In early April the news leaked out that President Ford had 'expressed interest' in attending the ceremony, and it was soon announced that he would deliver the principal address at Commencement. Rosemary therefore found herself an important actor in a huge pageant.

The President arrived by helicopter and was driven in a motorcade to the University's Museum, where 330 people attended a reception, followed by lunch. Afterwards there was a procession to the auditorium of all the students and honorands receiving degrees, with the band playing

Rosemary receiving the honorary degree of Doctor of Science at Leeds University from the Chancellor, the Duchess of Kent, in 1975.

Walton's 'Crown Imperial' in honour of the British delegation. Then came speeches, conferment of degrees and much applause, as well as a standing ovation from the women students when Rosemary and President Matina Horner of Radcliffe College received their degrees from the President of Penn. Rosemary's citation read:

> 'Cambridge University formed the prototype of the College that was transmitted to American shores ... As a scholar of chemistry, as President of New Hall, and as deputy Vice-Chancellor, the Vice-Chancellor elect of Cambridge has continued its magnificent inheritance.'[208]

Rosemary looks very serious in the photograph taken of her with President Ford. It was her first venture on to the international stage.

Rosemary and President Ford in 1975.

The admission of Rosemary as Vice-Chancellor took place on 1st October 1975 in a ceremony known as a Congregation of the Regent House (the voting members of the University), held in the Senate House. Rosemary was wearing a simple black cassock with white bands and a gown, a uniform she had designed herself since there was no precedent for a female VC. She was primarily concerned that it should be practical and unostentatious. She was met at the East Door by an Esquire Bedell and led up the length of the Senate House, through the assembly, followed by the Marshall. A gathering thunderstorm darkened the room, and as Rosemary took the Latin oath, there was a mighty clap of thunder, which some felt was appropriate to mark this momentous event. She was then conducted to the Throne, where she received the VC's rings and keys from the Proctors. Professor Jack Linnett, the outgoing VC, gave the customary address, reviewing the events of the past academic year[209]. He pointed out that by prudent planning the University had been able to avoid the more drastic economy measures taken by some other universities, but he deplored the government's cancellation of the quinquennial planning system, administered by the UGC, which had allowed universities to plan ahead with certainty that funding was assured. Thus Rosemary took over the reins at a time when Cambridge was in a difficult financial position and far-reaching changes were just beginning. Handing over to her, the

VC said, 'She knows and understands the University as very few other members of Regent House do ... The University will profit from her utter devotion to its well-being'.

The procession out of the Senate House only went as far as the Syndicate Room for its customary glass of wine, because New Hall was too far away. For the same reason, Rosemary decided that she must have an office in the Old Schools, whereas other VCs had worked in their colleges. The officials took their time deliberating, and when the Dome Room[210] was chosen as the location, appear to have dragged their feet deliberately because it would cut off a route through the building. Frustrated by the delay, Rosemary brought in her carpenter's tools one day and fixed the locks on the doors herself. This action gave the staff an idea of the sort of woman they had to deal with.

As one of her few luxuries, Rosemary bought herself a Sunbeam convertible, which she drove very fast, particularly when showing off to male passengers, but her everyday transport between New Hall and the city centre was her bicycle, and she naturally expected to park it in the yard of the Old Schools.[211] Alan Clark, VC's Assistant, remembers that she was very cross to find a notice on the bike asking the owner to put it elsewhere. Confronted by Rosemary, the offending porter quickly made amends by providing a stand labelled 'VC Only'. Rosemary was now sufficiently confident to indulge in slight eccentricity, especially when it showed her as one of the crowd. She had incorporated her Oxford doctorate in 1946, but still preferred to be known as Miss Murray. She made no secret of her carpentry and gardening activities and she liked her reputation as an intrepid traveller. Her choice of white-water rafting in the Grand Canyon as her 1973 Summer holiday must have raised a few eyebrows.

Rosemary had no intention of losing her grip on College matters. Over a year before her University appointment began she took to the College Council the suggestion that two officers should be elected to fill the gap when she was not present. The first would be the statutory Vice President, responsible for administration, of which the main items were Council business and chairing Council when Rosemary was absent, chairing most College committees, co-ordinating admission of affiliated, mature and research students and taking minor day-to-day decisions. Esther Welbourn, Director of Studies in Medicine was chosen.[212] It is clear that Rosemary was not intending to hand over much power to her deputy. She continued to be involved in the selection of undergraduates, and in the event she did not miss a single Council or Governing Body meeting during her two years as VC. The second officer, eventually known as President's Deputy, was to help her with social occasions, both College functions and the entertainment of official guests, a prominent part of the VC's duties. Elizabeth Rawson, a Fellow noted for taste and discretion, was elected to this post. She commented perceptively about Rosemary:

> 'Having been shy in youth and become more confident with success in late middle age only, all the social side which must be such a bore to most VCs was fresh and exciting to her'[213].

Lunches were held for the recipients of Honorary Degrees, visiting preachers and for the installation of the Chancellor, and Rosemary held regular formal dinner parties for Heads of Houses and Senior Members, mixing them up with visitors to the University, townspeople and those she met on her many external committees. The numerous thank you letters she received mentioned the happy and relaxed atmosphere at New Hall and the guests' curiosity to see inside the new buildings. Rosemary was complimented on presiding graciously. In this respect she became a role model for the Fellows, passing on her knowledge of etiquette, absorbed from an early age at Naval dinners with her father and practised at the High Tables of Oxford and Cambridge, to some of the younger Fellows who had less experience of entertaining. The cost of the official events was met by Trinity and St John's, though this was not public knowledge. The College grew up in these years, affirming its connection to the University and acquiring prestige among the other colleges.

Rosemary after her installation ceremony as Vice-Chancellor, 1975.

The Chancellor in the honorary degree procession, 1976, with the NAG demonstration in the background.

Rosemary in the procession.

– 12 –

Vice-Chancellor

THE FIRST MATTER ON THE AGENDA of Rosemary's first Council meeting as Vice-Chancellor was the nomination of the next Chancellor of the University. Lord Adrian, the current Chancellor, in failing health, had announced that he would resign on 1st January 1976. The Nomination Board, consisting of the Council and sixteen additional members, mostly Heads of Houses, met on 22nd November to consider eight names proposed by members of the Senate. After discussion, a shortlist of four was arrived at, and votes taken, eliminating the candidate with the least votes each time. As a result, Prince Philip, Duke of Edinburgh, who had not been a front-runner at the outset, was elected, with Eric Ashby, the former Vice-Chancellor, as reserve. Rosemary wrote immediately to the Prince because she was required to publish the name of the candidate by December 6th. Her Assistant delivered the letter by hand to Buckingham Palace. Recalling memories for Rosemary's 90th birthday, Prince Philip wrote: 'I still have a vivid recollection of the moment when I read your letter … I never dreamed I might occupy that position in Cambridge'[214]. He also joked in his resignation speech that it was 'like an approach from Al Capone: an offer I could hardly refuse.'[215] However, at the time he was unable to accept immediately. Rosemary received a personal reply on 3rd December, thanking her for the 'very flattering invitation' but saying that the deadline 'hardly gives me much opportunity to give this important matter any consideration, or to make any adjustments to my commitments'[216]. Prince Philip's Private Secretary revealed that he 'would love to do it' and would be very disappointed if the Council's timetable prevented the nomination going through. Rosemary had to keep this information confidential while asking Council to give the Nomination Board 'such extensions as they see fit'. She did confide in the legal adviser, Derek Bowett, President of Queens', who helped her to steer it through Council. It was not until November 1976, a year later, that the nomination was announced. Prince Philip became Chancellor immediately and his formal Installation was arranged for 10th June 1977. In preparation for the ceremony, Rosemary examined the Chancellor's embroidered robes (originally made for Stanley Baldwin) and found them in a poor state. It was typical of her thoroughness to check such a detail, and to take a hand herself in repairing the garments.

The programme for the Installation was arranged by Dr Alan Clark, Vice-Chancellor's Assistant, and Lord Rupert Nevill, the Prince's Private Secretary, under Rosemary's close scrutiny.[217] The Prince arrived by air at St John's College playing field, the first of numerous visits of his bulky red helicopter over the next thirty years. He was met by the Lord Lieutenant and civic leaders and conveyed to the Old Schools, where he was received by Rosemary and robed in scarlet. A procession formed up and walked to the Senate House, the Duke following a few minutes later with an Esquire Bedell. The new Chancellor took the oath, which was the same as Rosemary had taken as Vice-Chancellor: this time she was the questioner. Then the Prince was escorted to the Robing Room, emerging in the newly-mended robes, a female Page holding the train, to hear a speech of welcome in Latin from the University Orator and to deliver his address. The retiring procession walked up Senate House Passage in pouring rain to cars that would take them to New Hall for lunch. The programme had envisaged having a wine reception and the presentation of Fellows in Orchard Court, but in view of the weather the Walkway and Library were used instead. After lunch in the Dome, Rosemary proposed the Loyal Toast succinctly:

> 'This week we are celebrating the Queen's Silver Jubilee. Today we have installed our Chancellor and it is his birthday. For all these reasons I ask you to drink the health of Prince Philip, Chancellor of the University'.[218]

In the afternoon there was a second congregation for the Chancellor to admit Honorary Graduates to degrees, giving the public another chance to see the Duke in procession. The only woman among them was Mother Theresa, making a rare public appearance. Rosemary suggested her nomination and enlisted the help of a clerical friend to persuade her to accept.[219] Afterwards there was a garden party at Trinity College, fortunately in a marquee. Rosemary must have felt some relief when the helicopter took off at 5.30p.m., because her most prestigious event as VC had been entirely satisfactory. The Prince's Secretary confirmed that 'His Royal Highness thought the Installation and Presentation of Honorary Degrees could not possibly have gone better'[220] and he particularly mentioned the female Page, Jill Rumsey, a New Hall student hand-picked by Rosemary. It was a small innovation to have a woman, but indicative of Rosemary's intention to introduce parity for women whenever possible.

The incoming Vice-Chancellor always takes on a lot of business carried forward from his or her predecessor, and this was especially true when the period of office was only two years. Problems with the UGC have already been touched on. By October 1975 Council had to accept that the system of quinquennial grants had been effectively abandoned for the time being, and this was borne out when the allocation of the recurrent grant for 1976/7 was delayed, making it difficult to plan for the coming academic year. There had been a 6.4% increase in admissions in 1975; any further significant increase would mean a reduction in resources per student. Council was forced to examine student fee income, agreeing a level which would be adjusted with inflation, and to look into financial relations between the University and the Colleges. Amendments to Statute G II resulted in a substantial increase in the income of the Colleges Fund, whereby money was redistributed from the richer to the poorer colleges according to formulae relating to expenditure. New Hall greatly benefitted from this provision. Naturally the climate of financial uncertainty was a major topic of debate for the Committee of Vice-Chancellors and Principals (CVCP), a forum for discussion and consultation with the government and UGC, which Rosemary attended while in office. They persistently voiced anxiety about the level of recurrent grant provided by the government and the issue of tuition fees. For 1977/8 the government introduced significantly higher tuition fees, nominally 'discretionary', but since the government grant was based on the assumption that the fees would be levied, it was effectively a directive. The CVCP protested that the value of recurrent income per student had declined by more than 6% during the period 1972-7. They estimated that recurrent income for 1977/8 would be 1% less than that needed to meet inflation, and the equipment grant would only be half what was needed. They argued for financial provision sufficient to maintain standards, planning perspective, and commitment to maintaining the real value of grants. Cambridge was in a better position than many universities thanks to the level of donations and the wealth of some of its colleges; nevertheless development of the estate was held up. In Rosemary's time as VC several building projects which had already been funded were completed – the Music School (Stage 1), an Animal House and substantial refurbishment on the New Museums and Downing sites. The Hamilton Kerr Institute for conservation was approved by Council in 1975 because it was largely funded by Trusts and the charitable donation of a house. Similarly, the foundation of Robinson College was authorised as the result of a generous benefaction. In her Address to the Regent House at the end of her first year in office, Rosemary highlighted 'a rapidly and perhaps fundamentally changing situation', suggesting that 'the financial prospect for all who depend substantially on public funds – and this includes the universities – is likely to be extremely bleak'[221]. Academic staff vacancies had been carefully scrutinised during the year and the number of assistant staff reduced by 10% by not filling vacancies at a junior level.

Rosemary had been involved in discussions on Equal Opportunities since the government Green Paper appeared. Closely linked to the debate on discrimination against women was the movement to improve child care provision so that mothers could go back to work. In Cambridge the Nursery Action Group (NAG), led principally by academics, petitioned Council in May 1975 to provide funds for a nursery school and crèche facility. It could hardly have been a worse time to ask for new money. But when the request was turned down, NAG lived up to its name, continuing to lobby and organising a sit-in on 3rd June in the Senate House, the day before an honorary degree ceremony. To persuade them to leave, the then Vice-Chancellor made some promises, so Council, headed by Rosemary, was bound to reconsider and set up a Working Party. It took over a year to report. Meanwhile NAG staged a protest at the Installation of the Chancellor. Council, before coming to a decision, decided to refer the report widely, asking the Colleges for their views and offering a Discussion in the Regent House in the Michaelmas Term. It seems likely that many of the men on Council were strongly opposed to making a grant for this purpose, and that Rosemary, who must have been in sympathy with the proposal, used deferring tactics to allow the support to build. A compromise was reached, and Council agreed to give non-recurrent grants to assist existing nursery schools to expand, while encouraging the colleges to contribute as well.

Significant developments happened in the colleges during Rosemary's tenure as VC. The proposal from Sir David Robinson to found a new college (later named after him) first came to Council in 1973. It was received cautiously, because many felt that the University should not expand much further and there was also the question of providing land

and endowment, but ten Trustees were appointed, Rosemary among them. She was an obvious choice because of her experience in setting up a college. St John's College was persuaded to sell a site on Grange Road and assurances were obtained from the planning authorities that planning permission would be given. Rosemary was involved in the appointment of the architects, Gillespie, Kidd & Coia, chosen from submissions by five firms. She pointed out that 'Robinson College must be unique amongst the colleges of Oxford and Cambridge in having buildings before there was any college'[222]. It was the Trustees, soon in conjunction with a nucleus of Fellows, who determined the shape of the College, which became the first to be founded as a mixed society. Like New Hall it was first recognised as an Approved Foundation, which happened on Rosemary's watch, once Council were satisfied with the conditions of funding, education and discipline. The Trustees appointed the prospective Head, Jack Lewis, a Professor of Chemistry, and thanks to the persuasive University Treasurer, Trevor Gardner, prevailed on Mr Robinson to provide an endowment. Rosemary never met him, but thirty years later, when asked to provide her recollections at the retirement of the first Warden, she ended her speech with uncharacteristic asperity: 'I expect he thought an academic and a woman would not add anything worthwhile to his considerations'[223]. The first intake of research students was in 1977 and undergraduates followed two years later. Rosemary continued to take an interest in Robinson, and was made an Honorary Fellow in 1985, at the time when it became a full college.

Also making progress towards acceptance as a College of the University was Homerton, a College of Education which had been in Cambridge since 1894[224]. Rosemary was nominated by Council to the Board of Trustees in June 1974 in place of Robin Hammond, who resigned on her retirement. She felt strongly that Homerton should have closer ties with the University, and it seems no coincidence that only five months later the Head, Alison Shrubsole, wrote to the Council of the Senate seeking such links, possibly leading to the status of an Approved Foundation. There was considerable resistance to overcome, many academics feeling that teacher training was not an appropriate task for the University.[225] Council was still debating the matter in 1976, with further delay to investigate CNAA degrees as an alternative to awarding a B.Ed. from Cambridge. Finally Council's Report, 'Regulations for the Examination in Education and on Recognition of Homerton as an Approved Society',[226] was published and discussed by the Regent House and settled by a vote. In her VC's Address for 1976, Rosemary had hinted at her position, calling it 'One of the most important discussions of the coming year ... the decisions taken ... may well determine whether the University is, in the future, to play any part in the training of teachers'[227]. It was another example of the delaying technique which allowed time for consultation and persuasion, and it worked. Homerton became an Approved Society and the one-year B.Ed., introduced for the Colleges of Education, was replaced by a two-year B.Ed. for Homerton students only. Under a less sympathetic VC the outcome might have been very different. Rosemary remained a Trustee of Homerton and became its Visitor in 1990, always taking a close interest in its development into a College of the University.

There were changes afoot in other Colleges too. Girton's request to change its statutes to admit men was submitted to Council in 1970 and went through in 1971, and the first intake arrived in 1976. There is little doubt that Rosemary was shocked by this, although she made no pronouncement at the time. Much later she revealed that she considered it a betrayal of their founders and benefactors. Wolfson was recognised as a College for graduates in October 1976, and in 1977, together with Hughes Hall and Lucy Cavendish College, asked to increase its numbers. Council recommended no action at present. Sidney Sussex and Selwyn Colleges admitted women in 1976 and Trinity Hall in 1977. Trinity's statutes were changed in 1975 and the first women were taken in 1978. Fitzwilliam College, next door to New Hall, went mixed in the same year. There was an attempt to introduce a queuing system, vigorously opposed by Alan Cottrell, Master of Jesus, who also disagreed with Rosemary over the percentage of women a male college should introduce and said it could be lower than 20%. Despite all the requests for a phased approach, the tide of mixed colleges could not be held back: ten colleges began to admit women between 1978 and 1979, and as Rosemary had foreseen, the impact on New Hall's admissions was negative.

Rosemary's predecessor as VC, Jack Linnett, had begun discussions on the role and term of office of the Vice-Chancellor, prompted by Oxford's change from two to four years' tenure in 1969.[228] He consulted with four former Cambridge VCs, asking about the duration and run-up, run-down periods, whether candidature should be limited to Heads of Houses, and whether the VC should have an office in the Old Schools. The third question was settled before Rosemary took over, but the others rumbled on during her period of office and for a long time afterwards. A straw vote in April 1975 indicated a preference for a longer term of 3-4 years but no increase in the field of candidates. Since the VC was actually elected for a year at a time, there was nothing to prevent this happening, but the matter was shelved. Nomination of the next Vice-Chancellor in February 1977 raised the subject again. The two-year tenure was retained and Rosemary was asked to formulate her views for future discussion: she spoke at some length at the Council meeting on 30th May 1977. She outlined the job of the Vice-Chancellor in Cambridge, which she felt was very different from being a VC chosen from a wide field in a provincial University. First of all the VC spoke for the University to external bodies, after appropriate consultation with Heads of Colleges and academics and discussions in Council, and if necessary the Regent House. Secondly, the VC co-ordinated activities in the University by being Chair of the Council of the Senate, the General Board and the Financial Board. As a member of the CVCP, the VC reported back deliberations in other universities, reactions to government policy and national problems. At the same time she contributed the views of Council and her own opinions. Rosemary felt it was important for the Cambridge VC to be a Head of House because he/she needed to liaise with the colleges and be sensitive to their interests and thinking. A term longer than two years could mean that the VC would get out of touch with college affairs. Rosemary accepted that there had been shortcomings, due to the VC not progressing previous business, and suggested a longer involvement for the VC designate in University administration, such as two years' membership of the General Board before taking office[229]. It was a very conservative standpoint, and Council decided to follow her lead. Rosemary did not revise her views: she gave a very similar response when asked to comment in 1988.

Another idea of Jack Linnett's was the foundation of a Cambridge Society for all graduates of the University. Rosemary was an enthusiastic member of the Committee set up by Council at the beginning of 1975. The main aims of the Society were social and fundraising, keeping graduates in touch with each other and with University affairs, and consequently raising friends and potential benefactors. It was the shoot from which today's Development Office grew. The Society was launched in Cambridge and at a reception in the Guildhall, attended by the Lord Mayor of London. The Duke of Edinburgh was the Society's patron. Rosemary became the first President and when she left office as VC was

Vice-Chancellor's bike stand.

able to report that there were 2,000 members. An excellent Magazine was started and branches were set up all over the country. Rosemary was always prepared to go and speak at their functions.

The years as Vice-Chancellor offered several opportunities for travel which Rosemary was not slow to seize. The Conference of Executive Heads of the Association of Commonwealth Universities met in New Zealand in February 1976. Rosemary had never visited Australasia. In a letter of thanks she admitted, 'When I learnt ... the meeting would be in New Zealand I was determined that Cambridge should allow me to go'[230]. It was a gruelling journey in those days, taking two days to Wellington via Sydney. The conference occupied the first week, ending with a Farewell Dinner for over 200 delegates and wives at which Rosemary was placed on the top table. Then came a week's tour of South Island by bus and aeroplane. A long ride across the Canterbury Plains from Christchurch took them to beautiful Lake Tekapo: 'azure blue' noted Rosemary, and in the evening they enjoyed a boat trip by moonlight. Next day they took a chairlift 1400 feet up the cliff face of Mount Coronet and in the evening walked down a gorge as the setting sun coloured the rocky peaks. There was more spectacular scenery when flying over Milford Sound, a fjord, and visiting the magnificent waterfalls on foot. Finally the party toured Dunedin and the Otago University complex before flying to Auckland and home via Los Angeles. Rosemary was reported to have shamed unfit Vice-Chancellors by effortlessly clambering up hills at every stop, and to have surprised them by milking a cow. She greatly enjoyed the tour and made many international contacts. She would also have been pleased to have circumnavigated the globe.

At the end of March there was another official trip, sponsored by the U.S. Department of State and the American Friends of Cambridge University, to Chicago, Indiana, Washington, Philadelphia, New York and Boston. This was higher profile than her first visit to America and with an equally crowded itinerary: numerous tours, receptions, lunches and dinners in her honour, and a breakfast meeting with the media. Rosemary was continually annotating her programme with the names and key facts about the people she met. She got on particularly well with Gordon Williams, President of the American Friends, who hosted her visit to Washington and escorted her to the White House to meet the Advisor to the President for Women's Affairs. The themes running through the itinerary were Chemistry and Science generally; libraries, especially rare books and binding, for example at the Regenstein in Chicago and Lilly Library at Indiana University; women's education and medical facilities. At Bloomington, Indiana, Rosemary gave a lecture to the Faculty Women's Club entitled "Continuity and Change: Universities in the Modern World' and also taped a broadcast entitled 'It's about time', presumably about improved prospects for women. In Washington she made a speech at the Oxford & Cambridge Dinner and attended an Evening Dialogue at a Centre for International Scholars with the British ambassador. In New York the American ambassador invited her to dinner in Park Lane and in Chicago the British Consul-General gave a dinner party in her honour. It was a remarkable trip during which she experienced the full VIP treatment that America can offer. It may have been a lunch with Ella Keats Whiting, sometime Dean of Wellesley, on the final day that led to an invitation for a further visit later in the year to receive the degree of Hon. DSc. Ella was a woman of Rosemary's own stamp, and another administrator; they had much in common relating to their concern for women students. Rosemary received the degree at the end of May. The address from the President said that in the founding of New Hall Rosemary had 'recognised a great adventure' and devoted herself to helping a new college grow and flourish in venerable surroundings. On the same visit she gave the Commencement address at the University of Southern California and was honoured with the degree of Doctor of Laws. The oration at this ceremony was even more florid:

'As a distinguished educator, an exemplary administrator, and an innovative leader, she has pioneered in higher education, and is a stellar model of personal and professional achievement'.[231]

Less than a week after her return came the news that Ellen Murray, who had been suffering from dementia, had died. It was the day of the Honorary Degree ceremony and New Hall was holding a lunch for Elizabeth Schwarzkopf and others, so Rosemary was not able to go to Cadlington to make the funeral arrangements, but she attended the service on 16th June. Her mother was buried next to her father in the peaceful country churchyard at Blendworth, only a few hundred yards from her home. Eventually Rosemary's ashes would be placed in the same grave.

It was sad that Ellen did not survive to see her eldest daughter made an honorary Doctor of Civil Law at Oxford, her birthplace, because she would have been justly proud. So would her sister, favourite aunt Rosemary, who had died earlier in the year. Rosemary took her three brothers and their wives and children to the ceremony as guests and stayed with the Principal of LMH. The Encaenia was an elaborate occasion with a procession to the Sheldonian Theatre, lunch at All Souls and a garden party at Worcester College. In the evening she went to a gaudy at Christ Church, one of the grandest Oxford colleges. The Public Orator recalled Rosemary's career at Oxford and her achievement as first woman VC of either Oxford or Cambridge. Quoting Euripides' 'Medea' he recited,

'At last honour deferred, after too long delay,
Is accorded to womankind'.[232]

At the lunch, Rosemary sat next to Sir John Habbakuk, Vice-Chancellor, and opposite John Sparrow, the Warden of All Souls,

Rosemary receiving her Doctor of Laws hood at the University of Southern California, 1976.

a crusty old don who remarked, 'I suppose if we *have* to have women Vice-Chancellors, you are not doing too badly'. Rosemary was fond of repeating this back-handed compliment as it summed up the grudging acceptance by a male-centric university of women entering their ranks.

In her second year of office, Rosemary was again invited to the U.S.A. by the American Friends. This may have been the occasion when she travelled by Concorde, which she found a great thrill. She was hosted in Chicago by the philanthropist Gaylord Donnelly and his wife, spent a day or two at Notre Dame University and went on to Santa Barbara where she discussed 'reverse discrimination' – special quotas for women and minorities – and Women in administrative posts in Higher Education at the Center for the Study of Democratic Institutions. At the weekend she went birdwatching in the Ojai Valley and saw falcons. Next stop was San Francisco, where she was entertained by a friend of the Earl of Harewood, Mrs Robin Watt Miller, in her mansion, an architectural gem. Among the prestigious dinner guests was one of the Guggenheim family.

At Stanford University's Center for Research on Women, Rosemary gave a lecture on Women and Higher Education in Great Britain, which was followed by a reception and dinner. Two days later she spoke at the Seminar in British Studies at Austin, Texas and was taken round the University, meeting some of the chemists (Professor Buckingham from Cambridge happened to be there) and the President, Loren Rogers. Her second weekend was spent with a distant relative, Professor Crauford Goodwin and his family, in Durham, N. Carolina. Rosemary then flew to Indiana University and was met by Carleton Smith of the American Friends. Apart from a seminar on 'Conditions in England today', most of the engagements there were social ones, including a lunch in her honour for officers of the Lilly Endowment in Indianapolis. Finally she flew to New York for a meeting with the American branch of Cambridge University Press. Gordon Williams took her to see 'The King and I' on Broadway on her last evening. Clearly fundraising was one of the aims of these tours. Rosemary was not a good person to make a face-to-face 'ask': Robin would probably have done better, as she was worldly-wise and bolder. The American Friends were very generous to the University, but New Hall only benefitted indirectly. However, the American visits bolstered her self-esteem and she overcame the shyness which had been such a handicap, enjoying the publicity and the opportunities to speak out as an advocate for women.

There were several international conferences during this period; one sponsored by the Rockefeller Foundation on the education of women, was held at the opulent Villa Serbelloni at Bellagio, set on a promontory with a long terrace overlooking Lake Como. Rosemary had been to the first of these in 1965, as President of New Hall, and agreed to give a short survey of it, but she was unhappy about any off-the-cuff speaking and asked that someone else should make the formal comments on the lectures at the 1976 meeting. The International Council on the Future of the University, another American organisation, held annual conferences of a general nature. Rosemary went to those in Venice (1975) and Toronto (1976), representing the University, but was not a main speaker.

All these highlights, when Rosemary was honoured and fêted, were set against a background of VC and Presidential routine – meetings of the Council of the Senate and at least forty committees, consultations with the Registrary, Treasurer and Secretary General, and the conferring of degrees.[233] chairing Discussions of the Regent House, and attending

University and civic events. A columnist wrote, 'The VC's capacity for despatching University business with unprecedented rapidity is remarkable'[234], attributing the efficiency to her naval background. At New Hall the usual pattern of the College year involved her in admissions interviews, induction of Freshers, Council and Governing Body meetings, appointment of Fellows, presiding at dinners, entertaining and liaising with the Bursar and other Fellows and alumnae. In the City of Cambridge she was often called upon to preside at events such as the opening of a new Job Centre. She had cut down her J.P. work, but was still on the Bench. Whenever she was going to an event, she would prepare by checking out the guests in *Who's Who* and other sources, writing the briefest of notes to take with her, and sometimes a list of the people she particularly wanted to meet. She was 'networking' before that term was invented.

As usual, Rosemary took generous time out for holidays. In the Long Vacation of 1976 she did a tour of Abbeys in the North of England, making her way up to New Galloway for walking with Frances and Ian and then joined a larger group at Edsell. The Toronto conference in September 1977 was immediately followed by ten days in North Wales with her sister's family, the Crombies, climbing Cader Idris (2,000 feet she noted in her diary). In 1977 they all went to Shropshire, more gentle walking country. The nephews and nieces were by now in their twenties and starting their own families. Rosemary, whom they called 'Rumsey', had formed quite a bond with them all in their childhood, and did the same with the new generation, encouraging their enthusiasms and consulting on practical presents such as rucksacks and sheet music. After her mother's death she arranged weekends in Cadlington, where she was facing a massive clearance problem in advance of selling the house. She made endless lists of jewellery, silver, furniture and other items that were to be distributed amongst the extended family. Ellen Murray had always wanted a charitable cause to benefit from the house when she no longer needed it. In 1977 it was sold to Mencap for less than the market price, after an appeal on TV to raise funds to purchase it.[235]

Summing up her second year as Vice-Chancellor on the occasion of her retirement from office, Rosemary spoke of the severe financial restrictions and uncertainty about the future.[236] The Government was applying a stricter system of financing with no supplementation for rising costs. She expected the 1977-8 grant would probably show a cut of 4% in real terms. It was too risky to start long-term projects and building was almost at a standstill, apart from planning the new Clinical Medical School and two projects funded by donations, Stage 2 of the Music School and Robinson College. There was much concern about the effect of rising prices of books on libraries. Rosemary had been on the Committee of the College Libraries Fund, which subsidised the libraries of the poorer colleges to take the pressure off the University Library. She described the scheme as 'an effective, as well as economical, way of contributing to [undergraduate] need'. She also remarked on the increasing expenditure on the Computing Service.

One might gain the impression that in these difficult circumstances it had been impossible to achieve very much, but in fact there had been progress. Rosemary had been extremely supportive of Homerton and was pleased by its Approved Status and ability to award a B.Ed. (Cantab). It is unlikely that it would have happened without her. She had a deft touch in her dealings with students; patient, conciliatory but firm. She said that she welcomed the increase in student participation in the University and that Cambridge Students' Union (CSU) had been helpful and constructive, glossing over the unreasonable demands. The Library Syndicate was the next body to have student members, obviously so that concerns could be voiced before they escalated into protests such as the sit-in against reduction in opening hours. The important relations with the recently founded American Friends of Cambridge University were firmly consolidated, thanks to Rosemary's willingness to visit and establish personal contact, resulting in a steady stream of substantial benefactions. She also made a major contribution to improving relations between Town and Gown. As an experienced J.P. she already had an entrée into community affairs and she could see the benefits of co-operation. The Cambridgeshire Structure Plan was being developed at the time, and it was obviously sensible for the University to have an input. The Cambridge Joint Community Consultative Committee was set up before she took office. Rosemary held informal tripartite meetings between County, City and University representatives where people from these different spheres could get to know each other and tackle problems together. She invited townspeople to her VC dinners, and in return was asked to represent the University at many City functions. She probably meant it when she said it was 'a pleasure to attend them'.

When asked about the highlight of her career, Rosemary had no doubt that it was the period as Vice-Chancellor. She delighted in 'running the

Flight over Cambridge with Mr Barlow-Poole (centre).

University,'[237] as she saw it. She relished the challenges. She became a workaholic, happy to fill up her diary with meetings in Cambridge and elsewhere, and taking every opportunity to travel. At 62 she still had the stamina and the appetite needed to hold a position of command. On leaving office she spoke of 'the sense of privilege at having had the opportunity', and no doubt there was satisfaction too at having done the job so well, though she fought against the sin of pride. She had spoken in Ulster of 'achievement without self-satisfaction'[238] as an ideal. The people working with her and for her had responded to her charm and business-like approach. Ian Nicol, Secretary General of the Faculties, wrote and thanked her for making the work 'fun' and acknowledged that she had changed his thinking.[239] After the initial 'flutter in the dovecotes' consequent on the election of a woman, the assistant staff in the Old Schools found her one of the easiest VCs to work with, because she was clear and decisive and knew her way around the University. She had a reputation for being calm and unflappable. These men, who had little experience of women in positions of authority, sometimes fell back on the epithet 'schoolmistressy' to describe her. She could be demanding and impatient, but she led by example and got things done. The Old Schools was a male environment and Rosemary got on well with men. One of their treats was to accompany the Vice-Chancellor to London, when they would all enjoy a 'Big Fry' breakfast on the train to Liverpool Street. Towards the end of her tenure, knowing her taste for new experiences, some of the staff arranged with the OTC for Rosemary to have a ceremonial flight over the University. Adopting the custom for processions on the ground, she was preceded by her Esquire Bedell, Richard Barlow-Poole, in another plane.

Rosemary achieved her place in history by reaching the top job, but she did more: many thought she was one of the best Vice-Chancellors of recent times. It is no simple matter to control a committee of academics, all of whom love argument for the sake of it and think that their undoubted brilliance in one subject entitles them to make decisions on all others: it has been described as 'herding cats'. Rosemary developed into a professional chairman, who allowed everyone to have their say and then summed up succinctly, preferring to reach consensus rather than take a vote. 'She presided with a twinkle in her eye, easily deflating many controversies.'[240] 'She has a gift for settling matters – everyone goes away thinking they've won!'[241], said Ian Nicol, who worked closely with her. Part of her secret was the amount of preparation she put in, working long evenings in College when others were relaxing or with their families and mastering the details of each brief. She claimed hardly to notice that she was often the only woman in meetings. Beneath her calm exterior was a mixture of steely resolve and shrewd judgement. She was blessed with stamina and resilience, which enabled her to keep going in the face of difficulties, and according to Prince Philip, had "knock-out charm"[242].

One can understand why Rosemary had an immediate rapport with the Duke of Edinburgh: her adventurous temperament and naval background gave them much in common. Rosemary could also discourse on farming, because of her experience of the smallholding at Cadlington. A New Hall Fellow remembers that during an awkward pause at dinner she quickly asked what he was doing about set-aside land at Sandringham. The Duke also admired Rosemary's efficiency in managing every detail of his Installation as Chancellor and explaining the structure of the University to him. Though he may not have remembered, they had met before, at a Girton garden party, when he quizzed her about the setting up of New Hall. Looking back in 2004, he said in an interview, 'It's not the easiest thing in the world to start a new college ... It's a

Continued on page 217.

Rosemary and Robin holding the College Charter, 1972.

Frances and Ian Crombie with their children visiting partially built New Hall, c.1965.

The Vice Chancellor in the Dome Room.

Rosemary after receiving the honorary degree of Doctor of Laws at Cambridge in 1988.

Rosemary in Mendocino, California, with her brother David in 1997.

Rosemary and Frances reading on Mull in 1997.

Rosemary tending a herbaceous border in the Cranmer Road garden she looked after.

Rosemary, Frances and Ian in Dorset in 1998.

Rosemary with Prince Philip on the steps of New Hall in 2003.

Rosemary Murray and Anne Lonsdale at the New Hall Benefactors' Feast, 2003.

Robert Harkness, specialist rose breeder, presenting Rosemary with a basket of 'her' roses at the Chelsea Flower Show, 2004.

Rosemary in reflective mood at home in 2004, five months before she died.

Continued from page 208.

great tribute to Dame Rosemary that it's been such a success, because her influence in the early days was crucial. She had the sort of character that made it possible for a new development of that sort to get going'. In May 1976 Rosemary was invited to lunch at Buckingham Palace, no doubt in anticipation of the installation the following month. In April 1977 she stayed at Windsor, where she met Princess Margaret, and in June she was at the Queen's Jubilee Service of Thanksgiving at St Paul's in an official capacity. In July she attended a reception at Buckingham Palace. Elizabeth Rawson recorded that Rosemary 'specially adored hobnobbing with the Royal Family…'[243] She attended the Installation of Prince Charles as Chancellor of Aberystwyth University in 1977, in 1979 she stayed at Sandringham and in 1980 and 1981 she attended the Palace garden party. Of course there were many occasions when she met the Duke at formal events in Cambridge and occasionally also the Queen. The Royal couple officially opened Robinson College and Rosemary was among the guests hosted by the Vice-Chancellor, Professor Swinnerton-Dyer, Master of St Catherine's College, to a lunch. On one of Rosemary's last visits to Cambridge she was in the party that showed the Duke round New Hall. The photographs of the occasion reveal their relaxed and friendly relationship.

The crowning achievement of these years was the award of the DBE. Rosemary was asked in May if she would accept, and the honour was made public in the Jubilee Honours List, issued a few days after the Chancellor's Installation. Rosemary was inundated with letters of congratulation, and praise for the way she had conducted the ceremony[244]. 'I thought you were a Vice-Chancellor to be proud of in the Senate House last week, not only for the dignified and confident leadership of the proceedings, but also visually'. With her tall stature, powder white hair, which showed to advantage every time she doffed her cap, and piercing blue eyes, Rosemary stood out from the crowd. Dignity, competence and grace were the words which sprang to many people's minds. Her old friend Marjorie Verney wrote, 'I can't help thinking how Par would have loved to write to Dame Archi!'. A message from the Chair of the Governors at Downe said, 'Miss Willis would have absolutely purred with pleasure'. Rosemary must have been delighted to receive a personal letter from Princess Margaret, and a telegram from the Duke of Edinburgh: 'Many congratulations on your well deserved honour. Philip.' Other famous names were politicians

Shirley Williams and 'Rab' Butler and Ralf Dahrendorf the economist. The accolade was of course related to the successful completion of her term as Vice-Chancellor, and some colleagues took the opportunity to reflect on that in their letters. Professor Oliver Zangwill, a psychologist, wrote, 'I have been enormously impressed by the skill, patience, wisdom and good humour you have shown in managing the affairs of the University, small as well as great …'. Andrew Kennan of Jesus College complimented Rosemary on the major improvement in relations between students and senior members, mentioning 'the dedication with which you and a few colleagues continued to press for student participation in the government of the University'. The Vice-Chancellor of Birmingham University spoke of a wider audience: 'everyone appreciates what you have done in bringing a fresh look to the Cambridge scene'. It was Rosemary's single biggest pioneering act on behalf of womankind, though it led her to other 'firsts' for women. In quietly eliminating old prejudices and gently resolving conflict, she had demonstrated that women's talents could be just as relevant to the post as men's: in fact she would not have recognised her approach as particularly feminine. She wanted to be remembered as a leader, not a pretty face.

The investiture at Buckingham Palace took place on October 25th, not long after Rosemary had passed her keys and seal to the next VC, Alan Cottrell, who gave his opinion that the University was 'in excellent heart and shape, thanks largely to the good care and wisdom of my predecessor' and mentioned the cordial relations between the University, City and community generally, 'relations which Dame Rosemary herself has done so much to cultivate'[245]. Rosemary had in her diary 'Buck P.' sandwiched between other meetings: the AFPRB, the WRNS and the Harkness Foundation in London and the Colleges Committee and a memorial service for Lord Adrian in Cambridge. Cousin Ruth and her friend Verona attended the ceremony, and Ruth left a good account[246]. She described the throne room with cream and gilt panelled walls decorated with royal portraits, immense crystal chandeliers and gilt furniture upholstered in rose coloured brocade. A string orchestra was playing, pianissimo during the investiture, just a whisper of sound. The Beefeaters filed in and the band struck up the National Anthem as the Queen entered. She said a few words to each recipient, asking Rosemary what her work was, and pinned on the large enamelled medal. Miss Murray had become Dame Rosemary.

– 13 –

The final years at New Hall

Nora Barlow, New Hall's benefactor, writing to congratulate Rosemary on the D.B.E., asked, 'Life will seem a bit tame after September, won't it?'[247] Rosemary was determined not to slacken her pace. She was Deputy Vice-Chancellor, by custom, for the two years following her Vice-Chancellorship (1977-9) and continued as a member of the Council of the Senate until 1982. She found time to increase her activity in some of the external organisations she was involved in, and to add more, and she officially resumed the reins at New Hall again, not that she had ever let them slip.

Rosemary must have regretted being obliged to retire as J.P. at the age of 67 in 1980, as it had been a significant, albeit not very high profile part of her life. She had a long and distinguished career as a J.P., beginning in 1953 and graduating to the Lord Chancellor's Committee on J.P.s for Cambridgeshire in 1961. She officiated mostly in the juvenile and matrimonial courts. She chaired the Cambridge City Area Panel from 1970-74 and then became Chair of the Area Committee. The main responsibility was the appointment of J.P.s in the County. Many of those newly-appointed magistrates recall Rosemary's 'helpful hints and guidance, given with much sincerity and wisdom'.[248] Her sister Frances described her as very strict in court, and she could indeed cut a severe figure. She had a passion for fairness and a keen, almost forensic interest in people's characters and motivation. The court was a forum in which she could study the human personality and learn a great deal that was useful in her career. It also gave her training and practice in making judgements, which in early life she had found difficult, always agonising over decisions. This was of great importance in her University work: the only criticism being that she sometimes held too rigidly to her opinions.

Perhaps anticipating some gaps in her diary, Rosemary took on two new external committees in 1977, the London Committee for Harkness Fellowships of the Commonwealth Fund of New York and the Presidency of the National Institute of Adult Education (NIAE, later NIACE). The Harkness Fellowships were for British students wishing to study in the United States, complementing the Rhodes Scholarships for Americans

Retirement after 30 years as a magistrate, 1983. Rosemary was praised for her 'wisdom, fair judgment and humanity'.

coming to Britain. At that period they were not only for academics but were open to people in business and the creative arts and journalism. The field was always very competitive and the list of past alumni most impressive, so Rosemary would have enjoyed interviewing at this high level, and it was another link with America that she could follow up on her visits. NIAE was a charity promoting adult education and facilitating consultation and networking between the many organisations with this aim, especially local authorities and universities. One could say that Rosemary's interest was 'in the genes', because several of her ancestors had been involved in adult education – from Harvey Goodwin, who headed a Working Men's College, to Rosemary and Ruth Spooner, staunch supporters of Ruskin College Oxford. Ruth, despite having no formal qualifications, lectured on history and art in adult education colleges and gave free piano recitals all her life. The younger Rosemary had felt almost obliged to lecture for the Workers Education Association while she was at Girton, going out to the villages of Sutton and Stretham to teach small groups of five or six in the evenings. As VC she presided over the move of the Cambridge University Extra-Mural Service to Madingley Hall and the inauguration of residential courses. NIAE benefitted from Rosemary's extensive experience of education both at grass roots level and in the highest circles of decision-making. Her Presidency lasted three years and she served a further three as Vice-President.

Another organisation pleased to have Rosemary on board was the Council of the Winston Churchill Memorial Trust, which she joined in 1978, proposed by Sir Francis Pemberton, a Cambridge businessman and landowner who helped to found the Cambridge Science Park. The Trust awarded Fellowships for travel to people showing the potential to be leaders of society and the Council decided on the categories for each year. Rosemary's contribution was interviewing candidates in one or two of the categories along with two other members, and making the financial allotments. Right at the end of her period of office, in 1983, she was Chair of a Sub-Committee to write a survey of the work of the Trust during its first fifteen years. Distinguished fellow members included Sir Peter Scott, Lady Soames and the Duke of Marlborough. She had a number of disagreements with a recently-appointed Director General about this and other matters, but in any case had to resign, having reached the age of 70. A rather similar post was as governor of the English Speaking Union, an international educational charity promoting communication in the English language by awarding various types of scholarship to students in public speaking and debating and music. Exchange programmes with America at Secondary School and University level would have interested Rosemary, who had once hoped to win a scholarship to study there herself. At the Union's Diamond Jubilee in 1980, Rosemary had the honour of presenting a small group of distinguished guests to the Queen.

A new type of challenge, which she was only too pleased to take up, was an invitation in 1978 to be a non-executive director of the Midland Bank. She was particularly gratified to be the first woman on the Board, though determined not to be a token woman. At her first meeting there were 20 male directors and seven male managers and secretaries in attendance in the room; no other women. She soon involved herself in the interests of the female banking employees, their employment opportunities and the possibilities of mothers taking a career break to look after young children. In 1983 the Bank published the report of a Working Party entitled 'Equal opportunities for Women Staff in Midland Bank', admitting that there had been discrimination against women in the past. Fewer than 1% of their employees on management grades were female. The report suggested a 'returner' scheme for high calibre career women. The Midland also ran Women's Development Programmes in the 1980s. Rosemary's views were obviously very influential in this policy making. She would have pursued her aims at the Bank's luncheon and dinner parties as well as formal meetings.

Though naturally modest, Rosemary loved to reel off a list of posts she had held as the first woman, perhaps because she saw them as achievements for the cause of equality rather than personal successes. She took an impish delight in confounding expectations. Once she was introduced to a high (male) official as Vice-Chancellor, and was secretly amused when he looked around, bewildered, for a man. One of the 'firsts' for Rosemary was to be the first woman independent director[249] of the *Observer* newspaper, for twelve years from 1981. The five independent directors were briefly in the news themselves when asked by the paper's journalists to examine a dispute between the editor and the owner, 'Tiny' Rowland, over an article discrediting Robert Mugabe. They censored Rowland for 'improper proprietorial interference' in editorial freedom, and in return he threatened to cut their salaries[250]. Another breakthrough was becoming the first woman liveryman in the Goldsmiths' Company. The decision to admit women had met with some opposition. Admissions by patrimony (for daughters of freemen) had been allowed since 1954. 'Freeman by service', for those women who had completed a 7-year apprenticeship, remarkably was not brought in until 1983. Freemen had to be promoted to become liverymen, but in Rosemary's case election was by special grant, an honour reserved for royalty and distinguished persons, and she received the freedom and the livery on the same day in 1978. Having decided to admit women to the livery, the Goldsmiths were looking for those of national distinction. Rosemary had been helping them since the 1960s by reading the applications for their travel grants for schoolmistresses and preparing a shortlist, so she already knew several of their members, notably Fred Dainton of the UGC. Following Rosemary, they admitted Dame Cecily Saunders, founder of the hospice movement, and Lady Plowden, Chair of the Independent Broadcast Authority. Peter Jenkins, in his history of the Company, writes, 'There were mumblings of discontent from the general body of existing liverymen, but these did not amount to much and centred on the arcane pleasure which many men got from dining together without women…'[251] The duties of the Liverymen were ceremonial. Rosemary was invited to take part in the Trial of the Pyx, an annual meeting to assay the coins of the realm, dating back to the twelfth century. The coins are brought from the Royal Mint, counted and weighed and a selection put aside for the Assay Office to test the metallic content. In the post-war years the Company had added Education to its charitable aims. Rosemary joined the Education Committee at a time when they had some £45,000 p.a. to distribute. They met about eight times a year to short-list and interview for the awards. Annual receptions were held to keep the recipients in touch with each other and with the Company. Rosemary regularly attended the lavish dinners in Goldsmiths' Hall, at which the golden treasures of the Company were displayed as centrepieces on the dining tables, and having no spouse, took women guests, including her goddaughter, Alex Vlasto, and a number of Fellows of New Hall. Zara Steiner wrote to thank her for a 'fairytale evening' in the gilded hall with its coffered ceiling and massive chandeliers, remarking that her hostess was 'sharp as ever: your quick eye, superb judgement and clear vision still very much in evidence'[252]. The Company gave £10,000 in honour of Dame Rosemary to the 1992 New Hall Appeal with the intention of naming one of the major rooms in the proposed new building. Eventually it was agreed that the existing library would become the Rosemary Murray Library.

While Deputy Vice-Chancellor, and Chair of one of the Board of Education's committees, Rosemary was invited to conferences in South America and Africa. In 1980 she went to Mexico for a conference on 'The University of the Future', arranged by the Association of Universities and Schools for Higher Education, and chaired the session on 'The University and Teaching'. Early the following year she was able to attend a 5-day Seminar on 'Structure and Organisation in Higher Education in Nigeria' because the VC, John Butterworth, withdrew. The journey was difficult: it took two days to get to Kuru via Kano, 120 miles by road, and there was a 3-hour delay on her return to Lagos. The delegates stayed in guest chalets by a lake. Rosemary led a discussion on 'The Changing Concept of the University'. She was fascinated by Africa and wrote that she hoped that the visit would not be her last. Rosemary liked to extend the list of countries she had visited and at Easter she added another one, Portugal, when she attended the ICFU annual meeting, entitled 'Present Trends', held at the Gulbenkian Centre in Lisbon. It was in a beautiful parkland setting and Rosemary managed to slip out to see the cathedral and the Botanic Gardens. She chaired a session on 'Government and the University', a subject of great concern to her because she felt that the increase in bureaucracy and enforced compliance with reporting requirements was threatening the sense of community in universities as well as their autonomy.

Rosemary also made two more visits to the United States, in 1979 and

1980. In 1979 she spent a few days with her Goodwin relatives in Durham before a round of talks in Washington, Boston, Princeton and New York, organised by the Harkness Foundation. For four days Rosemary was followed about by a TV crew called PTV, probably a local or student network. They flew with her to Cambridge (Mass.) where she lunched at the Faculty Club and met senior women in Harvard administration. Among those she encountered was the young Bridget Kendall, daughter of a Cambridge don and a Harkness Fellow at Harvard. PTV also accompanied Rosemary to a wine and cheese party and a lunch with the Dean of Applied Science. She must have been glad when they returned to New York. Snow, blizzards and thunderstorms threatened her onward journey to Wellesley, but she arrived safely in Sherborn, to stay with Eleanor Webster, the Professor of Chemistry, whom she had made friends with on previous visits. Eleanor and her friend Dorothy had been on the Colorado River trip with Rosemary in 1973 and had visited her in Cambridge. She enjoyed doing some gardening for her hostess and attending one of her classes. Despite the honour Wellesley had given her, Rosemary did not have any official engagements and it was simply a social visit.

The 1980 trip was organised by the American Friends, and was of the same intensity as their earlier ones, regardless of Rosemary's age. Afterwards they wrote of her 'lightening visits to seven colleges and universities in five days'[253]. She did at least have three days' relaxation with Eleanor Webster on arrival, and caught up with Eleanor Keats Whiting at the Faculty Club. By this time the organisers, people like Gordon Williams, Gaylord Donnelley and especially Carleton Brown, had become friends who welcomed her back. Meetings at Harvard were focussed on fundraising, seeing the Director of the Alumni Relations Office and the Director of Development for Radcliffe College. Similarly at Yale, the AFCU Director, Wallace Tobin, introduced Rosemary to a senior Yale Officer on Alumni Affairs and his colleagues. At Barnard College she saw a senior representative of the Commonwealth Fund. A quick excursion to Princeton enabled her to meet the President, Director and Vice President of Development, and the Director of Annual Giving. She stayed one night at Goucher College, Maryland for discussions, returning to New York for meetings with Harkness Fellows and Cambridge University Press. On the final day of the visit she attended an AFCU Directors' Meeting at Harkness House. Gordon Williams reported that her presence was very helpful because she was able to comment on the background to funding requests from Cambridge bodies. It is surprising that she was allowed to do so, being an interested party. Among those awarded grants were the Department of Pathology, the Hamilton Kerr Institute, the Darwin project at the University Library and the Law Faculty for a prize in International Law. Rosemary must have been at her most persuasive. She also gave a clear explanation of the way Cambridge obtained financial support from the government and how this was allocated and used, and commented on British tax legislation and the way it affected charitable giving.

What amounted to a crash course in development and alumni relations came rather late in the day, because New Hall was badly in need of funds. The 'science' of development had not yet reached England: Rosemary was ahead of the game in looking to America for ideas and methods but she could have done with advice a year or two earlier. She was coming to the end of her Presidency, reaching the normal retirement age for senior members in July 1980, and there was an urgency in her efforts to leave the College on a sound financial footing. By the standards of most other colleges, New Hall was still poor. Although subventions from the Colleges Fund and gifts from St John's and Trinity had improved its endowment income, there had been major expenditure on additional buildings in 1978. Hammond and Clover Houses and the Vivien Stewart Room had cost £221,000.

The 25th anniversary of the arrival of the first students at New Hall fell in October 1979. For a long time some of the Fellows had been asking Rosemary to hold a Feast so that they could reciprocate the hospitality of colleagues in other colleges, but she always replied, 'When we are rich we will have a Feast'. There had been only one previously, in 1973, to celebrate the granting of the charter. The Silver Jubilee of the foundation was another landmark, and was identified as a good opportunity for making an appeal. A College committee was set up at the end of 1978 and quickly decided to hold three events: an Open Day for alumnae, a Benefactors' Feast and a large garden party, doubling as a farewell to the President. It was decided that the appeal would be aimed at getting continuous support from former students for recurrent expenses, development of the land that had belonged to The Grove, and bursaries and hardship funds. The final wording asked New Hall graduates to make a regular contribution 'as an act of faith in the role which New Hall should play in the future life of Cambridge and the nation'.[254] The first celebration was in fact an internal one, for all current members of New Hall, held as close as possible to the date of the first dinner in October 1954. For High Table Rosemary invited eleven senior Fellows and eleven students, signifying the more egalitarian nature of the College twenty-five years on. Patrick Wilkinson of King's, who had been a strong supporter since the inception of the Third Foundation Association, proposed the toast to the College, and Rosemary replied. The *New Hall Report* for 1979 announced the forthcoming festivities, but not the appeal. Robin Hammond, in retirement, contributed an entertaining article about the early days in Silver Street, 'Old New Hall'.[255] The students arranged their own Jubilee event in May Week, featuring a jazz band and rock groups.

Over 450 people attended the Open Day on 12th July for alumnae and their families. A variety of activities was provided for the 150 children of different age groups: there was an inflatable in the Fellows' Garden and football for 6-12 year olds on St Edmund's Field. It was necessary to have two sittings for lunch in the Dome and tea was served in a marquee in Orchard Court. On the Walkway, ice cream and soft drinks were on sale, together with memorabilia (T-shirts, mugs, bags and oven-gloves) and copies of Rosemary's book, *New Hall 1954-1972: the making of a College*, which she had written the previous summer. There was an exhibition of College silver in the President's Drawing Room and photographs from the 1960s were displayed in the Library. Guests were welcomed by Rosemary in the new Vivien Stewart Room, where she gave a speech designed to bolster the appeal, which had gone out in May with a questionnaire. After recalling the history of the College, she explained very clearly which expenses were not covered by College fees and why the College needed to build up an endowment to generate income. Keeping in touch with all old students, now numbering over one thousand, was a priority for the College and she urged them all to fill in the questionnaire with their contact details. She asked if the New Hall Society, run by the Librarian, would like to have a committee of alumnae. As a result four members volunteered, allowing the Society to organise more events.

The Silver Jubilee Feast was held in Michaelmas 1980. The guest list was designed to include all the categories of people who had helped New Hall over the years. Rosemary systematically divided it into Members of the College Council and Committees (many from St John's and King's); Third Foundation and New Hall Association members, some of them, like Mrs Burkill and Mrs Parsons, predating Rosemary's involvement; Dining Group members (Anna Bidder, Kay Wood-Legh and Margaret Braithwaite); some former Fellows, such as Elizabeth Rawson; Honorary and Emeritus Fellows, notably Robin Hammond; and The Visitor, Lord Devlin. The final category was 'Friends', mostly people who had worked for New Hall such as John Honer, representing Chamberlin, Powell and Bon, Victor Bugg, the surveyor, Bill Eason, the investment advisor, the College solicitor and the local bank manager. It was typical of Rosemary to include them among the academics and VIPs. Altogether 134 guests attended, filling the Dome. The menu was particularly exotic for New Hall, five courses including Saumon Trouvillaise and Sorbet Carribéan. On High Table Rosemary was flanked by the Vice-Chancellor, Sir Peter Swinnerton-Dyer, and Lord Devlin. A toast to Benefactors and Friends was proposed by the Visitor and Dr Boys Smith replied. The toast to the College was proposed by the VC with a reply from Rosemary. The event was a fitting commemoration of the combined efforts of the many people who had helped to establish the College and a tribute to Rosemary, who was acknowledged by everyone to be the kingpin. Among the many letters of thanks was one from Trevor Thomas, formerly Bursar of St John's, who had worked closely with Rosemary to bring about collegiate status and therefore understood the difficulties she had surmounted:

'The College has reason to be grateful to you for most splendid leadership, and those of us who were so glad to try and be supportive of your efforts are delighted that all should have turned out so well ... At the time, not many things seemed to fall into place: they had to be nudged – sometimes dragged - into their proper niches. But the completed scheme must make you very proud and happy and you richly deserve to be so.'[256]

The questionnaire sent to all Old Members was another attempt by Rosemary to leave the College in good shape for her successor. It was the first time New Hall had attempted to compile a complete up-to-date list of its graduates. Rosemary was well aware of the meticulous way in which Helen McMorran compiled and updated the Girton Roll, and realised that a list of alumnae was an essential tool of fundraising. The questionnaire also had elements of a sociological enquiry. What extra-curricular activities had students enjoyed at Cambridge, in the University, in College or student societies or elsewhere and what vivid memories did they retain? Marital status and number of children was requested, and a brief career outline with reference also to voluntary work. 'Present situation' gave them a chance to reflect on what they had achieved. Rosemary had investigated women's careers in the University, the armed forces and the banking world, but it was the first time she had studied the impact of a Cambridge education on her own students. She constantly puzzled over the difficulty of combining a career and motherhood, realising that she would not have achieved so much if she had married. As a single woman, living in an institution, she had been able to devote herself wholeheartedly to a career. She considered bringing up children to be a second career, meriting a long break. 'What we haven't yet made possible is for them [women] to come back again to their first career.' One suggestion was for returning women to change direction and go into administration, as she had done herself. At the Open Day she held a discussion on Families and Careers, asking for individual experiences; 'what the problems are and how some have solved them'. She collated the results of the questionnaire with great care, working out percentages. 29% of alumnae had replied, of whom 33 had achieved Ph.Ds. Teaching at various levels was by far the most popular career, followed by public service and industry. Nearly one quarter were doing some kind of voluntary work. Two thirds of the respondents were married, of whom 14% were working part time and 8% were no longer in paid work. She would have been pleased with some of the comments received about the College: 'relaxed', 'unstuffy' with 'friendly Fellows'.

The results of the Appeal were frankly disappointing, hence perhaps her dash to America to see if she could glean any new ideas. Ninety alumni responded quickly, but then the subscriptions slowed down. Rosemary's carefully argued request, that 'everyone should make a regular annual contribution to the college ... so that we can be sure of a yearly addition to income' did not have much effect, perhaps because it was presented in a very academic way at the end of a page of text with no illustrations.[257] The total raised only increased the College's income by £3,600 p.a.

The garden party, held at the end of June, was both a Jubilee celebration and a farewell to Rosemary on her retirement. Some 300 guests came; old friends of New Hall and Rosemary's colleagues from the University and City of Cambridge. It was just before her final appearance as President at General Admissions. She must have recalled the first occasion, in 1957, when she proudly led 16 students to the Senate House. A final public engagement as President of New Hall was the New Hall Society's dinner at the end of September for about 125 Senior Members and alumnae. A substantial sum of money had been collected and Rosemary was presented with a black leather briefcase and a cheque that she said she would spend on extending a visit to India that she was planning. In addition, a sundial was put on the South wall of the Darwin Building as a lasting memorial in College. Rosemary's speech to the Society has been preserved. It was quite a long one for her, going back over the early history, her initial involvement, interview for the post of Tutor-in-Charge and the appointment of Robin Hammond shortly afterwards. Robin, she said, often provided ideas and principles which Rosemary then implemented: New Hall was not the same without her. Rosemary was pleased to see that four of the first year alumnae were present that evening. Reminding her audience that New Hall was the first post-war College in Cambridge, Rosemary said that people often asked if she and Robin had a pre-conceived policy of making New Hall different. The answer was 'no', but because there was so much variation among colleges, there was plenty of scope for individuality. The nature of the College had emerged over the years from many different influences and individual decisions made by Council, individual Fellows – or even the President! The experience of an undergraduate depends largely on the interaction with other members of the College: the encouragement and teaching of supervisors and personal attention from Tutors down to the friendliness of the porters. She and Robin had applied any regulations with a light touch. 'Everyone contributes something to New Hall – very few in a negative sense – and so adds to what New Hall is able to give to each member. To me it gave the opportunity of being VC'. She spoke of the buildings and past, present and future members, all making up the College, but changing over time. The College was like a broom that could have new handles and heads but remained 'a fine old broom'. Rosemary was fond of this analogy and often used it to express the paradox of the College as a changing organism which in some way stayed the same. She recognised that she and Robin had set their stamp on New Hall[258]. As Prince Philip commented, 'Institutions do have characters and they retain that character even though individuals change'[259].

Rosemary left the College with a strong Fellowship that she had built up over the years. Being in close touch with the University she knew all about new appointments and was always on the look-out for bright young women who could teach. Some of them, like Ruth Lynden-Bell and Zara

The President and Fellows of New Hall in 1976.

Steiner were wives of academics and had no University posts. Thanks to association with New Hall they were able to continue research and reach the highest levels of distinction. In the 1970s quite a number of Fellows lived in, and communal meals provided many opportunities for discussion of College policy. Rosemary was always wanting to hear Fellows' opinions, so that she could crystallise her own views. She believed in being open and straightforward and consultative, but she made the ultimate decisions. Zara Steiner remarked, 'Rosemary ruled us with an iron hand, but we didn't notice it – she was so calm and kind'[260]. The small dining group learned a lot from her, just by watching and talking, and she certainly mentored some of them. Kate Pretty has described how Rosemary suggested she might like to swap her academic career for administration, as she herself had done. They worked closely together when Kate became Admissions Tutor, a useful training for future leadership. Rosemary still interviewed every candidate, summing them up in a few notes: for Kate, '...her instinctive judgement of the potential in students, her willingness to take risks, remain strong memories.[261]' Rosemary was elected into an Honorary Fellowship from October 1981. New Hall, led by the Vice President, had been searching for a new President throughout the year. Undoubtedly some colleagues were not sorry that Rosemary was retiring. She was perceived as rather authoritarian in her final years, always a danger for a chief who has been in post for a long while. She was considerably more experienced than anyone else, and in most situations the right course of action would seem obvious to her. The Fellows thought it was time for an academic to lead the College, and appointed Dr Valerie Pearl, a historian from London University. Rosemary lunched a few times with Valerie, hoping to be helpful, and produced a set of Notes for the President on two sides of foolscap, covering all the President's duties in and outside the College and indicating whether procedures were in the Statutes or the Ordinances. She was disappointed that Valerie was not very receptive. It was naturally daunting for her successor to follow such a legend. Rosemary was, however, able to pass on some of her wisdom to other colleges, as Trustee of Homerton and Robinson and a member of the Council of Hughes Hall. She was made an honorary Fellow of Robinson in 1985 and became Homerton's Visitor in 1990, remaining a source of wise counsel until her death. Kate Pretty became Principal of Homerton in 1991, and described herself as a hands-on President following Rosemary's example. She recognised that Rosemary's long connection with the Institute of Education helped to bring about a change of attitude to teacher training. Rosemary's relationship with Lucy Cavendish College was perhaps a little ambivalent, though in the 1970s she was on a committee guiding it towards full collegiate status. She gave some advice to Phyllis Bowden, the President, in 1981, but she turned down an invitation to help with fund-raising in 1983, presumably because she thought Lucy Cavendish would be in direct competition with New Hall. A further opportunity to impart her knowledge of the Cambridge system came when New Hall elected an Oxford graduate, Anne Lonsdale, as its third President in 1995. She asked if she might talk to Rosemary, and found her still very well-informed about Cambridge. Apart from keeping up with old friends from the corridors of power, Rosemary was still reading *The Reporter*[262]. She advised Anne to get involved in the University, because it would bring so many advantages to New Hall. Anne was happy to listen to her advice and Rosemary always stood back if Anne disagreed on a topic. They were soon firm friends.

September 1981 was a busy month, but Rosemary managed to fit in with a family holiday in the Lake District, based in a cottage at Ulverstone.

Frances and Ian arranged it, the party including three of their children, Nico, Andrew and Hugo, and wives and grandchildren. It must have reminded Rosemary of similar Murray gatherings when she was young. They walked on the shore of Lake Coniston and up the steep slope to the Old Man, had picnics and went on the Eskdale railway. Rosemary loved being with younger people and finding out about their lives. Shortly after her return she moved out of her College accommodation to a flat she had rented in Newnham since 1976. It was a major change, considering she had lived in institutions practically all her working life, but it was not difficult logistically because she had remarkably few possessions. She sorted her official papers into twenty boxes which, together with two scrapbooks of newspaper and other cuttings, she left with the Librarian, forming the beginning of the College Archive. Most of the furniture from her family, on loan to New Hall in public rooms and Fellows' studies, was finally given to the College. Among the notable pieces were a Serpentine chest of drawers bequeathed by Catherine Dodgson ('Aunt Cath'), a George IV armchair given by the Probys, a Chippendale oval mirror presented by Ellen Murray, and a seventeenth-century oak refectory table and oak coffer. These and many other smaller items - ornaments, clocks, silver - are still part of the College collection today.

– 14 –

Retirement

Rosemary had a long and active retirement, carrying forward much of the work she had started earlier and pursuing the same interests. In 1980 she was still a member of about 40 University and external committees and Councils. By 1983 the number had reduced considerably as she ceased to be a member of the Council of the Senate and was compulsorily retired from the AFPRB and the Justice service. Her thirty year stint as governor of Keswick Hall College of Education ended in the same year when it became part of the University of East Anglia. In 1981 the Vice-Chancellor asked her to continue as Chair of the Botanic Gardens Syndicate, certainly one of her favourite committees, and of Crane's Charity, the principal medical charity of the University, founded in 1651 for the relief of 'poor, sick scholars'. She also chaired at least four University Appointments committees, on which she remained alert to gender issues. She was known to ask, 'Why are there no women on the shortlist?' In 1978 she resumed her Chairmanship of the Institute of Education as the University representative and stayed on the committee until 1986, and she was also a valued Trustee of the Veterinary School, resigning only when she moved away from Cambridge. Since 1978 she had been on the committee of the Friends of the Scott Polar Research Institute, whose lectures she had attended since her arrival in Cambridge. Rosemary's book collection showed that she was a keen reader of accounts of polar expeditions. For many years after retiring, Chairmanship of the Cambridge Society took Rosemary all over the country. She was always 'on call' when a senior figure was needed to represent the University in Cambridge or elsewhere and she greatly relished stepping back into that rôle.[263]

Promptly as Rosemary retired from New Hall, her cousin Peter Proby, Lord Lieutenant for Cambridgeshire, wrote to enquire whether she would like to become his Deputy. He thought it would be very useful to have someone in close contact with the University, whom he could ask for advice. He went on:

'I also think that the time has come when it would be a good idea to have a Lady Deputy Lieutenant, and having been the first Lady Vice-

Old friends: the High Sherriff of Cambridgeshire, Sir Arthur Marshall, and Rosemary, the Deputy Lieutenant, wearing her WRNS uniform and DBE medal.

Chancellor, I wondered if you would like to be another "first" ... I cannot think of anyone who would be more suitable.'[264]

He explained that there would be certain occasions when she would be representing him, but the most helpful thing was to be a contact with organisations in the County, for example attending charity functions. He mentioned that ladies might wear any recognised uniform to which they were entitled. Rosemary was delighted to have the chance to dress in WRNS uniform again, and also pleased that she could still fit into it. She thoroughly enjoyed the rôle, and continued it when Peter Proby retired and even when she moved out of the County, often making the trip from Oxford for such occasions as Remembrance Sunday at Ely Cathedral and the commemoration of anniversaries at the American Cemetery.

The University was slow to honour its first woman Vice-Chancellor, but eventually LLD (Doctor of Laws) was added to her impressive list of honorary degrees in 1988, twelve years after the DCL from Oxford. Rosemary, who had presided over so many similar ceremonies in the Senate House, found herself in the rôle of recipient, in the company of Baroness Platt of Writtle, formerly Chair of the Equal Opportunities Commission and Dame Elisabeth Frink, the sculptor. She would have been pleased that women were now firmly on the list. The University Orator's presentation spoke of Rosemary's transformation from academic to administrator with an allusion to her naval connections.

> 'The skill of her captaincy [of New Hall] surprised no-one: she was an Admiral's daughter and had served as an officer in the Wrens … We invited her to take the helm of the whole University, as our first woman Vice-Chancellor. With what sureness of control she managed our affairs you all know; with what dignity she presided over our affairs you all have seen.'[265]

He praised her signal part in promoting women's achievements in recent years and her practical abilities. It was Robin Hammond who made sure these skills were included: she had written to the Orator about New Hall's 'early do-it-yourself years' when Rosemary was gardener, carpenter, electrician and plumber. Elizabeth Rawson added, 'she was splendid at mending fuses and mopping up floors, and … good on building committees.' Rosemary had much in common with Baroness Platt, another resourceful woman, said always to carry a screwdriver in her handbag. She had promoted technological training for women and opportunities for women with children to resume their interrupted careers.

Dressed in scarlet, with black and gold bonnets, the honorands processed to the Senate House and entered to a flourish of trumpets. A short recital by the choirs of King's and St John's preceded the main ceremony, and then each candidate was led forward and presented to the Chancellor, Prince Philip, by the Orator. On the dais, the Chancellor took the candidate's right hand and admitted her with a short Latin text. Again it was a rôle reversal for Rosemary, who must have recalled the occasion in 1976 when she admitted the Prince as Chancellor. More music followed and the procession left the building and proceeded down the length of King's Parade to Corpus Christi College, where they were to have lunch, hosted by the Vice-Chancellor, Michael McCrum. This was by no means Rosemary's last appearance in the Senate House. She continued to apply for tickets to honorary degree ceremonies for the next fifteen years and to walk in the processions and enjoy the Degree lunches.

Rosemary's high-pitched and by now slightly quavering voice could often be heard above the crowd at local City events. She was a regular helper on the Cancer Research Campaign Committee, not thinking it beneath her to serve at bazaars or to rattle a tin on flag days. She had been Chair of the WRNS Cambridge Branch since 1979 and also involved nationally, keeping in touch with a number of former colleagues. In 1980 she gave an enthusiastic speech about the life of Nelson to the WRNS Association: he was obviously one of her heroes. She was happy to devote more time to the Church of St Edward, King and Martyr, situated behind King's Parade, which she had been attending since she moved to Silver Street in 1954. It was an obvious choice, since her grandfather, Harvey Goodwin, had been vicar there. An annual service was held for Trinity Hall, the patrons of the church, and nearby colleges New Hall, St Catharine's and Clare. Rosemary was on the Parish Council and from the 1970s onwards acted as sidesman or sacristan. Her duties included preparing for Communion by laying the altar, lighting candles and preparing the bread and wine. During the service she took up the collection and afterwards counted it. The keys had to be fetched and returned to Trinity Hall. There was on-going friction between the Church and the College over funding, some of the Fellows wanting to be rid of the responsibility for spiritualities. Rosemary was sent as one of the ambassadors to meet John Lyons, when he became Master in 1985. They managed to negotiate a joint appointment of College Chaplain and Vicar of St Edward's, and later a trust fund was set up for both purposes. It involved 'much explaining', said Rosemary, and she needed patience to bring it about. She became one of the first Trustees, of whom three were from the Church and three from the College.

When attending meetings in London, Rosemary often stayed at her club, the University Women's Club, and used it as a base while travelling back and forth to other parts of England. Chairing the GPDST Court was a regular monthly fixture in the diary and in addition she attended their Education and Finance Committees. She was on appointments boards for more than twenty Headmistresses in the 1980s. Arising from this work was a close association with a number of girls' schools as governor or Trustee. In later years she took on special responsibility for Birkenhead High School and Belvedere Girls' School, both in the Liverpool area. This was not as inconvenient as it seems, because Rosemary was able to stay with her nephew Nicolas Crombie and his family in Norbury when she visited them. She would combine meetings at the schools with intensive periods of gardening for the Crombies. Letters show that she was valued by all concerned, and as a mark of thanks the Birkenhead Junior School was named the Murray Building in 1992.

Among the London meetings were visits to Toynbee Hall, an institution devoted to social reform based in Tower Hamlets. The original idea of the founders in the nineteenth century was to invite future leaders of the country to live in the East End and learn about the problems and conditions of the poor at first hand. Rosemary had a connection through teaching for the WEA, which was a spin-off from the settlement. She was invited to become a member of the Council of Toynbee Hall in 1982. With delay and confusion over her appointment, she eventually attended her first Council meeting in August 1983. She soon came to the opinion that there was little control over the finances: no proper budgeting for the various areas of work and money raised in the Centenary Appeal was not invested for endowment but used for current expenditure and to pay off the bank overdraft – unwisely, Rosemary thought. Various suggestions were made for raising funds, including selling off most of the site. Rosemary was involved in protracted efforts to revise the constitution and sort out the muddled administration, but eventually became so frustrated with the management team side-lining Council and taking decisions with which she disagreed that she resigned in 1989 – a rare instance of her giving up on an organisation. She was pleased to hear a few years later that administration and financial control had much improved.

Social and educational progress, particularly for women, came together in Rosemary's interest in the Cambridge Christian Brotherhood and its work in Delhi. This was another nineteenth-century foundation, started by a group of Cambridge clergy who were committed to the higher education of the poor in India. They established St Stephen's College in Delhi and it became part of the Anglican Church of North India, broadening its concern for the disadvantaged to include health care, skills training and schools. Rosemary seems to have visited it in a semi-official capacity, wearing her inspector's hat. In February 1983, in her 70th year, she set out for the trip of a lifetime, lasting five weeks. Although not as intensive as the American tours, the programme was quite demanding for someone of her age in temperatures reaching 100 degrees. The first week was spent at St Stephen's, seeing the College, Hospital and St Thomas's School and various projects around Seemapuri. She was made very welcome by the Brotherhood, took tea with the Vice-Chancellor of Delhi University and had an evening visit to old Delhi bazaars. She then travelled to New Delhi where she was to report on the education of women for the British Council. Rosemary had a meeting with the head of the women's unit of the National Council of Educational Research and Training and was rather critical of her management style, which was 'too centralised'. At the Adult Education Directorate she learned about vocational courses of a very basic kind for workers, and vocational courses for women who had finished formal education, in subjects such as textile design, housekeeping and secretarial work. She noted that the teachers were all graduates of the College and had no formal training. A trip to two villages gave an insight into courses in a rural setting: fifty women sitting in a courtyard with slates and notebooks were taking a literacy class in Hindi; in the village hall another group sat with sewing machines learning dressmaking; two more groups were being taught skills that would help them into work, having dropped out of school. Next day Rosemary visited a teacher centre which the British Council had helped to equip. It was designed for continuing professional development of all the teachers in the neighbourhood in both private and state schools. Rosemary felt the Principal needed 'help and guidance in the use of the centre'. She planned to send literature from the Cambridge Institute of Education and suggested sending teachers to do a PGCE course or at least have a taste of in-service training at Cambridge. Wherever she went she tried to help educators make contact with their British counterparts, and this was followed up at home by talking to people in authority, such as the Inspector of Schools for Cambridgeshire.[266]

From New Delhi Rosemary flew to Madras for a meeting with the Vice-Chancellor and a visit to the University's Department of Adult and Continuing Education. They too had programmes for literacy and useful skills in the rural areas: at one of the centres she picked up the course outline for bookbinding. She also had discussions on women's education at the YWCA and made day trips by taxi and train to schools and hospitals. The last fortnight of the visit was holiday, the extension she had spoken about when presented with a cheque from New Hall, and by good fortune she was able to visit her niece Clare, daughter of Frances, in Pondicherry. She left Madras on the Nellai Express, travelling overnight to Tirunelveli. It is said that she received a proposal of marriage on the train, from an Indian gentleman with whom she conversed about Shakespeare! Her mode

Rosemary at New Hall with Baroness Boothroyd and Dr Valerie Pearl, President in 1995.

of transport in Pondicherry was bicycle rickshaw, with Clare riding her bike alongside.[267] Rosemary continued to support the Brotherhood by contributing her expertise and raising funds, and in 1986 became Chair of the Cambridge Committee for Christian Work in Delhi. She was a generous contributor to the cause herself.

All these activities helped to fill the huge gap in her life without New Hall business to occupy her. She attended the annual dinner of the alumnae and delighted in seeing students she had admitted, and as an Honorary Fellow was invited to Feasts and other dinners, and she kept in touch with some of her former colleagues. Over the years her conversational skills had developed, along with her deep interest in people from all backgrounds, making her very talkative. She was always keen to hear about progress in the Rosemary Murray Library, and when it expanded into the basement she returned to open the Rawson Reading Area, housing Elizabeth Rawson's bequest of classics books. Few people knew that Rosemary had paid for the glass-fronted bookcases. In place of New Hall's garden she began to improve the communal areas around the blocks of flats where she was living, and she volunteered to look after the small garden of St Edward's Church, a rather public place for the former VC to be seen in her old clothes. Finding that a friend in Cranmer Road was having difficulty keeping up her large garden, Rosemary helped there too, achieving wonderful herbaceous borders in the style of Vita Sackville-West. Rosemary liked the traditional English garden flowers – roses, delphiniums, lavender, the giant *Crambe cordifolia* and clumps of daisies. She also had an interest in Alpines, going back to the time of expeditions with the Verneys in Switzerland, looking for wild flowers. In one of her portraits she is holding a gentian, *Gentiana verna*. This may have had an association for her with the name Verney and certainly with her many walking tours in the Alps.

Rosemary put gardening first in her list of hobbies in *Who's Who*. Next came bookbinding. She had taken classes at the Cambridge 'Tech.', taught by George Bolton who had learnt the trade of 'forwarding', i.e. the actual sewing and covering of books rather than 'finishing', which is lettering and decoration on the outside, as an apprentice to Grey's of Green Street. So Rosemary became a competent forwarder but always had problems with lettering. She was pleased that she could offer her skills in the service of the Florence restoration project. Another loss on leaving New Hall was the little workroom she had fitted up in a store of the Library, accessed from the same corridor as her rooms. There she could pop in and mend the Library books whenever she had time. After she left, she set up a bookbinder's bench in her flat and would come marching into the Library to collect and return bags of damaged books. When she moved to Oxford she did the same for LMH Library until failing eye-sight forced her to give up.

The third and fourth hobbies Rosemary listed were walking and travel and she had more time for both in retirement. Holidays with Ian and Frances took her to the Lakes, Wales and Scotland. In 1989 they explored Caithness and Sutherland by car, pausing for walks along the beach or in the mountains. In the usual Murray fashion they ate outdoors, even in poor weather. By 1991 the excursions had become a little less strenuous: a week with the Crombies in Wales and the Borders seeing Symonds Yat, Tintern Abbey, Chepstow and the Forest of Dean. From time to time Rosemary would spend a week with Robin Hammond at Essington Priors in Surrey, but she did not adopt Robin's leisurely life-style. She spent most of her visit gardening.

Robin would only occasionally stay at Rosemary's flat for a day or two. Rosemary also remained a keen sailor, well into her eighties, enjoying crewing for John and Lilias or Richard and Brenda, in the large yacht *Fulmar*, which the brothers bought in 1982 and kept on the West Coast of Scotland. In the mid-1980s, she spent a week nearly every year sailing with one of the couples round Lochs Melfort and Craiguish, and in 1988 had a three week holiday in the same area, taking in Megarry, Tobermory and several lochs around Oban. After *Fulmar* came *Martlet*, a similar yacht in which she sailed with various members of the family, including John's son, Michael, who was tragically killed in an accident a few years later. Her last Scottish holiday seems to have been in 1995, sailing in the Western Isles with Richard and David.

As commitments gradually diminished towards the end of the 1980s, Rosemary was left with the GPDST, the Wages Councils, the Goldsmiths' Company, the Board of the *Observer* and some School Governor and Trustee posts. The Wages Councils ceased to exist in 1993 and in the same year she left the Goldsmiths' Education Committee. Frances sensed that her sister was winding down and that the Cambridge-London axis was no longer so vital to her and made the suggestion that Rosemary should move to Oxford. She reported a bungalow for sale, just round the corner from her own home in Old Marston. A number of factors played a part in Rosemary's decision to move. The bungalow appealed to her: it had a room suitable for her bookbinding and was surrounded by a potentially attractive garden. There was the proximity to the Crombies and other relatives, the ready-made social life of Lady Margaret Hall, the local Girton Group, the Oxford Women's Lunch Club and the Oxford Society, and of the village. Perhaps, too she was already thinking of offering a home to her brother David, whose wife Diana had died in 1992.[268] She resigned from the rest of her Cambridge committees and prepared to move, giving away some of her furniture and a lot of her books (some to the Library of New Hall), making lists as ever, and on 26th October 1994, made the transition to 'the Other Place'. She was sorry to leave John and Lilias, but she knew that there would always be a bed for her at 16, Grange Road. It became a regular stopping-off place when she returned, usually taking the bus, to Cambridge for New Hall gatherings, Feasts, Honorary Degree ceremonies and Deputy Lieutenant duties. There was genuine disappointment in the upper echelons of the University when she sent out her change of address. Revd John Sweet summed it up when he wrote 'Cambridge will feel emptier without you'[269]. Rosemary was still an influential figure at the age of 81.

The bungalow was a great success. Ian Crombie helped her clear the garden, the first she had ever owned. She laid it out with a small greenhouse and vegetable plot near the back door and borders round the side and in front, bringing bags of leaves from LMH to enrich the compost heap. She planted flowers that had associations, such as gentians, which she had loved since first seeing them in their natural habitat, and the multi-petalled aquilegia bred by Nora Barlow. She kept a garden diary and all the plants were numbered and shown on a plan. Visitors would always be invited for a tour of inspection, with Rosemary checking what was in flower or needing special attention. Even when her sight failed she was able to identify the plants by touch and memory of their position. Anyone who showed an interest was given seedlings or cuttings. Rosemary quickly involved herself in village life, joining the WI and attending the ancient church of St Nicholas, only a few hundred yards away. She liked to go to the 8.00 a.m. Holy Communion, using the liturgy of the Book of Common Prayer.[270] She made herself useful, as sidesperson and deliverer of the parish magazine: she was one of the 'doers', said a neighbour. Rosemary brought many years' experience of jumble sales and bazaars and was always keen to run the Christmas Bookstall at Church. She was quite formidable, insisting on charging realistic prices and not allowing any bargains. It was not long before she joined the Parish Church Council (PCC). She prepared thoroughly for meetings, just as she had always done, having facts and figures ready. She would say innocently, 'I don't think I quite agree…' and out would come a logical and well-prepared argument. The vicar, Tony Price, became a huge admirer, even though she kept him on his toes.

> 'She used to drive me mad on the PCC with her searching questions (which so often discovered my ignorance, lack of preparation, or inefficiency) and requests for the fullest transparency and communication about everything. But I loved her for it too. It was all of a piece you see. The quality that really characterised her was a boundless curiosity about life and an interest in people…'[271]

Soon everybody in the village knew Rosemary and many became friends. There were often people dropping in to the bungalow for coffee or lunch, not only locals but New Hall alumnae and Fellows and colleagues who had worked with her in all her many spheres. She liked to entertain simply at home, but she still enjoyed grand dinners in the Colleges and in Goldsmiths' Hall and she continued to take up these invitations to the end of her life. Undeterred by her loss of sight she would arrange beforehand for someone to cut up her food.

RETIREMENT 243

Another focus was the village school, where Rosemary helped out by teaching children with reading difficulties. Although she had not taught this age group before, she took to it easily, bringing her usual encouragement and dedication. She kept notes on each child and was always looking out for books that would appeal. When asked what the children called her, she said 'Rosemary, of course'. Messages and drawings that she kept show how much they appreciated her. She continued until 2002 when she could no longer see to read.

Over in Cambridge a new generation seemed to have forgotten that their university had produced the first woman Vice-Chancellor. In 1998 there was a major celebration of the 50th anniversary of women receiving degrees with many elderly ladies returning to Newnham and Girton. An exhibition of photographs entitled 'Educating Eve: five generations of Cambridge women' was put together for the occasion. Several alumnae of New Hall were featured, Jocelyn Bell Burnell and Joanna MacGregor among them, and also the first President of Lucy Cavendish, Anna Bidder. There was no portrait of Rosemary, arguably the most outstanding woman of the past fifty years, because she was not a Cambridge alumna, so an opportunity was missed to celebrate her achievement. To add to the neglect, four years later the second woman Vice-Chancellor, Alison Richard, was elected with much publicity, and described by the journalists as the first woman. This wording was so ubiquitous that it must have been put out by the University Press Office, and was in fact defended by them when New Hall protested, saying that in the 1970s the VC was only a figurehead. This time Rosemary intervened and was quoted with the excuse 'I absolutely object to the notion that my job was a figurehead rôle'[272]. There was a quick *volte face* by the Old Schools, the Press Office producing an article entitled 'Sisters in Learning'[273] about both women.

Rosemary's appetite for travel did not diminish with age. In 1997 she visited her niece, Marion, who was living in California. Her brother David came with her, and Marion remembers it as a wonderful few weeks. As usual, Rosemary made herself useful: 'She was never happier than when faced with a hopelessly untidy workroom for sorting out, or a large pile of garden trimmings to burn up in a bonfire'[274]. She delighted to see her great nieces and nephews and talk about their enthusiasms. A final adventurous holiday took place in February 2000. Rosemary loved visiting places new to her, and when a friend in the village revealed that she had connections in the Falkland Islands it was soon fixed that the two of them would go over for a month. They flew overnight from RAF Brize Norton to the Ascension Islands, and thence to the Falklands. It is not surprising that the 87-year old was slightly disorientated after arrival, especially as they plunged straight into social activities and sightseeing. She kept a very detailed diary, noting all the people she met, their life histories, children and houses: everything interested her. There were a couple of invitations to Government House, otherwise one can guess that Rosemary found the social life of the Islands – mainly wives' tea parties and noisy evening gatherings – rather limited. However, she loved exploring and recording the flora, geological structures, animals and birds. She was thrilled to come across elephant seals basking on the beach, 'lying in a great heap throwing yellow sand over themselves in great yellow clouds. Much grunting and bellowing as they raised up against each other and then collapsed'. This was on Sea Lion Island, a haven for wild birds such as giant petrels, peregrine falcons, magellanic and other penguins and Patagonian crested ducks. Rosemary was in her element, marking on a map the birds and animals seen at more than twenty observation points that they reached by Land Rover. They came upon a group of sea lions, resting in tussock grass, and on two successive days spotted the black fins of killer whales. A highlight was Rockhopper Point, 'incredible great cliff covered with Rockhoppers which one could easily approach close to … hundreds all the way up … Also, an archway and boiling sea round the bottom'. As well as the wild scenery, Rosemary was interested in the recent history of the Falklands War, looking at wrecks and monuments and talking with a woman whose son had died on Tumbledown.[275] She made a note of rates of pay in the Air Force, as if she still worked for the AFPRB, and wangled an invitation to the Royal Engineers' depot for a demonstration of bomb disposal and an exhibition of mines, disarming devices, photos and 'pathetic' items of debris[276].

The journey home was not without incident. Half way along the runway there was a loud bang, and the plane staggered to a halt. After a 5-hour delay they departed again with 'much and many bangs of engine', managed to take off but were grounded at Ascension Island while a new plane was sent out. Basic army accommodation, sleeping in bunks in extreme heat, did not worry Rosemary; in fact she enjoyed the conversations with other passengers. After breakfast she found her way to the Officers' Mess and stayed there all day chatting to members of 2 Para regiment, who had all been in the conflict, she discovered.

Rosemary guided by a friend in the Honorary Degree procession, 2003.

Rosemary continued to be vigorous and energetic to the end of her life and to radiate enthusiasm for anything she undertook. In her late eighties she was still gardening, doing carpentry and bookbinding, and even varnished the hall floor in 2002, but she was increasingly handicapped by macular degeneration, an eye condition for which there is as yet no cure. It was an immense blow to find that she could no longer remain completely independent. Church friends suggested that she needed an extra pair of hands (and eyes) and recommended a retired nanny, Shirley Smith, whom she already knew. This capable lady, already in her seventies, came in for an hour twice a week. Rosemary saved up jobs for her, from sorting out her knitting to checking the fridge and medicine cabinet for out of date items. She acquired various aids; a telephone with oversize keypad, speaking watch, speaking scales, a special oven and talking books. Ordering the tapes, she was shocked to find that the New Testament had not been recorded and promptly arranged for it to happen. She was registered blind and used a white stick. Rosemary joined the Macular Society, encouraging her assistant to give a talk there and attending as a guest of honour. Whatever she felt in private, outwardly she remained cheerful and positive. A volunteer for the Oxford Association for the Blind wrote,

'Very quickly the visits [to Rosemary] became one of the highlights of my week. The tasks were varied and various. I began to learn about knitting, bookbinding, bread-making, the proper names of plants and to skim-read magazines and reports. It was sometimes challenging, always stimulating, and great fun. Rosemary's lively interest and kindly concern in all around her (not forgetting Coronation Street) and zest for life were infectious.'[277]

Rosemary was in good form for the New Hall Midsummer Feast in 2003, when she was guest of honour, to celebrate her forthcoming 90th birthday. At the reception she sat chatting in the Walkway, wearing a brightly-coloured blouse, her face lighting up as friends and acquaintances made themselves known, curious to hear their news. The Feast concluded with a personal signed message from the Chancellor, Prince Philip:

'It has given me the greatest satisfaction to serve Cambridge as Chancellor and I cannot thank you enough for your help and guidance in those early days and for your continued friendship ever since.'[278]

As a tribute to Dame Rosemary, £90,000 was raised as a matching gift to a donation in aid of repairs to the Rosemary Murray Library. Prince Philip visited the College a week later to see the refurbishment, and Rosemary was there to welcome him, alongside the President, Anne Lonsdale, and the Visitor, Dame Bridget Ogilvie. An upright figure, with shining white hair and twinkling blue eyes, she had not changed substantially since they first met, thirty years earlier. She still had that 'knock-out charm'[279] that he commented on in an interview for the College.

The New Hall Society decided to honour Rosemary's 90th birthday with a party at Wheatley. July 28th was a lovely sunny day and quite a large contingent of alumnae and thirteen members of the Murray family enjoyed lunch in a marquee, ending with a cake decorated with the New Hall Dome in icing. Rosemary, with straight short haircut and wearing slacks did not look her age and chatted vigorously. She was willing to make a speech on condition that she could do it before the meal, an indication that public speaking was still an ordeal. She reminisced on her life as a series of unexpected events. It was clear that she had never had a career plan but had seized and exploited opportunities as they came along.

New Hall celebrated its fiftieth anniversary in 2004 with a number of

Rosemary enjoying the company of young people at her 90th birthday party.

events, but also with the inspired idea of naming a rose in honour of its first President. What turned out to be Rosemary's last public appearance was a visit to Chelsea Flower Show for the launch. The yellow floribunda was displayed on the stand of the growers, Harkness, and was also chosen to go in a posy presented to the Queen. In the huge marquee, filled with the colours and perfume of flowers, Rosemary made a short speech of thanks to the growers and the College and was presented with a basket of 'her' rose.

Although there was a commitment not to reveal the news, the College was the recipient of a major benefaction, on a scale that would transform its operations in the long term. Rosemary had been the third person to know, after the President and Bursar, who had conducted the negotiations with the donors[280]. For the moment it was confidential, known only to the Fellows and a few close advisors, but Rosemary had the opportunity to meet and thank the donor, alumna Rosalind Smith (Edwards), at the 2004 Benefactors' Feast, as they stood on the Walkway admiring a replacement mulberry tree Ros had just planted. Rosemary must have felt that her life's work was completed, because she had been looking for a benefactor to put New Hall on a firm footing since it was founded, with a bland name that could be changed to commemorate such a donor. There had been the abortive effort to become Colston College, when the gift from a Trust was challenged and disallowed, and the appeal linked to the Silver Jubilee, shortly before Rosemary's retirement, which had not brought in the hoped-for level of support. As a result, she had left the College with unfinished business, and had looked on with some dismay as it went into debt to pay for repairs to the buildings she had so carefully overseen. The proposed name, Murray Edwards College, incorporating her own, pleased her, although she was naturally modest about being included: 'there's no need for that'. Ros Smith, who had grown a business herself, understood how difficult it had been to found the college and felt strongly that 'Murray' should be enshrined in its name.

Rosemary was unable to attend the New Hall alumnae dinner on September 25th, one of the high points of the fiftieth anniversary celebrations, because she had suffered a sudden arrhythmia or acute heart failure, leaving her short of breath and unable to walk. She needed an operation to replace a heart valve, obviously a risky procedure at the age of 91. It was carefully explained to her that there was only a 50% chance that the operation would be successful. The consultants were somewhat reluctant to perform it, but Rosemary was determined and persuasive. She immediately decided to take the risk, rather than be highly incapacitated for the rest of her life. At first things went well. After the operation visitors to the John Radcliffe Hospital found her in good spirits, surrounded by cards and flowers. In fact her vicar tells how she cheered all around her.

> 'I had one of those wonderful afternoons when a visit to a sick parishioner in hospital cheers you up so much, that you come home feeling a hundred times better than when you went'[281], he blogged.

But two days later Rosemary seemed distant, although she remembered to ask Anne Lonsdale if all was well at New Hall. It was the onset of a stroke, and the next day she was completely unresponsive, and slipped peacefully away on October 7th. Meanwhile some of her first New Hall students had been celebrating at The Hermitage after the unveiling by Robin Hammond of a blue plaque to mark the College's opening in Silver Street. It was exactly fifty years since the first dinner in New Hall.

The simple funeral at Old Marston parish church, with contributions by the younger relatives, was as Rosemary would have wished. The reading from *Pilgrim's Progress* on Mr Valiant for Truth would have been very familiar to her, though she would not have thought of applying it to herself[282]. In Cambridge flags flew at half mast and obituaries were written, all struggling to contain in a small space the many achievements of this remarkable woman. Frances received heartfelt letters of condolence, summing up what Rosemary had meant to so many people – her students, academic colleagues, fellow committee members, Headmistresses, J.P.s and Wrens, neighbours, and those who had worked for her. She had changed the course of many lives by her encouragement and personal example. One correspondent wrote, 'what a wonderful number of people there are who knew and valued her, and so many who loved her too'[283].

Cambridge University held a Memorial Service the following November in Great St Mary's Church, at which the second woman Vice-Chancellor, Dame Alison Richard, led the eulogies[284], saying that Rosemary 'understood Cambridge to the core' and 'carried people with her almost without their noticing how far they had come'. Former President Anne Lonsdale remarked that unlike some female leaders, Rosemary was always keen to mentor others and to pass on advice, so sincerely felt that it could never be resented. Kate Pretty added that she had observed Rosemary's passionate attention to detail and instinctive good judgement when managing College admissions. Following the service, the bell ringers rang a special peal in appreciation, noting that she had been the only Vice-Chancellor to visit their ringing chamber in the twentieth century. It was small acts like these that endeared Rosemary to people.

Rosemary was one of the great figures of post-war Cambridge, remarkable even by comparison with other Vice-Chancellors. She devoted nearly thirty years of her life to New Hall while maintaining a wider perspective by participating in numerous external bodies, mostly furthering the cause of education, especially of girls and women. Avoiding confrontation, she quietly worked to improve the position of women in society, slowly but surely. Her sustained effort to launch the college is quite unparalleled in the history of Cambridge University. As a result, thousands of women, of many different nationalities, have benefitted from a Cambridge education and have been enabled to give something back to their communities. New Hall is Rosemary's greatest memorial, and it is fitting that it now bears her name.

Rosemary with Anne Lonsdale, President (centre) and a group of alumnae of New Hall in Fountain Court.

– Endnotes –

Chapter 1: The Admiral's daughter

1. Pevsner, Nikolaus. The buildings of England: Cambridgeshire (2nd ed.) Harmondsworth, Penguin, 1970. p.202.
2. The principal duty of the two Esquire Bedells is ceremonial. They attend the Chancellor and Vice-Chancellor on public occasions, including Congregations and University Sermons.
3. Thus I give my word.
4. Women won the right to take degrees at Oxford University in 1920. In Cambridge it took until 1947.
5. Dame Myra Curtis had the distinction of being the first woman member of the Council of the Senate.
6. Ancient heroic Welsh tales first written down in the Middle Ages.
7. ARM Manuscript notes for a speech at Oswestry school, June 1974. NHPP 1/11/6/5.
8. Warden Spooner's Diary. Manuscript in New College Oxford Archive. PA/SPO1/2. Courtesy of the Warden and Fellows of New College.
9. Luke, Chapter 12, v.48.
10. Warden Spooner's Diary. William Spooner's description of his wife in 1881.
11. Canon Milford. Ruth Spooner: memorial oration. [1976]. NHPP 1/11/1/6.
12. Inge, Ralph. Diary of a Dean. London, Hutchinson, 1949. p.97.
13. Warden Spooner's Diary, December 23rd 1924.
14. In Arthur and Ellen's household the servants were treated liberally and the family worked alongside them in kitchen and garden. One dinner guest remarked, 'I was rather surprised at the familiar way Captain Murray was speaking to his parlourmaid', and then discovered that the other waitress, dressed in cap and apron, was his daughter Rosemary. (Quoted in Ruth Spooner's memories, p.27). There were several old retainers, and the children's Nanny, who left in 1929, was invited back to the family home in Cadlington during the War.
15. Warden Spooner's Diary, January 15th 1925.
16. Photocopy of one manuscript sheet of the play with cast list. NHAR 1/1/2/10.

Chapter 2: Early life and schooldays

17. Frances Spooner to ARM, [July 1934]
18. Catharine Spooner to Ellen Murray, June 21st [1915]
19. Frances Spooner ? to Ellen Murray, signed 'Fid', [June 21st 1915]
20. Ruth Spooner to Ellen Murray, 20.5.[1915]
21. Catharine Dodgson to Ellen Murray, [Undated]
22. Edward Roberts, Bishop of Ely to ARM, 1977. NHPP 1/11/4/15.
23. Mrs W.W. Campbell, quoted in Hayter, William. Spooner: a biography. London, W.H.Allen, 1977. p. 113.
24. The Maxwell Spooners, with their daughter Ruth, returned to Oxford in 1921, and great-grandmother Ellen King (Goodwin) spent her final years there with her unmarried daughter Mary, dying in 1926.

25. 'Aunt Cath' was the eldest daughter of Warden William Spooner.
26. DNB. Dodgson, (Frances) Catharine (1883-1954).
27. Quotations from Rosemary's school reports from Havant Preparatory School. Private collection.
28. Rosemary continued to read the historical novels of G.A.Henty as an adult. She had fourteen in her collection.
29. Quoted in Ridler, Anne. Olive Willis and Downe House. p. 101.
30. ARM to parents, 29.1.27.
31. Olive Willis to ARM's parents, 3.2.27.
32. Arthur Murray to ARM, 3.7.31.
33. Diana ? Hambro to ARM, 8.2.31.
34. Mary ? to ARM. 5.2.29.
35. Quotations from ARM's school reports from Downe House School. Private collection.
36. Dame Rosemary's 90th Birthday speech. *New Hall Review*, Winter 2003, p.2.

Chapter 3: Launching out: Neuchâtel and Oxford

37. The Seniors at Downe were the equivalent of prefects. There was no Head Girl.
38. Slang for interview or conversation.
39. Arthur Murray to ARM, May 1931.
40. Britain's industrial future: being the report of the Liberal Industrial Enquiry. [London], E.Benn Ltd., 1928.
41. Sir Harry Verney to ARM, 8.5.39.
42. Rosemary kept a separate journal of the six-month stay, and made a summary in another notebook, including a list of the numerous letters and postcards she wrote.
43. Report of the Royal Commission on Oxford and Cambridge Universities, March 1922. The commissioners left the question of women's status to the universities, but preferred that Cambridge should remain predominantly male.
44. Arthur Murray to ARM, 6.10.32.
45. William Spooner describes how he took a 'more or less leading part' in the Committee formed to oppose the admission of women to degrees in 1895. Warden Spooner's Diary. Manuscript in New College Oxford Archive. PA/SPO1/2.
46. Rules of LMH. Printed sheet. NHPP 1/11/3/2/ (File 2).
47. Gardner, A.D. Jean Orr-Ewing: obituary. *Journal of Pathology and Bacteriology*, Vol.58, Issue 1, 1946, p.149.

Chapter 4: Student days

48. Letter from ARM to Joyce ? 4.8.[1935].
49. ARM to Nancy Newman's daughter, Mo Laidlaw, 1991. Communicated by Anne Lonsdale.
50. Frances Spooner to Ellen Murray, [January 1936].
51. ARM to parents, 16.5.36.
52. Diary, 16.5.36.
53. Rosemary's diary makes clear that she was admitted because other members of her family were in the choir, not for her singing ability.

54. Ann Murray to parents, 29.12.36.
55. Testimonial from T.W.J.Taylor. Typescript. NHPP 1/11/3/2 (File 2).
56. NHPP 1/11/3/2 (File 1).
57. ARM's Lapland journal. Manuscript in private collection.

Chapter 5: Royal Holloway College and Sheffield University: the outbreak of war

58. Ruth Spooner's memories. Typescript. Autobiographical account of the life of Ruth Spooner. NHPP 1/11/1/6.
59. ARM to Rosemary Spooner, 2.10.38.
60. T.W.J.Taylor to ARM, 22.10.38. After the War he became the first Principal of the University of the West Indies and was knighted.
61. Murray slang for expedition.
62. T.W.J.Taylor to ARM, 3.5.39.
63. John had left Winchester a year early to take up fast track entry to the Navy.
64. Diana Hoare married David Murray in 1960.
65. Horace Barlow, son of New Hall's benefactor, Nora Barlow, interviewed by AMW, 5.5.2005. Oral history collection. NHPH 10/1/24.
66. Ann Murray to ARM, 18th May [?1943].
67. Oxford Letter section in *Brown Book*, LMH, 1940.
68. Ellen Murray to ARM. Undated.
69. ARM to Ellen Murray, 28.3.41.
70. Rosemary Spooner to ARM, 20.5.41.
71. Prof. Moore to ARM, 14.6.41. NHPP 1/11/3/2 (File 1).
72. Arthur Murray to ARM, 25.1.42.
73. Frances Murray to ARM. Undated.
74. Quoted in a letter from T.W.J.Taylor to ARM, 12.8.42: "Your phrase, subordination to stupidity, is apt. You won't escape all this self-seeking self-advertisement & narrow outlook even I imagine, in the WRNS". NHPP 1/11/3/2 (File 2).
75. ARM to Ellen Murray. Undated.
76 Arthur Murray to ARM, 2.5.42.

Chapter 6: Life in the WRNS

77. Laughton Mathews, V. Blue tapestry. p.191.
78. ARM's OTC notes. 2 notebooks. NHPP 1/11/7/1.
79. Profile by Joan Bakewell: Dame Rosemary Murray. *Illustrated London News*, June 1978, p.36.
80. Poem by S.Hassan, 1943. Typescript. NHPP 1/11/3/3.
81. 'Over paid, over-sexed and over here', as the popular slogan had it.
82. ARM to parents, 4.1.[1944].
83. ARM to Ellen Murray, 27.1.[1944].
84. ARM to Ellen Murray, 9.6.[1944].
85. Typescript dated 25.7.44. NHPP 1/11/3/2 (File 4).
86. ARM to Ann Murray, 4.1.[1946].
87. Notebook in private collection.

88. Mimi Josephson. Miss Murray, Principal of Cambridge's new college for women. *Homes and Gardens*, February 1955.
89 Laughton Mathews, V. Typescript reference for ARM, May 1946. NHPP 1/11/3/2 (File 4).
90 Laughton Mathews, V. quoted in Ursula Stuart Mason. The Wrens, 1917-77, p.119.

Chapter 7: The Girton years

91. Sir Robert Robinson again directed the course of ARM's career. Alex Todd, who had been an outstanding research student at the Dyson Perrins Laboratory, 1931-34, had asked his advice.
92. Rosemary may well have proposed him for the Honorary Degree he received from Cambridge University in 1979.
93. ARM to Ellen Murray. Undated [1946].
94. Letter of appointment to Girton, 3.6.46. Typescript. NHPP 1/11/3/2 (File 1).
95. Song by M.C.Bradbrook to the tune of 'Annie Laurie'. *Girton Review* No.142, Lent 1950, p.11. GCCP 2/1/4.
96. Cavalieri's 'Rappresentazione di anima e di corpo', translated and directed by Prof. Dent (1949) and Monteverdi's 'Orfeo' (1950).
97. Janet Harker interviewed by Kate Perry. Girton College, Cambridge archive. GCOH 2/3/22/5.
98. ARM to Ellen Murray. Undated, [January 1947].
99. Reprinted in ARM. New Hall, 1954-72. Appendix 1, p.47.
100. Marjorie Hollond.
101. Janet Harker interviewed by Kate Perry. Girton College, Cambridge archive. GCOH 2/3/22/5.
102. Note from Girton College Tutors' Office, 19.11.53. NHPP 1/11/3/2 (File 2).
103. Maureen Huse to ARM, 11.12.94. NHPP 1/11/3/1.
104. Anonymous rhyme, 19.11.53. NHPP 1/11/3/2 (File 2).
105. John Martin, Chemistry student 1950-1., in conversation with AMW.
106. *Journal of Chemistry*, August 1951, pp.1945-1950.
107. *Journal of Chemistry*, July 1951, pp. 1888-1890.

Chapter 8: The Third Foundation for Women

108. Greta Burkill's papers. NHAR 1/1/1/4/5.
109. Parsons, E.W. 'Notes concerning a possible third women's college'. Quoted in ARM. New Hall, 1954-1972, Appendix 3, p.49.
110. Report of the Council of the Senate. *The Reporter* 11.6.1952, p.1395.
111. The 'crisp and decisive chairmanship' of Boys Smith is mentioned in Linehan, P. St John's College, 2011, p.604.
112. Papers on Name of the Foundation. NHAR 1/1/1/4/2.
113. Dame Rosemary's 90th Birthday speech. *New Hall Review*, Winter 2003, pp.2-3.
114. *The Guardian*, 16.12.1953.
115. Packet of letters labelled by ARM 'Letters of congratulation on appmt as Tutor'. Private collection.

116. Reference from M.G.Lloyd Thomas. Typescript dated 26.4.1946.
117. Reference from K.T.Butler. Typescript dated 25.5.1949.
118. ARM to Robin Hammond. Undated [1954]. NHPP 1/14.
119. Anon. poem. Manuscript. NHPP 1/11/4/0.
120. Editorial by H.I.McMorran. *Girton Review* No.156, Michaelmas 1954, p.1. GCCP 2/1/4.
121. From 'Hail the Day' (an anonymous poem on ARM's appointment as Tutor-in-Charge of New Hall). Manuscript. NHPP 1/11/4/0.
122. Rosemary took morning prayers in college once a week for a few years. Students were also made welcome in Queens' College Chapel.
123. ARM. New Hall, 1954-1972. p.16.

Chapter 9: New Hall: early days as a Limited Company

124. The Darwins lived in Newnham Grange, celebrated in 'House by the river' by Margaret Keynes and 'Period Piece' by Gwen Raverat, both daughters of George and Maud Darwin. They also owned the Old Granary in the garden, which was later rented to New Hall.
125. Jenny Moody (Stanesby, NH 1954) in conversation with AMW.
126. *The Guardian*, 18.12.53.
127. *Times Educational Supplement*, 24.9.1954.
128. *Cambridge Daily News*, 6.10.1954.
129. In October 1961 three New Hall students staged a protest in the Cambridge Union. A month later one of them, Jenny Daiches, became the first female undergraduate to speak at a debate there, but a motion to admit women as members was unsuccessful.
130. RH in conversation with AMW.
131. Typescript of obituary by Pat Houghton (Slawson, NH 1955). NHRF 1/5/26.
132. RH to ARM 1.7.56.
133. This sum included fixed assets. NHAR 1/1/1/5.
134. Ellen Murray to ARM. Undated, [1955].
135. New Hall lives, p.35.
136. *The Times*, 16.10.54 and *Times Educational Supplement*, 22.10.54.
137. ARM. Manuscript notes. NHPP 1/11/6/5.
138. New Hall lives, p.121.
139. *The Guardian*, 2.11.1955.
140. New Hall lives, p.121.
141. *Cambridge Review*, 6.2.60
142. Alice Bacon to ARM. Undated.
143. New Hall lives, p.212. "I took my harp to a party" was a song performed by Gracie Fields.
144. *Cambridge Review* LXXVII, 1955. p.7.
145. Lewsey, Fred. Concrete Cambridge. *CAM Magazine*, 67, Michaelmas 2012, p.32, quoting Dr Marco Iuliano.
146. 'Arabia in concrete', was a headline in the *Financial Times*, 8.6.65.
147. RH to ARM, 27.10.62.
148. RH to ARM, Ibid.

149. ARM to RH, 3.11.62.
150. ARM to RH, 11.11.62.
151. RH to ARM, 7.11.62. Private collection.
152. W.W.Spooner to ARM, 6.11.60. NHPP 1/11/3/2 (File 2). He always signed himself 'Your affectionate uncle'.
153. Mrs Teichman stored it, but it has seldom been exhibited.
154. Gill Emberson, (NH 1962), to Frances Crombie, 9.10.04.
155. New Hall lives. Jenny Bacon, p.210.

Chapter 10: New Hall: from Approved Foundation to College

156. See Sica, A. and Wilson, A.M. The Murray Edwards Duse Collection, Milano, Mimesis, 2012.
157. Since 1998 known as the Girls' Day School Trust (GDST).
158. New University of Ulster. Addresses. Congregation... 6th July and 7th July 1972 NHPP 1/11/2/6.
159. Reply by ARM on behalf of the Honorary Graduates. Ibid.
160. AFPRB papers. NHPP 1/11/7/6-9.
161. John and Lilias spent their retirement in Cambridge in a house close to Rosemary's flat.
162. ARM in conversation with AMW.
163. Now in the New Hall Art Collection.
164. ARM to Helen McMorran. Undated manuscript. Private collection.
165. According to a later notebook, "Valentine for HM written with Robin". NHPP 1/11/1/10.
166. Helen McMorran to ARM. Manuscript preserved among ARM's letters. Private collection.
167. Now in the Girton Art Collection, hanging outside the Library.
168. Manuscript. NHPP 1/11/4/3.
169. Now Anglia Ruskin University.
170. ARM to Rosemary Spooner, Florence, 18.8.67.
171. King's College, Cambridge. Report on the Admission of Women, May 1969. Typescript. NHAR 1/1/1/16/1.
172. ARM Typescript marked confidential. 'Admission of women', February 1974. NHAR 1/1/1/16/2.
173. ARM. New Hall, 1954-1972. p.44.
174. Ibid. Plate XVII.
175. G. Kitson Clark to ARM, 7.1.74. '...colleges like Trinity and King's may get the cream of the women coming to Cambridge (but I am not certain of that), and certainly they may compete far too effectively for the exiguous number of women who manage to get senior posts in the University.' NHAR 1/1/1/16/2.
176. ARM to G. Kitson Clark, Dec. 1971. NHAR 1/1/1/11/1.
177. The design featured a friendly dolphin, an embattled border, referring to New Hall's location on Castle Hill and three 'mullets' or stars from the Murray crest. These stars are all the more relevant since the renaming of the College.
178. ARM. Papers concerning the winding up of the guarantee company. NHAR 1/1/1/11/1.

Chapter 11: University responsibilites

179. Eric Ashby to ARM, 17.10.68. NHPP 1/11/7/16.
180. The second one was New Hall Fellow Mrs Jenny Teichman.
181. Nevertheless the Cambridge men had a saying: 'Girton won't, Newnham might, New Hall will'.
182. Patricia Rogers (NH 1965) in conversation with AMW.
183. Robin Hammond, who retired, and Helen Clover, who died in a car accident in 1974.
184. Profile by Joan Bakewell: Dame Rosemary Murray. *Illustrated London News*, June 1978, p.36.
185. VC's speech. *The Reporter* 1.10.71, p.154.
186. Professor Owen Chadwick informed me that the Council wanted Rosemary as VC two years earlier, but it was too complicated to alter the rules.
187. ARM interviewed on BBC 'Woman's Hour'. 2.5.2001.
188. I pronounce Dr Murray, elected by you, Vice-Chancellor of this University for the coming year.
189. Packet labelled by ARM 'Letters re V/C + list' in private collection.
190. 'Gyp' is a name once given to college servants, in this case a cleaner.
191. Ellen Murray to ARM, undated [1973].
192. NH assistant staff to ARM, 31.5.73. Typescript signed by twelve of the staff. Private collection.
193. Charles Crawley to ARM, 24.5.73.
194. Muriel Bradbrook to ARM, 22.10.75. NHPP 1/11/4/0.
195. ARM to the Registrar, A.M.Currie, 28.7.77. Typescript. NHPP 1/11/2/7.
196. In 1973 she was specifically made VC's Deputy as Chair of the Institute of Education and in January 1975 Chair of the Appointments Committees for the Faculty of Clinical Medicine and the Department of Clinical Veterinary Medicine.
197. Peter Avery in conversation with T.G.B.Wilson.
198. Report of the High Steward. *The Reporter* 14.2.73. Special No.12.
199. Fred Dainton had gained a 1st in Chemistry at Oxford in 1937, overlapping with Rosemary at the Dyson Perrins Laboratory. He received an Honorary Degree from Cambridge University in 1979.
200. Council of the Senate. Minutes, 4.3.74.
201. ARM. Typescript marked confidential. 'Admission of women', February 1974. NHAR 1/1/1/16/2.
202. ARM to R.D. Gray, Fellow of Emmanuel College. NHAR 1/1/1/16/1.
203. NH Publicity Committee. Paper for discussion on the effect of co-residence on admissions. Typescript. Paper A for NH Council, 23.6.75. NHAR 1/1/1/16/3.
204. Teichman, Jenny. Typescript, 16.6.75. NHAR 1/1/1/16/3.
205. ARM. Paper D for NH Council, 23.6.75, on 'Long term alternatives'. NHAR 1/1/1/16/3.
206. Paper B for NH Council, 17.11.75 on' Future Policy of the College'. NHAR 1/1/1/16/3.
207. Prof.N.N.Greenwood presenting ARM. University of Leeds, 8.5.1975. NHPP 1/11/2/7.
208. Honorary degree citations. *Pennsylvania Gazette*, June 1975, p.17. NHPP 1/11/6/4.
209. Vice-Chancellor's address. *Reporter* 8.10.75, p.105.

210. The Dome Room began as a reading room of the original University Library. It is still the Vice-Chancellor's office today.
211. Cambridge was, even then, unusual amongst British universities in declining to provide its Vice-Chancellor with an official car.
212. New Hall Council minutes 24.6.1974. NHGB 3.
213. Elizabeth Rawson to Valerie Pearl, 6.3.88. NHPP 1/11/1/17.

Chapter 12: Vice-Chancellor

214. Prince Philip to ARM. Undated typescript, signed. Congratulatory letter read at the Feast commemorating ARM's 90th birthday. NHPP 1/11/1/12.
215. Prince Philip. Resignation speech as Chancellor of the University in Peter Richards' article , Prince of learning. http://www.alumni.cam.ac.uk/uploads/File/CAMArticles/CAM%2051/profile.pdf. A variant on this was his description of Rosemary as a cross between Al Capone and Mother Theresa.
216. Prince Philip to ARM, 3.12.75. NHPP 1/11/4/12.
217. Alan Clark. Programme for installation of the Chancellor. Typescript. NHAR 1/1/1/18/4.
218. ARM Typescript of speech. NHAR 1/1/1/18/3. The lunch menu was replicated 30 years on when Prince Philip retired as Chancellor.
219. Rosemary introduced more women into the Honorary Degree lists: Simone Weil and Elizabeth Schwarzkopf were two of her suggestions for nomination.
220. Lord Rupert Nevill to ARM, 14.6.77. NHPP 1/11/4/13.
221. VC's Address. *Reporter* 1.10.76, p.40.
222. ARM. Speech at Robinson College anniversary, 11.7.01. NHPP 1/11/3/3.
223. Ibid.
224. Homerton grew out of a dissenting academy in London, re-founded in 1850 for the training of men and women teachers. It became women-only after its move to Cambridge.
225. Homerton had a raft of other responsibilities and was part-funded by the DES for educating nurses.
226. Report on the recognition of Homerton as an Approved Society. *Reporter*, 6.10.76, p.14. Approval took effect from 1.9.77, *Reporter*, 20.7.77, p.934.
227. VC's Address. *Reporter*, 6.10.1976, p.42.
228. In Oxford the VC was not necessarily a Head of House, and if he were, could not hold another major appointment. However it was not until 1989 that Oxford elected a non-Head of House. See Harrison, B. ed. The history of the University of Oxford, 1994.
229. ARM. Notes for speech to Council of the Senate. Manuscript. NHPP 1/11/4/11.
230. ARM to the Vice-Chancellor of Victoria University, 2.3.76. NHPP 1/11/5/5.
231. University of Southern California oration. NHPP 1/11/2/6.
232. Oxford Encaenia oration. NHPP 1/11/2/8.
233. It was a great moment when she first conferred degrees on the New Hall women, although the Praelector, Elizabeth Rawson, cringed as Rosemary, in shaky Latin, admitted them in the name of the Father and the *Daughter* and the Holy Ghost.
234. Tom Howarth in Times Educational Supplement, 30.1.76.
235. Mencap partitioned the house into 52 rooms and owned it for 30 years, but it has since been divided into three luxury homes, with others adapted or built in the grounds.

236. VC's address. *Reporter*, 5.10.1977, p.33.
237. *Cambridge Evening News*, 7.1.2003.
238. Reply by ARM on behalf of the Honorary Graduates. New University of Ulster, 7.7.72.
239. Ian Nicol to ARM, 21.7.94. NHPP 1/11/3/1.
240. A.W.F.Edwards in the *Oxford Magazine*, Michaelmas 2008.
241. Ian Nicol interviewed by AMW. NH Oral history collection. NHPH 10/1/16.
242. Prince Philip in the film *New Hall: 50 years*, presented by Claudia Winkleman, produced by AMW. NHPH 10/1/21.
243. Elizabeth Rawson to Valerie Pearl, 6.3.1988.
244. Letters of congratulation. NHPP 1/11/1/17.
245. VC's address. *Reporter*, 2.10.78.
246. Ruth Spooner to Beatrice Hilton, 30.3.[1977]. NHPP 1/11/1/17.

Chapter 13: *The final years at New Hall*

247. Nora Barlow to ARM, 19.6.77. NHPP 1/11/1/17.
248. Brian Payne to AMW, 13.10.2004.
249. Similar to a non-executive director, but not allowed to hold shares in the company.
250. *The Times*. 25.4.1984 and 1.5.1984.
251. Jenkins, P. Unravelling the mystery, p.38.
252. Zara Steiner to ARM, undated. NHPP 1/11/3/1.
253. Gordon Williams, President, American Friends of Cambridge University, to Trevor Gardner, 8.12.80. NHPP 1/11/4/14.
254. Jubilee appeal. Printed sheet. NHAS 4/3/3.
255. Reprinted in New Hall lives, p.8.
256. Trevor Thomas to ARM, 5.10.80. NHPP 1/11/4/16.
257. Jubilee appeal. Printed sheet. NHAS 4/3/3.
258. In *The Cambridge Evening News*, Jon Hibbs reported, 'Nowhere else in Cambridge is one college so closely identified with one of its members'. 29.9.81.
259. Prince Philip. Interview for the film *New Hall: 50 years*, presented by Claudia Winkleman, produced by AMW. NHPH 10/1/21
260. Zara Steiner interviewed by AMW, 28.2.2004. Oral history collection. NHPH 10/1/16.
261. Kate Pretty. Eulogy at ARM's Memorial Service, printed in *New Hall Society Review* 2004, p.66.
262. Anne Lonsdale recalled: 'she taught me how to pick up subtleties from a reading of The Reporter which I would not have believed possible'. Eulogy at ARM's Memorial Service, printed in *New Hall Society Review* 2004, p.63.

Chapter 14: *Retirement*

263. Rosemary gave numerous talks, notably a series of three lectures at Bedford College London in 1982 on Women and Education, Equal Opportunities in Higher Education and Universities in Great Britain.

264. Peter Proby to ARM, 8.10.81. NHPP 1/11/3/3.
265. Oration at Cambridge Honorary Degree Ceremony, 1988. NHPP 1/11/2/9.
266. Papers concerning ARM's visit to India in NHPP 1/11/5/6 and Notebook in private collection.
267. Communication from Clare Crombie.
268. As David's health deteriorated, it became clear that he could no longer live alone. Rosemary invited him to stay and supervised his medical treatment closely, keeping notes and accompanying him to hospital appointments. He was with her for eighteen months until he died in 1998.
269. Revd John Sweet to ARM, October 1994. NHPP 1/11/3/5.
270. ARM was a member of the Prayer Book Society.
271. Revd Tony Price's blog, 'rosemary', 9.10.2004. http://www.godspell.org.uk/archives/2004_10_01_archive.html
272. ARM reported in *Cambridge Evening News*, 7.1.2003.
273. 'Sisters in Learning' in *CAM Magazine*, *40*, Michaelmas 2003, pp.6-7.
274. Communication from Marion Crombie.
275. Sgt. Ian Mackay of 2 Para.
276. As usual, Rosemary kept a journal of the trip, now in private hands.
277. Letter of condolence from Elizabeth Johnston to Frances Crombie. [2004].
278. Prince Philip to ARM. Undated typescript. Congratulatory letter read at the Feast commemorating ARM's 90th birthday. NHPP 1/11/1/12.
279. Prince Philip. Interview for the film *New Hall: 50 years*, presented by Claudia Winkleman. NHPH 10/1/20.
280. Rosalind (Smith) and Steve Edwards gave the College £30 million.
281. Revd Tony Price's blog, 2.9. 2004, 'Hospital tonic'. http://www.godspell.org.uk/archives/2004_09_01_archive.html
282. Bunyan, J. Pilgrim's progress. 'Then said he, I am going to my Father's; and though with great difficulty I have got hither, yet now I do not repent me of all the trouble I have been at to arrive where I am.'
283. Dr Judith Shakespeare, who had admitted Rosemary to hospital, to Frances Crombie. [2004].
284. The eulogies are reprinted in *New Hall Society Review*, 2004, p.62.

– Abbreviations –

AFCU	American Friends of Cambridge University
AFPRB	Armed Forces Pay Review Board
AMW	Alison Wilson
ARM	Alice Rosemary Murray
ARP	Air Raid Precautions
BFUW	British Federation of University Women
CSU	Cambridge Students' Union
CVCP	Committee of Vice-Chancellors and Principals
DES	Department of Education and Science
DNB	Dictionary of National Biography
EMM	Ellen Maxwell Murray
GPDST	Girls Public Day School Trust, later GDST
ICFU	International Council on the Future of the University
LMH	Lady Margaret Hall
MEC	Murray Edwards College
NAG	Nursery Action Group
NH	New Hall
NIAE	National Institute of Adult Education, later NIACE
NUWT	National Union of Women Teachers
OTC	Officer Training Corps
RH	Robin Hammond
UGC	University Grants Committee
VC	Vice-Chancellor
WEA	Workers' Educational Association
WRNS	Women's Royal Naval Service

– Bibliography –

Manuscripts

Collection of letters and photograph albums. Courtesy of the Crombie family.
Selection of ARM's diaries, 1921-95. Courtesy of the Crombie family.
Collection of papers sorted by ARM in New Hall Archive. Courtesy of the President and Fellows of Murray Edwards College.
Further papers and photographs filed in New Hall Archive. Catalogue on the Cambridge University Library Janus website, http://janus.lib.cam.ac.uk/. Courtesy of the President and Fellows of Murray Edwards College.
Papers and photographs in Girton College Archive. Courtesy of the Mistress and Fellows of Girton College, Cambridge.
Spooner, Archibald William. Warden Spooner's diary. Courtesy of the Warden and Fellows of New College, Oxford.

Books

Batson, Judy G. Her Oxford. Vanderbilt University Press, ?2009

Bertram, Kate. Lucy Cavendish College, Cambridge: a history of the early years. Cambridge, Lucy Cavendish College, 1989

Bradbrook, Muriel. That infidel place: a short history of Girton College, 1869-1969. London, Chatto & Windus, 1969

Brooke Christopher N.L. A history of the University of Cambridge. Vol IV, 1870-1990. Cambridge, C.U.P., 1993

Bruley, Sue. Women in Britain since 1900. (Social history in perspective) Basingstoke, Palgrave Macmillan, 1999

Carter, G.B. Porton Down: 75 years of chemical and biological research. London, H.M.S.O., 1992. Extract entitled Porton Down: a brief history at https://www.gov.uk/porton-down

Collett, D. Women in uniform. London, S.Low, Marston, [1946]

Dyhouse, Carol. No distinction of sex: women in British universities 1870-1939. London, UCL Press, 1995

Fletcher, Marjorie H. The WRNS. London, Batsford, 1989

Garfield, Simon. Our hidden lives. London, Ebury Press, 2004

Garfield, Simon. We are at war. London, Ebury Press, 2005

Girton College, Cambridge. Girton College Register, Vol.2, 1944-69. Cambridge, Girton College, 1991

Harrison, Brian, ed. The history of the University of Oxford. Vol VIII, The twentieth century. Oxford, Clarendon Press, 1994

Harwood, Elain. Chamberlin, Powell and Bon. London, R.I.B.A., c.2011

Hayter, William. Spooner: a biography. London, W.H.Allen,1977

Horn, Pamela. Women in the 1920s. Alan Sutton, 1995

Howse, Derek. Radar at sea: the Royal Navy in World War 2. Basingstoke, Macmillan, 1993

Hunt, Felicity. Women at Cambridge: a brief history. Cambridge, Press & Publications Office, 1998

Inge, Ralph. Diary of a Dean: St Paul's, 1911-1934. London, New York, Hutchinson, [1949]

Jenkins, Peter. Unravelling the mystery: the Goldsmiths' Company in the twentieth century. London, Goldsmiths' Company, 2000

Johnson, Audrey. Do march in step girls. Sandford, Audrey Morley, 1997

Keynes, Margaret Elizabeth. House by the river: Newnham Grange to Darwin College. Cambridge, Privately printed, 1954

Laughton Mathews, Vera. Blue tapestry. London, Hollis & Carter, 1948

Linehan, Peter, ed. St John's College Cambridge: a history. Woodbridge, Boydell Press, 2011

Martin, Ged. Hughes Hall Cambridge, 1885-2010. London, Third Millennium, 2011

Mason, Ursula Stuart. The Wrens, 1917-77: a history... Reading, Educational Explorers, 1977

Mason, Ursula Stuart. Britannia's daughters: the story of the WRNS. London, Leo Cooper, 1992

Murray, Rosemary. New Hall 1954-1972: the making of a college. Cambridge, New Hall, 1980

Postgate, Caroline et al., ed. New Hall lives: the Silver Street years. Cambridge, New Hall Society, 2005

Raverat, Gwen. Period piece: a Cambridge childhood. London, Faber & Faber, 1952

Ridler, Ann. Olive Willis and Downe House: an adventure in education. London, John Murray, 1967

Robinson, Jane. Bluestockings : the remarkable story of the first women to fight for an education. London, Viking, 2009

Spooner, Ruth. Ruth Spooner's memories. Privately published (typescript)

Thomas, Lesley. WRNS in camera. Stroud, Sutton, 2002

Tullberg, Rita McWilliams. Women at Cambridge. 2nd ed. Cambridge University Press, 1998

Turner, Mary. The women's century ... 1900-2000. Rev.ed. Richmond, The National Archives, 2003

Walton, Karen Doyle. Against the tide. Bloomington, Ind., Phi Delta Kappa Educational Foundation, 1996

Williams, Robert Joseph Paton, et al. Chemistry at Oxford: A History from 1600 to 2005. London, Royal Society of Chemistry, 2009

Wilson, James. Rose Castle: the residential seat of the Bishop of Carlisle. Carlisle, Charles Thurnam and Sons, 1912

Zweiniger-Bargielowska, Ina, ed. Women in twentieth-century Britain. Harlow, Longman, 2001

Periodicals, Websites, Film

BBC WW2 People's War. Wartime reminiscence website http://www.bbc.co.uk/history/ww2peopleswar/categories/
Cambridge Daily News (to 1962)
Cambridge News 1962-9 (continued as Cambridge Evening News)
Cambridge Review, 1955 and 1960
Cambridge University Reporter, 1946-2004
Council of the Senate, University of Cambridge. Minutes, 1972-80
Dictionary of National Biography. OUP, 2004 http://www.oxforddnb.com/
The Dolphin, 1990-2001 publ. Friends of New Hall and 2002- NH/MEC Development Office
Girton Review, 1946-54

Lady Margaret Hall, Oxford. Annual Reports, 1931-35, 1936-40.
Lady Margaret Hall, Oxford. Brown Books, 1931-33, 1934-36, 1937-39
Lady Margaret Hall, Oxford. White Register
New Hall Oral History collection. A collection of filmed interviews in the New Hall Archive
New Hall Report, New Hall Society, 1967-95
New Hall Review, New Hall Society, 1996-
Price, Revd Tony. Blog, 2004.
　　http://www.godspell.org.uk/archives/2004_10_01_archive.html
The Times Archive. http://www.thetimes.co.uk/tto/archive/
Todd, Alexander Robertus. Lord Todd interviewed by Prof. Louis Wolpert (Interviews with Nobel Prize Winning Scientists) recorded 1985. www.bbc.co.uk/archive/scientists/10601.shtml

Articles

Anon. Jills of all trades on top of the hill. THES, 12.12.80
Anon. Dame Rosemary Murray: scientist who went on to found New Hall… *Daily Telegraph*, 8.10.2004
Avent, Catherine. Dame Rosemary Murray, DBE, DL. LMH Brown Book, April 2005, p.76
Bakewell, Joan. Dame Rosemary Murray. *Illustrated London News*, June 1978, p.36
Connell, Brian. Dr Rosemary Murray: the admiral's daughter takes over. *The Times*, 6.12.76
Downe House. Dame Rosemary Murray:1913-2004. *DHSA Magazine*, 2005
Edwards, A.W.F. Notes from Cambridge. *Oxford Magazine*, Noughth week, Michaelmas Term, 2008
Hammond, Robin. Old New Hall. *New Hall Report*, 1979
Harker, Janet. Transcript of a recorded interview with Kate Perry. Girton College Archive. GCOH 2/3/22/5.
Holgate, Beth. A great Dame. *Stop Press with Varsity*, 13.6.81
Houghton, Pat. Obituary of Robin Hammond (typescript)
Houghton, Pat. Robin Hammond, dynamic lecturer who helped to establish a new women's college at Cambridge. [Shortened version of obituary] *The Times*, 16.3.2011
Jones, John, et al. The Dyson Perrins Laboratory and Oxford Organic Chemistry 1916-2004. Oxford, J.Jones, 2008
Josephson, Mimi. Miss Murray, Principal of Cambridge's new college for women. *Homes and Gardens*, February, 1955
Knowles, Jeremy. The Dyson Perrins Laboratory at Oxford. *Organic and Biomolecular Chemistry*, 2003,1, p. 3625
　　http://www.chem.ox.ac.uk/history/DP-History/index.html
Lewsey, Fred. Concrete Cambridge. *CAM Magazine*, 67, Michaelmas 2012, p.32

May, Alex. Murray, Dame (Alice) Rosemary (1913-2004). Oxford Dictionary of National Biography, O.U.P., 2008

Murray, (Alice) Rosemary. Dame Rosemary Murray - what else? [ARM's 80th birthday speech] *New Hall Review*, 1993

Murray, (Alice) Rosemary. Dame Rosemary's 90th birthday speech., 28.7.2003. *The Dolphin*, Winter 2003, Issue 26, p.2

Murray, (Alice) Rosemary. The first year of New Hall, *Cambridge Review*, Vol.77, October 1955, p.7

Murray, (Alice) Rosemary. Opening of the Elizabeth Rawson reading area. *The Dolphin*, 1996

Murray, (Alice) Rosemary. The Third Foundation for women in Cambridge, *Girton Review*, Lent, 1954, p.3-4

New Hall. Refoundation: New Hall becomes Murray Edwards College. New Hall, [2008]

Phillips, Lucy. Dame Rosemary Murray: first female V-C. *Varsity*, 15.10.2004

Sinker, Philip. The Esquire Bedells. *Cambridge*, No.8, 1981, p.60

Soames, Strahan. New Hall expands. *The Guardian*, 6.2.57

Tullberg, Rita McWilliams. (Mary) Lynda Dorothea Grier (1880-1967) Oxford Dictionary of National Biography, O.U.P., 2004

Watts, Janet. Light blue stocking. *The Guardian*, 15.10.75

Wilby, Peter. And Rosemary for remembrance of order and moderation. *TES*, 24.10.75

Wilson, Alison M. Dame Rosemary Murray: first woman to be Vice-Chancellor… *The Independent*, 18.10.2004

Wilson, Alison M. Dame Rosemary Murray: a celebration.*The Dolphin*, Winter 2004, Issue 28, p.4

Wilson, Alison M. Dame Rosemary at ninety. *The Dolphin*, Summer 2003, Issue, 25, p.2

Woodward, Susan. Sisters in learning. News from Cambridge, 2003, p.6-7

Wykes, Ursula. The University women's Lappland expedition. *Oxford Magazine*, 3.11.38

– List of Illustrations –

The author and publisher would like to thank all those individuals and companies who have supplied images. 'Family photos' indicates illustrations reproduced courtesy of Rosemary's extended family, especially her sister Frances Crombie and nieces and nephews in Oxford. Every effort has been made to identify copyright holders. Any errors and omissions are entirely unintentional, and if reported will be rectified in any future edition of the book.

Front cover. Rosemary as Vice-Chancellor (© Lafayette Photography, Cambridge.)
Back cover. Preparing for a ceremonial flight over Cambridge (© Cambridge Newspapers Ltd.)
Frontispiece. Portrait by Patrick Phillips. (Julia Hedgecoe, photographer, courtesy of Murray Edwards College)
Title page verso. W.W. Spooner (Private collection)
p.7 Prince Philip (NASA, Wikimedia commons)
p.14 Installation of the Chancellor (© Cambridge Newspapers Ltd.)
p.19 Frances and William Spooner (Family photos)
p.22 'Henry Ford' (Family photos)
p.25 Ellen and Arthur Murray (Family photos)
p.26 Rosemary, Frances, Ann and John (Family photos)
p.30 Rosemary Spooner and Rosemary Murray (Unknown photographer) Ellen and Frances, Rosemary aged about 9, The Murray children (Family photos)
p.37 Downe House (From a postcard, courtesy of Downe House School Archive)
p.40 Massed dancing (courtesy of Downe House School Archive)
p.46 Sir Harry Calvert Williams Verney, 4th Baronet. (1930s vintage print by Elliott and Fry, © National Portrait Gallery, London)
p.54 Rosemary's matriculation photograph (courtesy of the Principal and Fellows, Lady Margaret Hall)
p.57 Student sitting-room in Deneke, LMH (courtesy of the Principal and Fellows, Lady Margaret Hall)
p.63 The Dyson Perrins Laboratory, Oxford (© Dr Karl Harrison, Chemistry Department, Oxford University)
p.64 Passport photo of Rosemary aged 25 (Family photos)
    Finstergrun Castle (courtesy of Austrian National Tourist Office)
p.79 Rosemary sailing with Felicity (Family photos)
p.80 Cadlington House (© Bryan Jezeph)
p.83 Rosemary sailing with her father (Family photos)
p.85 Chemistry Laboratory, Royal Holloway College (William Davis, General Photographic Agency © Getty Images. Courtesy of the Archives, Royal Holloway College)

LIST OF ILLUSTRATIONS

p.98 Wren ratings (Unknown photographer)
p.106 Rosemary as Wren officer (Unknown photographer)
p.113 Olive Willis (courtesy of Downe House School Archive)
Lynda Grier (courtesy of the Principal and Fellows, Lady Margaret Hall)
Dame Myra Curtis (courtesy of the Principal and Fellows, Newnham College)
Helen McMorran (courtesy of the Mistress and Fellows, Girton College, Cambridge. © Lafayette Photography, Cambridge)
p.116 The Chemistry Laboratory, Cambridge (Unknown photographer)
p.131 Rosemary and Robin in the sitting room (Estate of Antony Barrington Brown, by permission of the Master and Fellows of Gonville & Caius College, Cambridge)
p.134 Leaving party (courtesy of the Mistress and Fellows, Girton College, Cambridge, © Lafayette Photography, Cambridge)
p.135 The Hermitage in 1954 ((Estate of Antony Barrington Brown, by permission of the Master and Fellows of Gonville & Caius College, Cambridge)
The front door (Photographer Edward Malindine. Published in *Illustrated*, which has not been identified)
p.136 The first dinner at New Hall (Estate of Antony Barrington Brown, by permission of the Master and Fellows of Gonville & Caius College, Cambridge)
The first year at New Hall (Daily News)
p.138 The Hermitage in 1954 (Photographer Edward Malindine. Published in *Illustrated*, which has not been identified)
p.139 Rosemary with two students (Daily News)
p.140 Jenny Stanesby (Photographer Edward Malindine)
p.148 A section of the Dome (courtesy of the photographer, R.A.Douglas Noble)
p.149 Construction of the Dome (courtesy of the photographer, R.A.Douglas Noble)
p.154 The Queen Mother with Rosemary (© Cambridge Newspapers Ltd.)
p.156 The Queen Mother arriving at New Hall (© Cambridge Newspapers Ltd.)
The Queen Mother on the Walkway (© Cambridge Newspapers Ltd.)
p. 158 The Dome in 1966 (Photographer Edward Leigh. © Lafayette Photography, Cambridge)
p.161 Attempting to clean off footprints on the Dome (Daily News)
p.163 The Lockwood Committee (Unknown photographer)
p.172 The New Hall Council in 1969 (Stearn and Sons, © Lafayette Photography, Cambridge)
p.173 Rosemary in the new Library (© Cambridge Newspapers Ltd.)
p.174 Dr T.W.J.Taylor (courtesy of Brasenose College, Oxford)
Sir Robert Robinson (Reproduced courtesy of the Library of The Royal Society of Chemistry)
Alexander Robertus Todd, Baron Todd (Estate of Antony Barrington Brown, by permission of the Master and Fellows of Gonville & Caius College, Cambridge)
Revd Dr John Sandwith Boys Smith (Photographer Bassano Ltd. 1960, © National Portrait Gallery, London.)
p.187 Rosemary at Leeds University (Unknown photographer)

p.188 Rosemary and President Ford (Frank Ross Photography)
p.191 Rosemary in procession (© Cambridge Newspapers Ltd. Courtesy of *The Telegraph*)
p.192 The Chancellor in the honorary degree procession, 1976 (© Cambridge Newspapers Ltd.)
      Rosemary in the procession (© Cambridge Newspapers Ltd.)
p.200 Vice-Chancellor's bike stand. (© Cambridge Newspapers Ltd.)
p.203 Honorary degree in Southern California. (Unknown photographer)
p.207 Ceremonial flight, 1977 (© Cambridge Newspapers Ltd.)
p.209 Rosemary and Robin with the charter (Unknown photographer)
Ian and Frances Crombie and their children (Family photos)
p.210 The Vice-Chancellor in the Dome Room (Unknown photographer)
p.211 Rosemary as Honorary Doctor of Laws, Cambridge University (Unknown photographer)
p.212 Rosemary in Mendocino, California (Family photos)
      Rosemary and Frances reading on Mull (Family photos)
p.213 Rosemary tending the garden (Unknown photographer)
      Rosemary, Frances and Ian in Dorset (Family photos)
p.214 Rosemary and Prince Philip (courtesy Julia Hedgecoe, photographer)
p.215 Rosemary with Anne Lonsdale (Unknown photographer)
      Robert Harkness at Chelsea Flower Show (courtesy of Harkness Roses)
p.216 Rosemary in old age (© Katz Pictures)
p.220 Retirement as a magistrate (© Cambridge Newspapers Ltd.)
p.230 The New Hall Fellows in 1976 (Ramsey and Muspratt, courtesy of Cambridgeshire collection)
p.234 Rosemary with Sir Arthur Marshall (Unknown photographer)
p.239 Rosemary with Baroness Boothroyd and Dr Valerie Pearl (courtesy of Julia Hedgecoe, photographer)
p.245 Rosemary guided by a friend, 2003 (courtesy of Pat Houghton, photographer)
p.247 Rosemary enjoying the company of young people (courtesy of Pat Houghton, photographer)
p.250 Rosemary with a group of New Hall alumnae (© Cambridge Newspapers Ltd.)

– Index –

Note. Women are listed under their maiden name, if known, with married name in brackets. References to pictures are in italics. For abbreviations see page 261.

Adrian, Lord, Chancellor 193, 210
AFPRB 16, 164, 233
Agar, Delia 128, 130
American Friends of Cambridge University
    sponsor ARM's 1976 tour, 201
    sponsor second visit 203
    Gordon Williams, President 201, 203, 224
    Gaylord Donnelly 203, 224
    Carleton Brown 203, 224
    relations with Cambridge University 205-6
    ARM attends Directors' meeting 224, 225
Anscombe, Professor Elizabeth 171, 185
ARP
    at RHC 86
    ARM as ambulance driver 90, 92-3
    RHC committee resigns 93
    in the WRNS 99
Ashby, Sir Eric, Vice-Chancellor 175, 186
Association of Commonwealth Universities
    ARM visits New Zealand 200-1
Association of Universities and Schools
    for Higher Education 223
Avery, Peter 180

Bacon, Alice 145
Bacon, Janet, Principal of RHC
    ARM's first meeting 86
    congratulates ARM 89
    preparations for war 92
    and ARP committee
Balfour, Annabel (Rathbone)
    first President of NH JCR 137
    on television 139
    experience of NH 143
Balfour, Arthur, Prime Minister 29
Barlow, Professor Horace 90
Barlow, Lady Nora *see* Darwin, Nora (Barlow)
Barlow-Poole, Richard, Esquire Bedell 207
Barrington Brown, Antony 137
Baxter, Kay 139
Belsey, Catherine
    on Women's Appointments Board 182
    campaigns for non-UTO's salaries 184
Belvedere Girls School 236
Benians, Mrs S.M. 128, 129, 133
Bertram, Kate 129, 143, 180

BFUW 117, 123, 143, 168
Bidder, Anna, 143, 227, 243
Bibas, Elizabeth 167
Bibas, Henriette 167
Birdwatching
    at Emsworth 28
    around Oxford 59, 73
    in Lapland 78-9
    around RHC 87
    interview topic 144
    with Ann Murray 165
    in Ojai Valley 203
    in the Falklands 244
Birkenhead High School 236,
    Murray Building 237
Blackwell, Miss, 90
Blendworth *see also* Cadlington House
    grave of Arthur and Ellen
    Murray and ARM 202
Board of Trade 128
Boat-building
    at Winchester 60, 82
Bombing raids
    disruption on railways 90
    on Portsmouth 92, 93, 94
    on Weybridge 92
    on Egham 93
Bookbinding
    in Florence 169-70
    classes 240
    ARM binds books for NH and LMH 240
Boothman, Mary 133, 137, 160
Botanic Gardens Syndicate 16, 233
Bowett, Derek, President of
    Queens' College 193
Boys Smith, Revd Dr J.S.,
Vice-Chancellor 127
    at opening of NH new buildings 155
    Chair of NH Council 155, 171
    speaks at the NH Jubilee Feast 227
Bradbrook, Muriel, Mistress of Girton College
    composes College song 115
    reference for Robin Hammond 130
    congratulates ARM on
    Honorary Fellowship 180
Brasenose College, Oxford 59

Brewer, Dr 59-60, 61, 62
   ARM's examiner 72
British Council 238
Brookfield 27, 31
   packed up and rented 69
   Murrays move back 72-3
Building projects
   at New Hall 147-9
   in the University 195-6, 205
Bullough family 159
Burkill, Mrs Margarete 123
   meets Vice-Chancellor 124
   on the meeting in Lady
     Whitby's drawing room 124
   suggests The Orchard as a site for NH 125
   suggests the name Queen
     Elizabeth College 125
   at Jubilee Feast 226
Butler, K.T., Mistress of
   Girton College 111, 131
Butler, R.A. ('Rab') 146, 217
Butterworth, John, Vice-Chancellor 223

Cadbury, George 151
Cadlington House *80*, 81
   purchased by Murray family 80
   possible war hospital 84
   ARM works on house
     requisitioned 84, 91-2
   army moves out 93
   commercial smallholding 165
   sale to Mencap
Cains, Antony, bookbinder 170
Cam, Professor Helen 119
Cambridge Antiquarian Society 116
Cambridge Christian Brotherhood 237-8
   ARM chairs Committee for
     Christian Work in Delhi 239
Cambridge, City 204, 206
   relations with Cambridge
     University 206, 218
Cambridge Philosophical Society 117
Cambridge rapist 157
Cambridge Society 199
   ARM first President 199-200
   ARM Chair and speaker 233
Cambridge University Extra-mural Service 220
Cambridge University Institute of
   Education 177, 196, 231, 233, 238
Cambridge University Musical
   Society (CUMS) 116
Cambridge University Music School

building Stage 1 195
building Stage 2 205
Cambridge University Press Office 243
Cambridge Students' Union (CSU) 205
Cambridge Union 141
Cambridge University Press 203, 224
Cambridgeshire Structure Plan 206
Camping 27, 34
   at Falmouth 67
   by Chichester Harbour 118
Cancer Research Campaign Committee 236
Cartwright, Mary, Mistress of
   Girton College 121, 124, *134*
Chadwick, Professor Owen,
   Vice-Chancellor 178
Chamberlain, Neville, Prime Minister 83
   ARM sees his return from Munich 85
Chamberlin, Peter ('Joe')
   visits to NH Building Committee 148
   complaints about contractors 148-9
   neglects UGC standards 152
   ARM confronts over defects 159
   plans for a chapel 176
Chamberlin, Powell and Bon
   appointment 147
   problems with building 159-60
   represented at the Jubilee Feast 227
Chancellor of Cambridge
   University 13, 193-4, 235, 246
   robes 193-4
Charteris, Margaret ('Aunt Peggy') 82
Chateau d'Oex, Switzerland 45
   ARM with the Verney family 48
   ARM with parents 51
   Ann convalesces 76
Chelsea Flower Show 247
Chemical weapons 91
Chemistry Department, Cambridge *116*
   Tea Club 121
   ARM's first visit 111
Churchill College, Cambridge 147, 153
Clark, Dr Alan 189, 194
Clarkson, Christopher, bookbinder 170
Clinical Medical School, Cambridge 205
Clover, Mrs Helen 171, 176, 182, 226
Coaching, by ARM at Oxford 73, 75, 77
Coates, Sheila 145
College Libraries Fund 205
Colleges Committee 142, 150
Colleges Committee Working
   Party on Co-residence 182
   Report 184

Colleges Fund 195, 225
Colombiers 45
ARM sees autogyro on the Planeyse 49
Army exercises 51
Colston, Sir Charles 146
Committee on Long Term Development 181
Committee of Vice-Chancellors
    and Principals (CVCP) 195
Commonwealth Fund of New York
    Harkness Fellowships
    London Committee 217
Coronation of George VI 75
'Coronation Street' 158, 246
Cottrell, Sir Alan, Vice-
    Chancellor 179, 198, 217
Council of the Senate 16
    women eligible 119
    ARM elected 177
Crane's Charity 233
Crawley, Charles W. 127, 180
Crombie, Clare 238-9
Crombie, Ian 166, *209*, *213*, 241,
Crombie, Marion 243
Crombie, Nicolas 232, 237
Crum, Mary 73, 82, 88
Crum, Michael 73
Curtis, Dame Myra, Principal of
    Newnham College 15, *113*, 124
    Chair of Third Foundation
    Committee 126
    retirement 130

Darwin family 126
    Sir Charles Darwin 125, 128
    Ida and Horace Darwin 145
    Emma Darwin 146
    Ida Darwin (Rees Thomas) 126
    Nora Darwin (Lady Barlow) 125, 126, 219
DBE 16, 208, 217
    investiture 217-18
Deane, Phyllis 180
Demobilisation 110
Devlin, Lord Patrick
    Report 181
    Visitor, NH 227
Dining Group 124, 143, 227
Dodgson, Campbell 29, 75
Downe House School 35-8
    parents welcomed 39
    Frances Murray at school 39
    massed displays 39, *40*
    dining and boarding groups 39
    shooting 41
    'flu epidemic 42
    ARM represents, presented
    to Queen Elizabeth 44
    ARM leaves 46
    ARM homesick for 49
    Seniors weekend 53
    ARM visits 60
    Old Seniors Association started 89
    ARM attends meetings 117
    ARM as Governor 123, 162
Dresden 66
Dubied, Mme. 49
    teaches ARM French 49
    helps ARM with a talk 50
Du Cane family 17, 92
    Alicia (Nonna) 33
    Isabel 33, at Finstergrun 65
    Julia 33
    Nela 69
    Louis 46
Dufton, Miss 131, 179
Duke, Alison 114
Duke of Edinburgh *see* Prince
    Philip, Duke of Edinburgh
Dunkirk 91
Dyson Perrins Laboratory, Oxford 67,
    ARM's first visit 43
    women outnumbered 57
    ARM's routine 68
    explosion 68
    ARM says goodbye 84
    Prof. Robinson invites ARM back 91

Elizabeth Nuffield Foundation 152, 157
Elton Hall 32, 55, 117
Emsworth 27, 53 *see also*
    Brookfield and Sailing
English Speaking Union 213
Equal Pay Act 159, 184
Equal opportunities 181, 182, 196,
    in Midland Bank 221, 235
Esquire Bedells 13, 188, 179

Fairlie, Alison 114, 132, 167
Falkland Islands 243
Finstergrun Castle, Mautendorf 65, *64*
First Aid
    at Oxford 73
    at RHC 90
    at LMH 92
Fitzwilliam College

acquires part of The Grove land 146
Lasdun's design 147
hospitality to NH 153
Floud, Jean, Principal of Newnham College
Chair of the Sub-committee on
the Admission of Women 184
Floud Report 184

Gardening
at Brookfield 73
at Cadlington 90
at NH 137
for Eleanor Webster 224
with Nicolas Crombie 237
around Pinehurst 239
at St Edward's Church 239
at Cranmer Road 240
for Robin Hammond 240
Who's Who entry 240
garden of ARM's bungalow 241
Garrod, Professor Dorothy 112
Gartland, Jenny 147
Gibraltar
visit to Home Fleet 52-3
Ann Murray passes by 69
Gill, Roma 143
Girl Guides
ARM troop leader 40-1
at Downe House 42
in Horndean 46
Girton College
ARM at 14-15
ARM interviewed 111
ARM appointed College Lecturer 112
history 112
Pig Club 114-5
entertainment 115
Fellowship 116
becomes a College 119
Queen Mother's visit 119-20
ARM Director of Studies 120
ARM on the College Council 120
ARM as Tutor 120-1
represents Girton on Women's Appointments Board 123
Girtonians and additional places for women 124
allows NH to contact applicants 127
The Grange 130
ARM's final term at 131
Girton poems 115, 132
ARM's leaving party 132, *134*

Helen McMorran's career at 167, 169
ARM Honorary Fellow 180
decision to admit men 198
Goldsmiths' Company
ARM first woman Liveryman 222
Trial of the Pyx 222
ARM on Education Committee 222-3
Dinners in Goldsmiths' Hall 241, 242
Goodwin, Catherine (Spooner)
moral welfare 19, 21
Goodwin, Crauford 203, 224
Goodwin, Ellen *see* King, Ellen
Goodwin, Frances Wycliffe
(Spooner) 17, 18-19, *19*
at Chateau d'Oex 51
social life at Canterbury Road 54
ARM to meals 58
ARM lives with 67
letter to Ellen Murray about ARM and brothers 70
Goodwin, Henry, Bishop of Carlisle 17-8
Vicar of St Edward's 236
Goodwin, Mary 28
GPDST
ARM forges links with 161
ARM on committee 162
Helen McMorran a member 168
ARM Chair of Court 236
Gray, Ronald D. 183
Great St Mary's Church 117,
ringing chamber 249
Grier, Lynda, Principal of LMH *113*
Ellen Spooner visits 44
interviews ARM 43
as administrator 58
consoles ARM for failing to get a First 72
ARM prefers to Miss Butler 111
visits NH 143
The Grove
attempt to buy for NH;
University purchase 146
drive used for Queen Mother's visit 155
development of land 225
Guest, Lady Charlotte 17

Hall, John 185
Hamilton Kerr Institute 196
Hammond, Robin 15, *131*, *136*, *209*
works for Board of Trade 114
applies to be Tutor at NH 130
ARM congratulates on appointment 131
helps ARM with speeches 150, 200

INDEX

in charge in ARM's absence 150
hears intruders on the Dome 160
relationship with ARM and R. Syfert 167
building named for her 176, 225
announces retirement 180
resigns from Homerton Council 197
'Old New Hall' article 226
at Jubilee Feast 227
ARM's gratitude to 229
Adds to ARM's degree oration 235
ARM visits 240
Harker, Janet 115, 132, 133, *134*
Harkness Foundation 219, 224
Heather, Lilian 42, 44, 73
Heffer, Reuben 180
Hellenic tour 75
Hessey, Wilma 58, 61, 63
The Hermitage 126, *131*, *138*
preparation for NH 130, 133-4
students arrive 137
crowded dining room 144
Hoare, Diana
helps at Cadlington 90, 91
accompanies Ann to S. Africa 117
marries David Murray 90 (endnote)
death 241
Hollond, Marjorie 120
Homerton College 197
becomes an Approved Society 197
2-year B.Ed. 198
ARM as Visitor 198, 231
ARM as Trustee 231
Honer, John 148, 227
Honer, Peter 148
Horton, Mrs A.C. 128
Huang, Professor C. L-H. 171

Inge, Catherine 28-9
Inge, Kitty *see* Spooner, Catherine (Kitty)
Inge, Paula 28-9
Inge, Ralph, Dean of St Paul's 20
his portrait 32
Inge, Richard 107
International Council on the Future of
the University (ICFU) 204, 223
Isostilbene research 61, 70, 76, 77

James, Vera H. 131
Jenkinson, Rosamund 59, 68
John Murray Publishers 17
Joint Standing Committee on
Student Numbers 179

Justice of the Peace (JP)
ARM appointed 16
congratulations on appointment 121
assignments 158
cuts down while V-C 204
on Lord Chancellor's Committee
for Cambridgeshire 219
retires 233, *220*

Keats Whiting, Ella 201, 224
Kennan, Andrew 217
Keswick Hall College of Education
ARM Governor 157
Retired Principal, Miss
Duff on NH Council 172
Amalgamated with University
of East Anglia 233
King, Ellen (Goodwin) 17, 28
on ARM as a child 29
'Armoo' 28, 29
Kitson Clark, G. 127, on women's rights 172

Lady Margaret Hall (LMH)
ARM decision to apply 42
examination and interviews 43
Warden Spooner one of the founders 55
convenience of location for ARM 54
rules 56
Deneke 56, 57
Settlement in Lambeth 59
science students 83
ARM Honorary Fellow 171
ARM returns in old age 241
Lapland expedition
ARM ornithologist 78
Lake Torne Träsk 78
buzzard pellets 79
tourists 79
ARM writes up research 84
Laughton Mathews, Vera, Director WRNS 99
considers ARM an exceptional officer 106
talent spotting ability 106
commends ARM 110
speeches 110
congratulates ARM on
appointment to NH 129
League of Nations, Geneva 47
Leishman, J.B. 159
Levack, George 171
Lewis, Jack, Master of Robinson College 197
Linnett, Jack, Vice-Chancellor
V-C elect 178

outgoing V-C 188
  on role and term of V-C 198
  suggests Cambridge Society 199
Litt, Nancy 58, 61, 63
Lockwood Committee 162, *163*
Lodging Houses Syndicate 177, 181
Londonderry 102
  Belmont 102
  Western Approaches Command 102
  Ebrington Barracks 103
  Christmas in 104
  Lockwood Committee in 162
  Magee College 162
Lonsdale, Anne, President of NH
  215, 231, 246, 248, 249, *223, 249*
Lord Lieutenant *see* Proby, Peter
Lucy Cavendish College 231
Lupton, Patricia (Peter) 58, 63
Lynden-Bell, Ruth 229

MacDonald, Inez 159
Macklehose, Alec 66-7
McCrum, Michael, Vice-Chancellor 235
McMorran, Helen I. *113, 134*
  friendship with ARM 168-9
  career 167
  Valentine from ARM 168
  Valentines to ARM 168, 169
  holidays with ARM 169
  administers Girton Roll 227
  death 169
Macpherson, R.E. 152
  on NH Council 172
Macular degeneration 245
Magdalene College 143
Marshall, Arthur *234*
Martin, Sir Leslie 147
Megaw, Helen 116
Midland Bank 221
Miller, Edward, Master of
  Fitzwilliam College 185
Moore, Professor at RHC
  ARM meets 78
  advises on research 86
  invites ARM to tea 87
  thanks ARM for her assistance 89
  keen to have ARM back after the War 94
Mill Hill Central Training Depot 99
Mother Theresa 194
Murray, Alice Rosemary
PERSONAL LIFE (ARM)
  family and ancestors 17-21, 31-3, 54-5

family life 20-6, 31
letter-writing 24-5, 108
accent 25
not a Feminist 26, 177
birth 27-8
childhood in Emsworth 27-8
childhood visits to Oxford 23, 28-9
favoured by parents and family 29
leader of the Murray children 29-30, 34
moral sense 33
at school in Havant 33-4
at Downe House School 35-44
relationship with Olive Willis,
  headmistress 35, 36, 37
relationship with Miss Nickel 38
dislike of dancing 39, 53, 103
'flu epidemic 42
presented to Queen Elizabeth 44, 120
School Certificate 41
Oxford Entrance exam and interview 42-4
etiquette at dinners 46
friendship with Marjorie Verney
  and family 40, 45, 47-8, 72
at Chateau d'Oex 48, 51
in Neuchâtel 49-52
relationship with Pasquier family 49, 50-2
takes courses at University
  of Neuchâtel 50, 52
visits Gibraltar 52-3
matriculation at LMH 54, *54*
allowance from father 55
in love at Oxford 57
relationship with Dr Brewer 60, 62, 72
relationship with research supervisor,
  T.W.J.Taylor 61, 67-8, 86, 87-8
Oxford Part II examinations 61-3
at Finstergrun Castle 65
lodges with grandmother 67
takes care of Nancy Newman 68
looks after brothers in
  mother's absence 69-70, 73
coaching 73, 75
appendicitis 74-5
lodges at Polstead Road 76
moves to Cadlington 80-1
helps with boat-building 82
considers war work 82, 89
has poor relations with Dr Plant 89, 93
milks goats 90
misses John 96, 105
takes charge of emergency centre 132
friendship with Helen McMorran 167-9

INDEX

clears Cadlington 205
moves to Oxford 241
retirement activities 233-47
celebrates 90th birthday 246
chooses heart operation 248
death 248

PROFESSIONAL LIFE (ARM)
  First woman Vice-Chancellor
    13, 16, 179, 217, 243
  first woman to install a Chancellor 13, 194
  experience of women's colleges 14-15
  joins Third Foundation Association 15
  Tutor-in-Charge of New Hall 15
  at Girton College 14-5
  service in the WRNS 14,15
  J.P. 16, 121, 130, 211
  member of AFPRB 16, 164-5
  member of Lockwood Committee 16, 162
  applies to RHC and is accepted 77-8
  passes D.Phil viva 823,
  degree conferred 88
  at RHC 84-87, 89-91
  volunteers at Dyson Perrins Laboratory 91
  drives lorries and ambulances 92-3
  moves to Admiralty Signal School 94
  at Sheffield University 95-7
  joins the WRNS 97
  WRNS career 99-110
  promoted to WRNS Officer 101
  leadership skills 101
  at WRNS Headquarters 105-7
  at Donibristle Air Station 107-9
  at Chatham 109-10
  interviewed and appointed
  at Girton College 111-2
  Fellow of Girton 120
  Tutor 120-1
  publishes papers with Herchel Smith 122
  joins Third Foundation
  Association committee 126
  member of two Third Foundation
  sub-committees 126
  appointed Tutor-in-Charge, New Hall 129
  organises The Hermitage 133-4
  demands high standards at
    NH 137, 138, 141, 145
  interaction with students 141-2,
    145,150, 175-6, 177, 181
  promotion of NH 142
  as interviewer 144
  relationship with CPB 147-8, 159
  first President of NH 153
  organises move to
    Huntingdon Rd. 153, 157
  organises visit of Queen Mother to NH 155
  supports B.Ed degree 157, 197-8
  routine at NH 157-9
  speeches 161
  member of Wages Councils 163-4
  elected to Council of the Senate 177, 180
  Deputy Vice-Chancellor 180
  admission as V-C 188-9
  appoints two deputies at NH 189-90
  entertaining 190
  negotiations with Prince Philip 193
  thoroughness 194
  chooses female page 195
  attends CVCP 195
  supports Robinson College 197
  supports Homerton as
    Approved Society 197
  thoughts on tenure of V-C 198-9
  supports Cambridge Society 199-200
  fundraising 146, 150, 151, 203, 226, 227
  networking 204
  guides student representation 205
  relationship with staff 158, 206
  efficiency in meetings 204, 207
  DBE 208, 217
  Supports adult education 220, in Delhi
    238 *see also* NIAE, Harkness Foundation,
    Council of the Winston Churchill
    Memorial Trust, English Speaking Union,
    Goldsmiths' Company Education
    Committee 222
  survey of NH alumni 227-8
  seeks solutions for women combining
    careers with children 221, 229
  retirement party 228
  relationship with Fellows 230-1
  friendship with Anne Lonsdale 231
  first woman Deputy Lord Lieutenant
    for Cambridgeshire 233-4
  honorary degree from
    Cambridge University 235

INTERESTS AND ACTIVITIES (ARM)
  family games, plays and charades 20, 22
  films 22, 59
  reading 22-3
  Scout movement 34
  tennis 39, 53, 75
  Girl Guide movement 40-1, 43, 46
  teaches brothers 53
  canoeing and punting in Oxford 58

church and chapel attendance
  58, 87, 117, 236, 242
walking 59, 65, 67, 87, 96,
  105, 201, 205, 232, 240
cycling 59, 73, 87, 90, 92, 103, 117, 189
attendance at concerts 59
plays clarinet 74, 87
visits Settlements 44, 47, 59, 147
21st birthday 59
rowing 66, 103
sailing 53, 66, 73, 75, 82,
  86, 114, 118, 133, 240-1
First Aid 73, 90
birdwatching 28, 73, 78-9, 87, 203, 244
singing 74, 87, 115, 116
skiing 74, 77, 118
Lapland expedition ornithologist 78-80
stage manager 115
member of orchestra 87, 115
climbing 165, 205
bookbinding 169-70, 240
see also camping
see also gardening
see also New Hall
CHARACTER, OPINIONS
AND IDEAS (ARM)
  ideal of service 16-7, 21, 31
  prone to home-sickness 49, 91, 95-6
  shyness 50, 56, 101, 102,
  116, 121, 142, 204
  signs of snobbery 87, 96, 110
  shocked by American attitude 104
  aware of career restrictions on women 123
  reluctant to apply for Tutor-
  in-Charge post 128
  delighted to have Robin
  Hammond as Deputy 131
  comparison with Robin Hammond 141
  shyness 116, 142, 190
  first impressions of America 151
  on University education 163
  attachment to father 166
  enjoys breaking gender barriers 142-3
  wants NH to remain single sex 171
  satisfaction as NH becomes a college 172
  interested in the workings
  of the University 175
  good judgement 175
  equable disposition 175
  firmness and clarity 178
  no ambition 179
  supports equal opportunities

for women 182
suggests phasing in of co-residence 183
concerned about lack of good
  women candidates 183
not anxious for more postgraduate
  places for women 183
wants more non-UTOs 186
sets out options for NH's future 185
practical ability 186, 235
stamina 165, 207, 208
charm 122, 207, 208
leadership 100, 110, 132, 235
Murray, Ann Olivia
  birth 29
  in Wei Hai Wei, China 68-9
  in Vent 74
  success in Oxford Entrance exam 75
  sailing Zelda 75
  at Lausanne clinic 76
  continued ill health 76
  saw Cadlington for sale 81
  Exhibitioner at LMH 75
  helps at Cosham Emergency Centre 93
  living in Cambridge 117
  departs for S. Africa 117
  at Cadlington. Illness and death 165
Murray, Anne Helen 70, 72
Murray, Arthur John Layard, Admiral 17
  serves in *Montrose* 46
  advice to ARM on travelling abroad 47
  serves in *Nelson*
  salary and pay-cut 52
  advice to ARM starting at Oxford 55
  saves lives with ARM 58
  commanding HMS *Dorchester* 60, 69, 75
  in Wei Hai Wei with Eastern Fleet 69
  in Hong Kong 71
  sails into Portsmouth 73
  at Admiralty Signal School, Portsmouth 75
  party held by Frances Spooner 76
  helps John to build *Calliope* 82
  preparations for war 84
  Rear Admiral 89
  enquires about work for
  ARM at Admiralty 89
  posted to Red Sea 91
  returns to Signal School 93
  attempts to get ARM a
  job at Signal School 96
  ARM visits him in Yarmouth 97
  invalided out as Vice Admiral 107
  convalescence 165

INDEX

founds Horndean Community
    Association 165
    death 165-6
Murray, Arthur David
    birth 29
    in Gibraltar 53
    looked after by ARM 69-70
    refuses Christmas stocking 89
    marries Diana Hoare 90 (endnote)
    at school in Winchester 93
    helps at Cosham Emergency Centre 93
    at Oxford 96
    climbing with ARM 105
    career 166
    sailing with ARM 241
    visits California with ARM 243
Murray, Barbara 17
    runs St Margaret Settlement 47
    spends Christmas with
    ARM and family 69
    visits Emsworth 82
Murray, Betty (Proby) 17
Murray, Ellen Maxwell *see* Spooner,
Ellen Maxwell (Murray)
Murray Edwards College 248
    see also New Hall
Murray, Ellen *see* Spooner, Ellen (Murray)
Murray, Frances Marion
    (Crombie) *26, 30, 209, 212, 213*
    birth 28
    at Downe House 39
    School Certificate 41
    in Chateau d'Oex 51
    at Ruskin College 51
    holiday in Scotland 66
    in Wei Hai Wei, China 68
    at Chelsea School of Art 77
    studio at Cadlington 81
    decides to be a nurse 84
    at Abbots Langley Hospital 92
    writes to ARM about Sheffield 85
    receives condolences on ARM's death 248
Murray, John Hallam
    birth 29
    sailing 66
    companion to ARM 73
    building *Calliope* 73
    gunnery training, HMS *Erebus* 89
    prepares Cadlington for Army 92
    passed for National Service 92
    ARM visits in Newcastle 96-7
    Norfolk Broads holiday 118

surveying with ARM 118
career and retirement 166
Bursar of Cambridge
    Technical College 166
sailing in Scotland with ARM 240-1
house in Cambridge 241
Murray, Richard Wycliffe 18
    birth 29, 34
    in Gibraltar 53
    sailing 66
    looked after by ARM 69-70
    at Shepway 70
    wins race sailing with ARM 82
    at school in Winchester 93
    visits ARM in Cambridge 117
    Norfolk Broads holiday 118
    career 166
    sailing in Scotland with ARM 240-1

National Institute of Adult
    Education (NIAE) 219-20
National Union of Women
    Teachers (NUWT) 123
Neuchâtel, University of 45
    vacation courses 50
    Piaget lectures 50
    ARM receives certificates 52
New College, Oxford
    Lodge 20, 31-2
    Chapel 20, 18,32
    Choir 74
    choirboys 74, 75
New Hall
    name 128, Colston College 146
    ARM appointed Tutor in Charge 128-9
    Council 130
    Limited Company 130, 137, 175
    Recognised Institution 130
    gate hours 137-8
    Poppy Day participation 139-40
    students form Women's Union 141
    first cohort at General Admissions 143
    entrance paper 143
    admission interviews 144
    hostels 144
    Building Committee 147
    Appeal Committee 146, 150, 225-6, 228
    ARM President 153
    Approved Foundation 155
    takes B.Ed. students 157
    flood 160
    footprints on Dome 160, *161*

Constitution Committee 170
co-residence debate 170-1
stays single sex 171
Charter of Incorporation 173, *209*
Coat of Arms 173
Working Party on Economies 176
rent strike 176
concern about numbers 183
Publicity Committee paper 184-5
explores twinning 185-6
Silver Jubilee 225-9
questionnaire 227-8
Fellowship 229, 230
ARM Honorary Fellow 230
furniture from ARM's family 232
50th Anniversary 246-7
New Hall Archive 232
New Hall Association 142, 227
New Hall Feminists 177
New Hall Society 226
dinner for ARM's retirement 228
ARM's speech at dinner 229
annual dinners 239
ARM's 90th birthday party 246, *247*
50th Anniversary Dinner 248
Newman, Nancy 67, accident 68
Newman, Sarah 153, 226
Newnham College 112, 128
Nickel, Maria 38, 147
Nicol, Ian 206
Nomination Board (for Chancellor) 193
Norman, Tony 147
Nursery Action Group (NAG) 196

Observer Newspaper 222, 241
Odgers, Mary
student friend of ARM 59
canoe trip 62
ARM visits in Norfolk 82
Ogilvie, Dame Bridget, New Hall's Visitor 246
The Orchard
Mrs Burkill suggests the site 125
donation of house and land to NH 126
NH moves to 144
demolished 152
Orr-Ewing, Jean
interviews ARM 43
ARM's Tutor 57-8, 60
writes to T.W.J. Taylor 61
opinion of RHC 78
Oxford Bach Choir 74
Oxford Encaenia 202

Oxford University
entrance exam 41, 44
ARM matriculates 54, 54
degrees for women 54, 118
ARM takes Finals 60-2
ARM writes up thesis 73
ARM's D.Phil. viva 82-3,
degree conferred 88
ARM's Honorary Degree 180
Oxfordshire Association for the Blind 245

Parsons, Mrs E.W. 124, 125, 226
Pasquier family 49-52
Pearl, Dr Valerie, President of New Hall 231
Penson, Dame Lilian, 119, 178
Phillips, Patrick, artist 152
Plant, Dr
ARM meets at RHC 78
welcomes ARM 85
approves lecture plan 86
poor relations with ARM 87, 89
leads economy campaign 90
argument with ARM 93
Platt, Beryl, Baroness Platt of Writtle 235
Porton Down 91
President Ford 186-8, *188*
Pretty, Kate 230
Principal of Homerton College 231
eulogy for ARM 249
Price, Tony, Vicar of St Nicholas
Church, Old Marston 242, 248
Prince Philip, Duke of Edinburgh
elected Chancellor 193
installation as Chancellor 194-5
patron of Cambridge Society 199
relationship with ARM 208
congratulates ARM on DBE
on institutions 229
message for ARM's 90th birthday 246
visits NH 246
Princess Margaret 208, 217
Privy Council 172
Proby, Claud 32,
at Finstergrun 65
at Goodwood ball 69
Proby, Peter, Lord Lieutenant 32
invites ARM to be Deputy 233-4
Proby, Sir Richard, 17

Queen Elizabeth (later Queen Mother) *154, 156*
Honorary degree 119
at Girton College 119

Visitor, Girton College 120
suggested as name for NH 125
opens new buildings 155

Radar 94
Rawson, Elizabeth
   Leverhulme Fellow 152
   President's Deputy 190
   former Fellow 227
   ARM's degree oration 235
   Rawson Reading Area 239
Richard, Alison, Vice-Chancellor 243, 249
Robbins Report 177
Robinson, Sir Robert 61, *174*
   requests ARM's help for war work 91
   recommends post in Sheffield 94-5
Robinson College 196
   ARM a Trustee and Honorary Fellow 197
   architects 197
   opened by the Queen
     and Prince Philip 208
   ARM becomes Visitor 231
Rosemary Murray Library, NH 239, 246
   donations to 159
   professional Librarian 169
   Rawson Reading Area 239
Rosemary Murray rose 247
Royal Holloway College (RHC)
   ARM's interview 77
   ARM's first visit 78
   ARM moves in 84-5
   ARP preparations for war 86
   Chapel services 87
   entertainment 87
   economy campaign 90
   explosion in laboratory 93
   ARM decides to leave 94
Rumsey, Jill, page 194-5

Sailing *79, 83*
   Arthur Murray's passion for 24
   Hayling Regatta 53, 73
   in Scotland 66
   at Emsworth in *Kelpie* 73, 81, 114
   in *Zelda* 75
   in Spinnaker Cup race 84
   in *Calliope* 114, 118
   in Scotland in *Fulmar* 240-1
   in Scotland in *Martlet* 241
St Anne's College, Oxford
   twinned with NH 143
St Edward's Church, Cambridge 236

Harvey Goodwin, Vicar 18
   ARM a Trustee 236
St Nicholas Church, Old Marston 242, 248
St Nicholas Primary School, Marston 242-3
St Stephen's College, Delhi 237
Salter, F.R. 127
Sandringham 208
School Certificate 41
Schools
   Havant Primary 33-4
   Downe House 35-44
   see also Downe House School
Schwarzkopf, Elizabeth 151, 202
Scott Polar Research Institute 116, 233
Scout movement 34
Selwyn, Lucy 45, 49, 50, 69
Senate House 13, 120, 143, 179, 188, 194, 235
Servants 20, 24
   Nanny 20, 31, *30*
   Maids' outing 67
   Ethel 69
Shaw, J. Byam, artist
   Christmas with the Dodgsons 69
   School of Art 152
Sheffield University
   ARM Assistant Lecturer 95
   ARM discontented and leaves 96
   ARM's Honorary Degree 180
Shrubsole, Alison, Principal
   of Homerton College 197
Signal School, Portsmouth 94
Silver Jubilee Appeal, NH 225, 226, 228
Silver Jubilee of George V 61
Smith, Herchel 122
Smith, Rosalind (Edwards) 247, 248
Smith, Shirley 245
Sparrow, John, Warden of All
   Souls, Oxford 202-3
Speeches
   ARM helped by Robin Hammond 142
   ARM in America 151
   to GPDST 161
   to Cambridge Society 200
   at retirement dinner 229
   at 90th birthday party 246
Spencer-Booth, Yvette 171
Stewart, Vivien 171, 176
Spooner, Catherine (Dodgson) 20
   letters to Ellen Murray 24, 29
   with Arthur Balfour and ARM 29
   house in Montagu Square 32-3
   as artist 35

finances ARM 52
takes ARM to Royal Academy 53
Christmas with 69
Lends ARM etchings 86
Spooner, Catherine (Goodwin) *see*
Goodwin, Catherine (Spooner)
Spooner, Catherine (Kitty) (Inge) 19
Spooner, Ellen Maxwell ((Murray) 17, *25, 30*
   Bible study 21
   marriage 27
   car driver 23
   letter-writing 24
   in Neuchâtel 48
   warns ARM she may have
    to leave Neuchâtel 52
   organises trip to Gibraltar 53
   preparations for war 84
   suggests ARM do war work 90
   packs up Brookfield for army 91
   J.P. 121
   visits NH 143
   describes opening of NH's
    new buildings 155
   widowed 166
   on ARM as V-C 179
   death 202
Spooner, Frances Wycliffe see Goodwin, Frances Wycliffe (Spooner)
Spooner, Maxwell 19-20
Spooner, Rosemary *30*
   local councillor and OBE 21
   letters to Ellen Spooner 24
   visits Murrays 31
   friendship with ARM, her niece 39
   helps Ruskin College, Oxford 55
   managing finances of the Murrays 69
   letter from ARM about RHC 84
   meets Mrs Robinson 94
   visit of ARM for MA ceremony 96
   death 202
Spooner, Ruth 19-20
   On ARM as a child 29
   helps Ruskin College, Oxford 55
   ARM moves to Polstead Road 71
   friction with ARM 73
   asks ARM to move out 76
   visit of ARM for MA ceremony 96
Spooner, Revd Dr William Archibald *19*
   Warden of New College 17, 18-21
   Spoonerisms 18
   Founder of LMH 56
   against degrees for women 56

Spooner, William (Bill) 58, 107
Spooner, William Wycliffe
   photo title page 4
   Visits to Oxford 58-9, 76
   wife Maidie 58
   sets up Spooner Charitable Trust 152
   Spooner Building, NH 152
   Commissions Patrick Phillips
    to paint ARM 152
Squirrel, Wren Officer, 103
Stainer, Alice 53
Stanesby, Jenny (Moody) *140*
Steiner, Zara 160, 229, 230
Stewart, Vivien 171
   Vivien Stewart Room 226
Student representation 175, 176, 181
Swinnerton-Dyer, Peter, Vice-Chancellor 185, 227
   Master of St Catharine's College 208
   attends Jubilee Feast 227
Syfret, Rosemary
   congratulates ARM on becoming
    Tutor-in-Charge 129
   approached to be Tutor,
   suggests Robin Hammond 130
   friendship with J.B. Leishman 159
   friendship with Robin Hammond 167
   congratulates ARM on becoming
    Honorary Fellow of LMH 171

Tait, Archibald Campbell,
   Archbishop of Canterbury 17
Taylor, Dr T.W.J., (later Sir Thomas) *174*
   agrees to supervise ARM 61
   over-familiar 67-8
   ARM considers a good supervisor 68
   recommends ARM for D.Phil studies 70
   testimonial for ARM 76-7
   visits RHC 86
   reads joint paper to Chemical Society 87-8
   visits Galapagos Islands 88
   at Porton Down 91
   running Operational Research
    Division in Ceylon 105
Taylor, Mrs Georgina 71, 72, 73, 77
   in ATS 90
   letter to ARM about
    working in Ceylon 105
Teichman, Jenny 185
Third Foundation Association 15, 125-9
   founded 125
   ARM elected to Committee 126

INDEX

NH recognised as Approved
   Foundation 155
   work completed 173
   members at Jubilee Feast 227
Thomas, Trevor, Bursar of
   St John's College 172
   on NH Council 172
   drafts Statutes of NH 172
   thanks ARM 227
Thomson, David 127, 145
Thorpe, Lady Sibyl 159
Tindle, David, artist 152
Todd, Prof. Alexander, Lord
   Todd of Trumpington 174
   headhunts ARM for Girton 111
   ARM dines with 117
   encourages ARM to apply for
   Tutor-in-Charge, NH 128
Toynbee Hall 237
Trinity Hall 236

University Grants Committee
   (UGC) 152, 181-2, 183, 195
University of Leeds *187*
   ARM receives Honorary Degree 186
University of Southern California *218*
   ARM receives Honorary Degree 202
University of Ulster
   Lockwood Committee 162
   ARM receives Honorary Degree 162
University Women's Club 236

V.E. Day 197
Verney, Sir Harry, 4th Baronet *46*
   and Lady Rachel 45
   ascends the Salève with ARM 47-8
   walks with ARM in Chateau d'Oex 48
   emotional departure 48-9
   at Rhoscolyn 72
   congratulates ARM 171, 179
   interest in Alpine flora 240
Verney, Marjorie 40, 48, 209
Veterinary School
   ARM a Trustee 233
Vice-Chancellor
   women eligible 119
   ARM a candidate 178
   ARM's installation 188, 189, *191*
   office in the Dome Room 189
   V-C's bicycle 189, *200*
   entertaining 190
   rôle and term of office 198-9

routine as V-C 204
staff 206
ceremonial flight 207, *207*
not a figurehead 243
see also Ashby, Sir Eric, Vice-Chancellor;
Boys Smith, Revd Dr J.S., Vice-Chancellor;
Butterworth, John, Vice-Chancellor; Chadwick,
Professor Owen, Vice-Chancellor; Cottrell,
Sir Alan, Vice-Chancellor; Linnett, Jack,
Vice-Chancellor; McCrum, Michael, Vice-
Chancellor; Richard, Alison, Vice-Chancellor;
Swinnerton-Dyer, Peter, Vice-Chancellor

Wages Councils 163-4, 241
WEA 117, 129, 220, 237
Webster, Professor Eleanor 224
Welbourn, Esther 171, 189
Wellesley College
   ARM's Honorary Degree 201-2
   ARM visits Eleanor Webster 224
Westfield College 99
Whitby, Lady
   hosts meeting about a third
   foundation for women 124
   Chair of NH Council 130
   Chair of NH Appeal Committee 146
Widdowson, Eva 95
Wigram family
   ARM joins skiing holidays
   in Vent 74, in Aosta 77
Wilkinson, L.Patrick 127, 129, 226
Willis, Olive *113*
   sets up Downe House School 35-7
   eccentrics 38
   dancing and gymnastic displays 39, *40*
   in Athens 73
   donation to NH 129
   belief in consultation 176
Windsor Castle 208, 217
Winston Churchill Memorial Trust 221
Wolfson Foundation 147
Women's Appointments Board 123, 139
   ARM appointed to Committee
   ARM chairs Committee 182
Woollcombe, Jocelyn, Deputy
   Director WRNS 103, 106
Wrens see WRNS
Wright, Margaret 157
WRNS 14, 15, *98*, *106*
   ARM applies and is accepted 97
   ARM's career in 98-110
   OTC 100-1

WRNS *contd*
    Pay and Registry Office 100
    Supplies 100
    Guard of Honour 101
    Ordnance Board 101
    ARM 3rd Officer 101
    Admiralty Fleet Orders 102
    ARM at HMS *Ferret* 102
    drill 104
    Christmas in Londonderry 104
    ARM 2nd Officer 105
    ARM Acting 1st Officer 105
    at HQ, Queen Anne's Mansions 105
    Officers Appointments Branch 106
    at Donibristle Air Station 107-9
    ARM Chief Officer at
    Chatham RN Barracks 109
    WRNS uniform 234, *234*
    discharged 114
WRNS Association 117
    ARM Chair of Cambridge Branch 236
    ARM gives speech on Nelson 236
Wykes, Ursula 58, 63, 78

YWCA 96

Zangwill, Oliver 209